Lacan and Education Policy

Also available from Bloomsbury

Foucault and School Leadership Research, Denise Mifsud
Deleuze and Guattari, Politics and Education, edited by Matthew Carlin
and Jason Wallin

Lacan and Education Policy

The Other Side of Education

Matthew Clarke

BLOOMSBURY ACADEMIC
LONDON • NEW YORK • OXFORD • NEW DELHI • SYDNEY

BLOOMSBURY ACADEMIC
Bloomsbury Publishing Plc
50 Bedford Square, London, WC1B 3DP, UK
1385 Broadway, New York, NY 10018, USA

BLOOMSBURY, BLOOMSBURY ACADEMIC and the Diana logo
are trademarks of Bloomsbury Publishing Plc

First published in Great Britain 2019
Paperback edition first published 2021

A catalogue record for this book is available from the British Library.

A catalog record for this book is available from the Library of Congress.

ISBN: HB: 978-1-3500-7055-4
PB: 978-1-3502-0135-4
ePDF: 978-1-3500-7056-1
eBook: 978-1-3500-7057-8

Typeset by Newgen KnowledgeWorks Pvt. Ltd., Chennai, India

To find out more about our authors and books visit
www.bloomsbury.com and sign up for our newsletters.

This book is dedicated to Liz and Ella for all their love and support and to Ted and Mary Clarke, who live on in the fond memories of their family.

Contents

Figures

Acknowledgements

I would like to thank Mark Richardson at Bloomsbury for his interest and enthusiasm during our initial conversation about this project and to Maria Giovanna Brauzzi for working with me and answering my questions over recent months. I also thank a number of colleagues whose friendship and conversation has contributed to my thinking. Specifically, I owe a large debt of gratitude to Dean Garratt, Charlotte Haines Lyon, Ray Misson and Kalervo Gulson, for their generosity in reading and responding to drafts of various chapters as they developed and to Ansgar Allen, Peter Bansel, Emile Bojesen, Jeff Buckles, Jordi Collet, Rob Creasy, Linda Hammersley-Fletcher, Sajad Kabgani, Tony Leach, Helen Lees, Margaret Lo, Michael Michell, Alex Moore, Gary Peters, Anne Phelan, John Schostak, Sam Sellar, Julian Stern, Greg Thompson, Jonathan Vincent, Margaret Wood and Terry Wrigley, for fruitful and rewarding debates and discussions around issues related to this book over a number of years.

Education in the Neo-liberal Era: Crisis and Impasse

In today's world, higher standards are demanded than were required yesterday and there are simply fewer jobs for those without skill. Therefore we demand more from our schools than did our grandparents.

James Callaghan, Speech at Ruskin College, 1976

If an unfriendly foreign power had attempted to impose on America the mediocreeducational performance that exists today, we might well have viewed it as an act of war. As it stands, we have allowed this to happen to ourselves.

National Commission on Excellence in Education, 1983, p. 7

If Australia is to rise to these challenges, we need a revolution in the quality of our education outcomes, the nature of our investment in education and in the collaboration between governments and the education and training sectors.

Commonwealth of Australia, 2008, p. 5

[T]his so-called crisis. It does not exist, it could not ... In psychoanalysis, there are no immediate answers, but only the long and patient search for reasons.

Lacan, 1974

Introduction: Education in a time of crisis

It is no accident that the language of policy, indeed of politics more broadly, frequently deploys the language of crisis. Crisis discourse has always been one of the key 'mobilizing passions' (Paxton, 2005, p. 41) for politicians and policymakers seeking to bring about radical change. As this suggests, the invocation of crisis involves a substantial element of strategic rhetoric. This is not to say that all crises are fabricated or false. But any discourse of crisis assumes certain values, it asserts particular narratives and enables and encourages particular questions. It privileges certain diagnoses, while foreclosing others, and promotes preferred solutions that 'fit' the chosen diagnoses.

Crisis has become a pervasive discourse in education policy. If we look back to 1976 and UK Prime Minister James Callaghan's Ruskin College speech, we can see the privileging of links between education and the economy that have only intensified in the intervening years, so that writing in 2007, Ball noted how 'education is increasingly, indeed perhaps almost exclusively, spoken of within policy in terms of economic value and its contribution to international market competitiveness' (p. 185). Callaghan's speech provoked outrage, though not so much for its content, as for the perception that his government was seen to be interfering in what had traditionally been the domain of education professionals. Indeed, in terms of its content, Callaghan's words seem anything but inflammatory: 'The goals of education, from nursery school through to adult education, are clear enough. They are to equip children to the best of their ability for a lively, constructive, place in society, and also to fit them to do a job of work. Not one or the other but both.' The same can hardly be said of *A Nation at Risk* (National Commission on Excellence in Education, 1983), the publication of which in the United States, initiated an identifiable and persistent line of attack on education in media and political discourse, accusing schools of being not just pedagogically ineffective but also morally negligent:

> Our concern, however, goes well beyond matters such as industry and commerce. It also includes the intellectual, moral, and spiritual strengths of our people which knit together the very fabric of our society. The people of the United States need to know that individuals in our society who do not possess the levels of skill, literacy, and training essential to this new era will be effectively disenfranchised, not simply from the material rewards that accompany competent performance, but also from the chance to participate fully in our national life. A high level of shared education is essential to a free, democratic society and to the fostering of a common culture, especially in a country that prides itself on pluralism and individual freedom. (pp. 8–9)

This purported state of crisis clearly had profound implications, threatening to undermine and undo not just the economic, but the moral and political fabric of American society.

In the past forty years, a purported state of crisis in education has been used by politicians and policymakers to legitimate radical, if not revolutionary, measures intended to remedy and rectify education's perilous state. It is not accidental that this line of thinking coincides with the rise of neo-liberal politics in Western societies, and the ascendancy of neo-liberal policies in education; for as numerous commentators have observed, the narrative of crisis is very much part and parcel of neo-liberalism, generating and justifying a perpetual state of relentless revolutionary reform (Cahill and Konings, 2017; Gamble, 2014; Klein, 2007; Lipman, 2014; Mirowski, 2013). But, of course, the term 'revolution'[1] has multiple meanings and, in addition to signifying radical change, also signifies turning full circle, and returning to the tried and trusted approaches of the past. We see this in cultural politics more broadly, with the forceful assertion of various forms of 'fundamentalism', including (heteronormative) 'family values' (Cooper, 2017) and autarkian nationalism (Fekete, 2018; King, 2017), as well as in education with the growing popularity of 'traditional' models of curriculum (Wrigley, 2017, 2018; Zipin, 2017), authoritarian behavioural policies (Sullivan, Johnson and Lucas, 2016) and autocratic management models in schools (Courtney and Gunter, 2015).

Crisis and impasse

At the same time as being locked in crisis, education, like society more broadly (Monbiot, 2016), is increasingly experienced and understood, especially by educators, as being in a state of impasse, in the sense of being stuck in a bad place (Ainley, 2016). On the one hand, this sense of being simultaneously in crisis – something requiring change and action – yet also in impasse – implying the impossibility of both change and action – may appear something of a contradiction, akin to a paradox or double-truth. On the other hand, however, crisis and impasse may be seen as two sides of the same coin insofar as we would not be in crisis if we were not already at an impasse, while being in an impasse constitutes something of a crisis.

This book sets out to engage with the mutual entanglements of neo-liberal politics and education policy and offer new insights into the relationship between politics and policy by viewing this relationship through the lens of Lacanian psychoanalytic theory. As part of the background to this analysis, I argue that education and society are each riven by tensions, contradictions and paradoxes – something captured in the notion of crisis-impasse. Society ostensibly values

---

[1] Jodi Dean reminds us, as I have noted elsewhere (Clarke, 2012), that the term 'revolution' is one that the left has abandoned and the right embraced, pace the 'Thatcher revolution', the 'Reagan revolution' and the 'tea party revolution'. More recent examples include the Trump revolution (Mercer, 2016) and the 'Brexit revolution' (https://mainlymacro.blogspot.com/2017/11/the-brexit-revolution-and-its-source-of.html).

individuality but promotes conformity. Education simultaneously declares its allegiance to exclusivity and individual excellence on the one hand and to inclusivity and communal solidarity on the other. Lacanian psychoanalytic theory, I argue, is particularly helpful in thinking paradoxically. For example, as we shall see, Lacanian psychoanalytic theory views the origin of the subject as *neither* purely individual, or intimate, *nor* entirely social, or external, but as *both* intimate *and* external, or 'extimate'. Similarly, the realm of language and the symbolic order is seen as at one and the same time as regulatory and constraining yet also as site of potential freedom and creativity (McNulty, 2014; Ruti, 2012, 2017). The signifier itself – the basic unit of meaning within the symbolic realm – is at once characterized by the flickering alternation of presence and absence (Eagleton, 2001). In these and other instances, what are otherwise seen as two separate realms are viewed in Lacanian psychoanalytic theory as continuous and indistinguishable, a symbiosis symbolized by the Möbius strip, in which inside flows seamlessly into outside and vice versa. Similarly, Lacanian psychoanalytic theory does not share the neo-liberal meritocracy's view of the individual as someone who has complete agency, or control, in relation to his or her actions and life outcomes and whose desire is encapsulated in objectified commodities to be consumed for gratification, accumulation and advantage – what Teresa Brennan (1993, pp. 90–102) describes as 'the foundational fantasy'. But nor does it view the individual as completely at the mercy of social forces, as do some (albeit caricatured) versions of theories that stress the social determination of, and constraints upon, the subject, such as classic Marxism. Instead, rejecting the opposition between individual agency/freedom and social determination/ constraint, Lacanian psychoanalysis recognizes the agency of language, as part of the symbolic order, and of the unconscious. Paradoxically, it also views the individual, insofar as s/he remains a slave to the (assumed) desire of the Other, as the source of her or his own limitations. It is important to state at the outset, however, that the book adopts a broad reading of psychoanalytic theory, and hence I draw on the work of scholars, thinkers and writers from a range of disciplines, including political economy and cultural, literary and film studies, all of which provide evidence, if any were needed, of the growing relevance and take-up of psychoanalysis beyond the clinic (Frosh, 2010). But back to crisis . . .

Crisis? What crisis?

The period in the last century from 1914 to 1945 is often viewed as the quintessential era of crisis (Hobsbawm, 1994), dominated by the demonic figures of Hitler, Mussolini and Stalin, but it can be argued that it was equally linked to the developments and contradictions of capitalism (Anievas, 2014). The connections between capitalism and crisis were identified long ago by Marx, who highlighted the contradiction implicit in the capitalist's twin imperatives of maximizing production, while also minimizing wages and consequently reducing the capacity of labour to purchase the fruits of capitalist production. As Piketty argues in his critique of a return to 'patrimonial' capitalism, 'this inequality expresses a fundamental logical contradiction. The entrepreneur inevitably tends to become a rentier, more and more dominant over those who own nothing but their labor. Once constituted, capital reproduces itself faster than output increases. The past devours the future' (Piketty, 2014, p. 571). Examples of the many other contradictions of capitalism include its simultaneous promise of abundance and its reliance on scarcity, its promises of satisfaction and its dependence on unfulfilled desire, its valourization of competition and its tendency to produce monopolies (think of Google, Amazon ...) and its elevated rhetoric regarding the sanctity of private property rights and the dependence of these same rights on the power of the social state, including state-supported and enforced legal systems, contractual obligations and infrastructural provision (Harvey, 2014; McGowan, 2016).

Yet, crises are not just a matter of logical contradiction – they can also be read dialectically, as forms of creative destruction that are fundamental to the ongoing renewal and extension of capitalism as a system of social relations (Harvey, 2014; Klein, 2007; Mirowski, 2013). Moreover, to the extent that neo-liberalism – and even more so its most recent variant, austerity – represents an intensification of capitalist relations (Panitch and Gindin, 2012; Seymour, 2014), crises are even more central to social, economic and political reproduction in the neo-liberal era. This centrality generates an intensified need for narratives that frame crises as extraordinary events. Within such narratives, it is all too easy to conflate crises with natural disasters, as if they occurred with no connection to human activities and policies. Indeed, the promotion of ignorance, or 'agnotology', in relation to politico-economic crises has been one of the hallmark strategies of neo-liberal politics (Mirowski, 2013). However, as Gamble notes, 'within a discourse perspective, crises are not like natural disasters which are beyond human capacity to control. Crises are instead socially constructed within language and discourse ... out of particular interpretations and beliefs ... A crisis exists when enough people believe that it exists and act on that belief' (2014, p. 41; see also Gamble, 2009). In this sense crises have strategic dimensions, all too easily obscured behind populist and objectivist ontological assumptions, both in terms of their construction (Clarke and Newman, 2010) and their exploitation (Lipman, 2014).

Given the fundamental role of crises in the political economy of capitalism, and given 'the simple fact that investment in education and training is a sine qua non for capitalism's competitiveness' (Harvey, 2014, p. 184), the enduring presence of crises, manufactured or otherwise, as a recurring feature of the educational landscape should come as no surprise. And as in economics, so too in education, crises are used to foreshorten lines of thought and truncate possibilities for action. Hence, in response to repeated narratives about 'failing' public education, new hybrid forms of school, including 'charter schools', 'free schools', and 'academies', have been introduced, involving the benefits of state funding minus the inconvenience of responsibility to state regulation, on the assumption that, as a result of increased competition, the market's invisible hand will bring about greater educational success for all (Blacker, 2013, p. 34).

From crisis to impasse

Crises, however productive they may be for a minority of individuals and groups, are traumatic for the majority of society and for most of us, repeated crises lead to impasse. My use of this word is quite specific and is indebted to the work of Lauren Berlant, who describes it in the following terms:

> I offer impasse both as a formal term for encountering the duration of the present, and a specific term for tracking the circulation of precariousness through diverse locales and bodies. The concept of the present as impasse opens up different ways that the interruption of norms of the reproduction of life can be adapted to, felt out, and lived. The impasse is a space of time lived without a narrative genre ... the impasse is a cul-de-sac – indeed the word impasse was invented to replace cul-de-sac ... An impasse is a holding station that doesn't hold securely but opens out into anxiety, that dogpaddling around a space whose contours remain obscure. (2011, p. 199)

For many educators, enduring the 'terrors of performativity' (Ball, 2003) that have such a stranglehold on education and schooling, the stuck-ness suggested by the notion of impasse will have resonance. For hand in hand with the pervasive sense of crisis surrounding education has come a pandemic of policy initiatives, driven by 'beatific' fantasies of ever-improving exam results and improved performance in the international league tables that tests like the Organization for Economic Cooperation and Development's (OECD) *Programme for International Student*

Assessment, or PISA, have fed (Sellar, Thompson and Rutkowski, 2017), as well as 'horrific' fantasies of terminal educational decline, which policymakers threaten will ensue unless the reforms of the day are adopted (Clarke, 2012b). Yet, such policy hyperactivity has done little to empower or improve the lot of teachers and educators and has instead led to a sense of 'spinning wheels' (Hess, 2011) – an apt description of the state of impasse. For example, in their study of policy enactments in schools, Ball, Maguire and Braun found an absence of discourses beyond the dominant scripts of standards and accountability, while school staff clearly felt little ownership of, or derived much sense of empowerment from, the predominant neo-liberal performativity regime, with any resistance expressed 'only in asides, and occasional discontents and murmurings' (2012, p. 68). Indeed, we might describe today's educators as suffering a sense of 'policy alienation' (Tummers, 2013; Tummers, Bekkers and Steijn, 2012) in the face of an onslaught of policy reforms in which they have little stake or say.

The dynamics of this pervasive policy alienation is considered in this book in terms of Lacan's four discourses – introduced in the next chapter – and in particular, as a consequence of the dominance of the two authoritative discourses: the discourse of the master and the discourse of the university. One consequence of the prevalence of these discourses for educators has been a relative loss of 'voice' (Couldry, 2010); and this silencing can be considered constitutive of alienation, stymying opportunities for cathartic processes of symbolic sublimation through participation in conversations that matter (McAfee, 2008; Oliver, 2004). Ironically and paradoxically, this alienation on the part of educators – and one might argue of parents and students too – has occurred in a context in which education has been elevated to unique status as *the* pathway to individual realization and societal development, ushering in a world of unfettered freedom and undreamt of abundance for all.

Education, Education, Education . . .

As noted already, media and political concern with education has never been greater. Education policies, frequently legitimated by notions of crisis in public education and marketed under the label of education reform, have proliferated in recent decades in a range of global settings. Each instance, while characterized by significant contextually related differences, also manifests striking similarities reflecting the existence of a global neo-liberal imaginary (Rizvi and Lingard, 2010). Significantly, in relation the concerns of this book with psychoanalytic notions of fantasy, in each case education is paradoxically positioned as at once the perennial problem *and* as the potential panacea on the road to social and economic utopia.

In the UK, for example, 'Education, Education, Education' was how Tony Blair characterized his party's 1997 election priorities, though, despite hopes to the contrary, this largely amounted to a consolidation and extension of the previous conservative government's agenda of increased central control of curriculum coupled with an increased emphasis on marketization, 'choice' and competition under the New Labour 'mantra of modernization' (Forrester and Garratt, 2017, p. 16). In the United States, George W. Bush vowed that No Child would be Left Behind in his government's quest to raise standards in all US schools, through the tight coupling of eligibility for federal education funds and demonstrable achievement of minimum levels of proficiency as evidenced by the results of mandatory testing; less than a decade later, Barack Obama's administration announced a Race to the Top – an annual competitive funding round requiring state compliance with a number of specific requirements, including annual performance reviews for teachers and principals, implementation of standards-based core curricula, maintenance of data systems to track educational performance of all schools and students, removal of caps on charter schools and strategies to address the problem of low-performing schools. Meanwhile, on the other side of the world, in 2008 the Australian Labor party announced the need for a focus on 'quality education' as part of 'the case for an education revolution in our schools' (Commonwealth of Australia, 2008), though this largely amounted to a managerialist revolution involving an increased emphasis on performative accountability and transparency (Reid, 2009). At the international scale, in the year 2000, the United Nations Educational, Scientific and Cultural Organization (UNESCO) announced the Education for All Movement, involving 'a global commitment to provide quality basic education for all children, youth and adults' (UNESCO, 2000) – though this and other similar developments by global institutions have been critiqued for their embedded neo-liberal assumptions regarding the economic rationale for education and for their 'business as usual' donor perspectives masquerading behind pious rhetoric about the emancipatory potential of education (McKenzie, 2012; Opolot, 2003; Rutkowski, 2007). All the while, the pages and websites of both corporate and social media are regularly occupied by prognoses and prescriptions for education, posing problems and suggesting solutions to the purported shortcomings of schools, students and, in particular, teachers. Education has clearly been overburdened, tasked with onerous responsibilities and loaded with unrealistic expectations (Bridges,

2008), but at the same time, perhaps this is in part because education seems capable of meaning all things to all people – an omnipresent, omniscient and omnipotent phenomenon that is always at fault but at the same time able to right all wrongs and compensate for past and present shortfalls in efficiency, justice and equity. This raises the question of what do we mean by the signifier, 'education'?

Education as an empty signifier

In thinking further about this question of what we mean by education, it is helpful to be mindful of the connections between sociopolitical ideologies and educational provision in modern society and the ways in which education policy is inextricably linked to the social, economic and political imperatives of the time. Thus, we can see links between a conservative political ideology and an emphasis on education as the instillation of correct moral values, the transmission of a revered cultural canon and the preservation of time-honoured traditions. We can trace the connections between a social democratic orientation in politics and an emphasis on education policies deemed to promote increased equality of opportunity and enhanced social integration. Likewise, to take an example with particular contemporary salience, we can identify the links between a neo-liberal insistence on sustained growth and increased productivity as the only legitimate economic values and the competitive, instrumental and atomistic logics of neo-liberal education policy (Clarke, 2012b).

But beyond these considerations, I want to suggest that 'education' is a classic example of what, following Laclau (1996), we can describe as an 'empty signifier'. Such a signifier, as Gunder and Hillier (2009, p. 3, n2) note, is not really empty since a signifier cannot be without signification; rather, the empty signifier is emptied of specific, concrete meanings in order to embody an aspiration (necessarily fantasmatic) towards completeness, fullness and harmony, a yearning for an ideal social order. In this sense, empty signifiers are also floating signifiers insofar as 'floating requires a tendential emptiness' and vice versa (Laclau, 2014, p. 20). As such, empty signifiers are not an aberration but a fundamental aspect of the (political) order of discourse. As Žižek puts it, 'in every set of signifiers there is always "at least one" which functions as the signifier of the very lack of the signifier. This signifier is the Master Signifier: the "empty" signifier which totalizes ("quilts") the dispersed field – in it, the infinite chain of causes ("knowledge") is interrupted with an abyssal, non-founded act of violence' (2008 [1992], p. 119). Empty signifiers thus serve to bind together and articulate a range of other signifiers within a particular discursive formation (Laclau, 1996, p. 44). They also serve, despite their enigmatic nature, to bind together members of a community:

> Suffice it to recall how a community functions: the master signifier that guarantees the community's consistency is a signifier whose signified is an enigma for the members themselves – nobody really knows what it means, but each of them somehow presupposes that others know it, that it has to mean 'the real thing', and so they use it all the time. (Žižek, 2002, p. 58)

An example of an empty signifier from political discourse is the term 'freedom', which was emptied of any concrete, specific meaning, while simultaneously binding together and articulating a number of other signifiers such as 'democracy', 'capitalism' and 'us' (the United States), in order to represent an idealized universal value for the Bush regime and the community that identified with it and thus serve to legitimate the regime's 'war on terror' waged against those who were deemed to threaten this value. In similar fashion, empty signifiers such as 'quality', 'standards' and 'reform' articulate the discourse of neo-liberal education policy and bind together members of the education community in a shared sense of (un)knowing.

In order to disguise the gap between the idealized state and current realities, as well as to provide the mechanism for a continued campaign to turn the latter into the former, the discursive production of empty signifiers typically relies on various forms of fantasmatic support. These can be of two contrasting types (Glynos and Howarth, 2007): the positive, 'beatific' fantasy – *if we improve standards in education we will ensure our economic competitiveness in the global marketplace* – or the negative, 'horrific' fantasy – *unless we ensure the maintenance of our traditional national identity through a common core curriculum, society will fragment leading to destructive social upheaval.* In each instance, the empty signifier can only fulfil its function through the support of fantasy: 'the other side of semiotic emptiness is fantasmatic fullness' (Stavrakakis, 1999, p. 81). This 'other side' of the semiotic emptiness of the signifier education – this fantasmatic fullness – is one of several meanings suggested by this book's subtitle, *The Other Side of Education*, in that I seek to foreground the reliance of recent neo-liberal policy discourses in education on fantasy in its various guises.

In surveying the education policy reforms of various national governments, briefly sketched above, a number of common themes are evident. Accountability and transparency, standards-based or core curriculum, high-stakes testing, teacher quality and professional teacher standards, choice and competition – such are some of the policy foci that characterize the education policy-scape in a range of international contexts. These recurring themes, and the education policy proliferation in which they are embodied, can be read as manifestations of Toulmin's (1990) three pillars of modernity, that is, *certainty*, formal rationality, or *systematicity*, and the absence of memory, or *the clean slate*. That is, neo-liberal education reforms – perhaps like all policy – are never couched in the sort of tentative modality that might admit self-doubt or be open to uncertainty; for example, policymakers all too often exhibit a blind faith that increased competition between schools and choice for (some) parents will drive up standards across the board. This certainty is underpinned by assumptions about the systematic alignment of various phenomena, such as achievement in test scores being an accurate measure of student learning and hence a true reflection of teacher quality. We can see both certainty and systematicity at work in the following quote from England's former Secretary of State for Education, Michael Gove: 'We need to create more new schools to generate innovation, raise expectations, give parents choice and drive up standards through competition' (Gove, 2012). At the same time, neo-liberal education policy typically exhibits a wilful failure to learn from, or even acknowledge, the lessons offered by temporally or spatially distant experiences of policy failure. We can see this, for example, in the Blair and Obama regimes' intensification rather than reversal, let alone amelioration, of the policies – and hence of the numerous problems stemming from them – of their predecessors; we also see it in the Australian government's borrowing, in the accountability regime associated with their education revolution, of policies developed and implemented by their counterparts in England and New York, without paying sufficient attention to the differences in histories, contexts and cultures between borrower and lender (Lingard, 2010) or, as significantly, to critical evaluations that cast doubt on their effectiveness.

In many ways, the neo-liberal hegemony in education policy amounts to a managerialist takeover of education. This new version of education is underpinned by the same individualistic ontology and objectivist epistemology that shore up much traditional social science and has been influential in policy studies – of which more below – while management-derived understandings of growth and productivity, audit and risk management, accountability and transparency, reside at its core, thus furthering the conquest, commonly described as neo-liberalism, of all other aspects of life by economics. Against neo-liberalism's managerialist revolution, this book counterposes the 'ongoing revolution' of psychoanalytic thought, drawing inspiration from the 'adventure of insight' (Felman, 1987) that this body of thought potentially provides, as a tool with which to rethink and resist neo-liberalism's colonization of education policy in recent years. That is not to say that psychoanalytic thought provides all the answers or that it represents a pure 'good' in contrast to neo-liberalism's 'bad', but merely that it offers an alternative framework within which to conceptualize education with which to counter what Fielding and Moss (2011) characterize as the 'There is no alternative' hegemony of neo-liberal education policy. The psychoanalytic revolution Felman refers to asks us to rethink fundamental questions, such as: *What does it mean to be human? What does it mean to think?* (1987, p. 9). Following this line of thought, this book draws on psychoanalytic theories to ask fundamental questions, such as: *What is education? How is it currently (and how might it be differently) constructed as an (ontological) object? What are its current and potential purposes? What does it mean to educate? What does it mean to be educated? What are the implications for education – for schools, teachers and students – and for society of dominant, and potential alternative, policy directions?*

These questions may seem somewhat abstract and philosophical, but policy is deeply bound up with philosophical questions about the nature of education – it is 'at least partly about the overall aims that a society has for itself and about how these aims are realised in practice. It cannot, therefore, be a neutral, technical exercise, but is invariably a deeply ethical, political and cultural one bound up with ideas about the good society and how life can be worthwhile' (Winch and Gingell, 2004, p. vi). This book draws on ethical, political and cultural ideas and insights from Lacanian psychoanalytic theory, in order to offer critical insights into recent and contemporary directions in education policy and suggest, if not fully developed concrete alternatives, then at least glimpses of alternatives – glimpses of what I am calling, in another of the title's several meanings, 'the other side of education'.

Education policy studies

In order to further locate this book's project for the reader, I offer the following brief and somewhat simplified sketch of policy studies in education. As Rizvi and Lingard note, policy studies is a relatively recent discipline (2010, p. 1) and in the case of critical policy studies this is even more so. As recently as 1985, for instance, Prunty outlined the contours of a social theory informed, critical approach to policy studies, expressing the hope that 'the ideas presented in this article may stimulate others to consider the prospects of a critical perspective, and serve as signposts to such pursuits' (1985, p. 138). The predominant tendency prior to this was, as Prunty notes, the 'policy science' approach, which sought to limit policy analysis to either descriptions of the status quo or offer technical recommendations for enhancing policy's efficiency, while downplaying its ethical dimensions and obscuring its political implications.

Illustrative of the policy science approach is the functionalist paradigm, which was grounded in an objectivist, rather than a social constructionist, worldview.

> The functionalist paradigm is based upon the assumption that society has a concrete, real existence, and a systemic character oriented to produce an ordered and regulated state of affairs ... The ontological assumptions encourage a belief in the possibility of an objective and value-free social science in which the scientist is distanced from the scene which he or she is analyzing through the rigor and technique of the scientific method. (Morgan, 1980, p. 608, cited in Prunty, 1984, p. 14)

As Prunty notes in the same paper, policy science was steeped in functionalist assumptions about the nature of policy and approaches to its analysis. From this perspective, policy studies are largely conceived as a technical, scientific endeavour reflected in the term policy science. Such policy science targets and seeks to solve 'problems', which are seen as enjoying a distinct and independent existence in relation to their analysis and solution. The most well-known advocate of this highly rational and systematic approach was Harold Lasswell (1951). Within this policy science approach – which went on to have its heyday in the 1960s, the age of Sputnik and of unbridled confidence in the progressive potential of science, but which still remains influential with politicians and policymakers and underpins contemporary 'evidence based' approaches to policy – the process of policy studies is conceived in terms of a series of stages that constitute the policy 'cycle', including the rational analysis of the policy context, the identification of competing policy options, the determination of which option was most likely to meet the objectives of the relevant policy agenda, followed by its formulation, implementation and evaluation as policy (Kay, 2011; Rizvi and Lingard, 2010; Tribe, 1972). There was little sense that the problem might be constructed through the very formulation of its solution, that is, that the policy process as practised was as much solution-led as it was problem-driven. There was little awareness of the location of specific policy fields, like *education* within a unique array of historical, social, cultural, political and economic discourses and practices; rather, education policy was more an applied version of a generic field of policy studies. And there was little sense that policy analysts' situated subjectivities influenced their perception of the 'issues' they studied or recognition that policy (facts) and politics (values) were mutually imbricated. The guiding principles of such an approach, particularly its adherence to 'two constricted conceptions [that] may be termed, respectively, objectivism and instrumental rationality' (Dryzek, 1993, p. 213), can be read as a reflection of traditional social science's status anxiety in relation to the natural sciences and its consequent adoption of the assumptions presumed to underpin the latter (Flyvbjerg, 2001), as well as perennial anxieties on the part of policy analysts and policymakers regarding the relevance and transfer of policy research (Ozga, 2007).

In more philosophical terms, policy science presumes an ontology of the purely rational and fully conscious mind and 'depends on, indeed axiomatically assumes, a positive, rationalist, realist epistemology' (McSwite, 1997, p. 57). In this sense, policy science approaches to policy studies resonate with what Kamberelis and Dimitriadis (2005) refer to, in relation to qualitative research in education, as the chronotope of 'objectivism and representation', embracing a correspondence theory of truth and an objectivist perspective on knowledge, while discounting the constitutive role of language and the influence of interpersonal relations. In the context of policy studies, such an approach asserts the possibility of analysis mapping, directly and unproblematically, onto the facts of an objectively conceived world in a one-to-one fashion in order to produce valid and reliable knowledge, with scant suspicion that knowledge might be partial and interested, or that language might be anything other than 'a neutral medium for accurately *representing* observed relations in the external world ... [as] unmediated, uninterested transmission of facts' (Kamberelis and Dimitriadis, 2005, p. 29, emphasis in original).[2]

In contrast to this scientifically conceived world of objective facts and solutions, pragmatic approaches reflected in the work of figures like Lindblom (1959, 1979), and Wildavsky (1979), highlighted the messiness of the policy process, including deliberation but also debate, consultation, critique and contestation, all in the context of unpredictable political environments and complex interpersonal relationships. Far from being a rational science, policy from this perspective was a matter of 'muddling through' to use Lindblom's memorable expression. More recently, critical approaches to policy studies,

---

[2] Space does not permit a detailed exploration of Kamberelis and Dmitriadis's chronotopes approach to qualitative research studies but it is worth noting the parallels between their framework and Jones's (2013) four orientations framework in relation to policy analysis, as well as between these two and Lacan's four discourses.

pioneered by figures like Prunty and influenced by developments in social theory and continental philosophy, particularly poststructuralist insights into the mutually implicated nature of power and knowledge that have shaken naïve faith in reason and unsettled assumptions about progress, underline the impossibility of direct and unproblematic representation of social reality. Here the separation of facts and values, ends and means, and policy from politics is problematized. The policy process is recognized as complicated by the multiple, conflicting interests at stake and the inevitable gaps between policy intention and policy enactment. Here the analyst's subjectivity, bias and experience, along with theoretical framings and language choices, are all recognized as complicating factors that inevitably mediate the relationship between policy problems and their analysis. Here, rather than policy analysis being viewed as separate and distinct from the objects it studies, the former is now seen as crucial in the construction of the latter. Overall, power – something that was either off the radar or conceived in mechanistic, zero-sum terms in the world of scientifically conceived policy studies – is now recognized, in both its repressive and its productive dimensions, as inseparable from the formulation of either policy problems or policy solutions.

These changes and complexities in the nature of policy studies have been given further impetus by what Ball refers to as 'the changing form and modalities of the state' (2008, p. 9). While space does not permit a detailed treatment of these changes, it is important to note how a range of developments in the social and economic sphere have all contributed to the increasing prominence of the global as a scale and a modality in the practice and analysis of policy. These developments include the exponential growth of computing power and development of digital technologies, the increasingly multinational nature of business enterprises along with the associated 'flows' of capital and people. They also include the growth of quasi-governmental bodies such as the World Bank, the International Monetary Fund and the Organization for Economic Cooperation and Development – the latter body playing a particularly significant role in the creation of a global space of educational commensurability and comparison through technologies such as the PISA testing regime (Grek, 2009; Lingard, Martino and Rezai-Rashti, 2013; Sellar and Lingard, 2013; Sellar et al., 2017). And while this newly prominent global scale has by no means replaced or supplanted the national scale, its increasing prominence has undoubtedly involved a reframing of the nation's responsibilities and capacities, altering the very nature of social, political and economic life for countless millions of individuals – for some, for the better, for many, for the worse. This reframing, and the consequent radical changes in the very fabric of social endeavours, including education, is also the fruit of the ideational, ideological and institutional project known as neo-liberalism.

> Just as a social imaginary of neoliberal globalization has been a central component in the creation of the global market, so it has been within the global field of education policy. A global field of education policy is now established ... as a global commensurate space of measurement of educational performance. (Rizvi and Lingard, 2010, p. 67)

As Rizvi and Lingard suggest, there are complex ties between the changes associated with globalization and the 'open-ended and contradictory process of politically assisted market rule' that has unfolded in a range of global contexts over the past three decades and which we can describe as 'neoliberalization' (Peck, 2010, p. xi). Indeed, as Larner notes, 'neoliberalism appears to have usurped globalisation as *the* explanatory term for contemporary forms of economic restructuring' (Larner, 2003, p. 509, emphasis in original). This ubiquitous if complex and troublesome, phenomenon, including its origins and its manifestations in education policy are explored in the following chapter.

This book approaches policy in a way that foregrounds its textual and discursive nature, which is not to downplay the significance and complexity of the processes by which texts and discourses emerge and are enacted in institutional contexts (Ball, 1993; Ball et al., 2012). In foregrounding this book's approach, it is also important to emphasize that texts and discourses, far from merely embodying abstract meanings, directly act upon the world by promoting certain lines of thought and action as reasonable and others as unintelligible. In Lacanian terms, discourse forms a social link grounded in language. But a Lacanian approach to policy and policy discourse also highlights the gaps and slippages between communicative acts and unconscious thought processes (Nobus and Quinn, 2005). These ideas are explored further in the following section.

Psychoanalysis and the other side of education

> Psychoanalysis, whether Freudian or Lacanian, is a thoroughgoing form of philosophical, ontological critique.
>
> Žižek in Irwin and Motoh, 2014, p. 139

An obvious question that arises in relation to a book such as this is what psychoanalytic theory, and specifically a Lacanian lens, has to offer in thinking about the challenges facing education and education policy. In addressing this question below, I will briefly introduce some of the specific concepts and tools which will be explained in greater detail in the next chapter before being mobilized in the critical analysis comprising the subsequent four chapters which are structured in terms of Lacan's four discourses.

At first glance, education policy and Lacanian psychoanalytic theory may seem strange bedfellows. After all, education is public, institutional and mandatory whereas psychoanalysis is private, personal and discretionary. Yet, common ground between psychoanalysis and education can be identified on a number of fronts. Both mass schooling and psychoanalytic practice are symptoms of the rise of modernity and the development of urban industrial environments; both educational and psychoanalytic practice involve interpersonally mediated processes of generating insights through a dialectic between inner and outer worlds, knowledge and ignorance, conscious and unconscious; and both educating and psychoanalysing are instances of what Freud referred to (along with a third, governing, the domain of politics and policy) as 'impossible professions' (Bibby, 2011; Britzman, 2009; Freud, 1937).

Alongside these common dimensions, however, significant differences exist between the rationalities of policy and Lacanian psychoanalytic thought. As noted earlier, education policy tends to be framed in terms of a search for solutions to problems (even though, as also noted earlier the 'problem' is often identified in order to legitimate the solution) and is underpinned by a logic of reconciliation, requiring adaptation between individual and society, and between psychic and social reality, in order to ensure that in each case the former is made to 'fit' the latter. By contrast, Lacanian psychoanalytic theory foregrounds the irreducible difference characterizing the social subject, whose non-self-coincidence manifests in a series of divisions: between conscious and unconscious; knowledge and desire; imaginary, symbolic and real registers of the psyche. From a Lacanian psychoanalytic perspective, then, we are all irredeemably 'misfits', implying a view of education as helping us in understanding and come to terms with our lack-of-fit, rather than coercing, shaping and suppressing psychic realities in order to ensure these conform to societal demands and adapt to institutional requirements (Clarke, 2018a; Donald, 1992; Ellsworth, 1997).

An objection may be raised with regard to the transference of psychoanalytic ideas, developed in the clinical setting, to wider social contexts including their deployment in academic work. Here I would follow Frosh (2010) in arguing that notions such as the unconscious, desire and fantasy are of too great a significance to be ignored when they clearly have insights to offer beyond the clinical encounter. The challenge then becomes 'not that of justifying psychoanalysis, but rather of deploying it creatively and yet with integrity' (Frosh, 2010, p. 4). In relation to this point, it is important to stress at the outset that my engagement with psychoanalytic theory does not involve the 'application' of its ideas to education policy, for to attempt to do so would be to do both violence and injustice to each domain; rather, one can use such theories 'only as enabling metaphorical devices, not as extrapolated, preconceived items of knowledge' (Felman, 1987, p. 11). Indeed, given the extralinguistic dimension that Lacanian psychoanalysis presumes – a dimension involving objects we can point towards but cannot reach, objects that resist symbolization and lie beyond signification, objects in relation to which language is always insuperably inadequate – the very notion of 'application' appears reductive and simplistic. In this context, I view psychoanalytic theory as offering glimpses of what I am referring to as 'the other side of education' in order to consider what possibilities and perspectives this might open up for education policy. That is to say, I see psychoanalytic theory as capable of illuminating education policy in particular and distinctive ways, affording fresh insights and suggesting creative possibilities to contrast with the grandiose but moribund certainties of neo-liberal education policy. But critically, this is not the same as offering a set of recipes or blueprints for educational policy and anyone seeking such is bound to be disappointed. Rather, as implied in the book's subtitle *The Other Side of Education*, I seek to explore potential insights and implications that a Lacanian psychoanalytic reading of the other and otherness, including the otherness residing within each of us as individuals and groups, as a form of irreducible difference within the same, might hold for 'the very thought of education'.[3]

The following chapter introduces key elements of Lacanian psychoanalytic theory, including the key role of desire and fantasy, and outlines Lacan's theory of the four discourses. The subsequent four chapters each takes one of Lacan's four discourses as the starting point for thinking about 'the other side of education' in various guises. Specifically, on the grounds that education and education policy can only be understood in light of the political developments shaping wider society, Chapter 3 offers a critical genealogy of neo-liberal politics, read in terms of Lacan's discourse of the master and the dominance of particular economic master signifiers – money and the market. Here the critical role of would-be 'masters of the universe' (Stedman Jones, 2012), such as Friedrich Hayek and Milton Friedman, the networking activities of the 'neoliberal thought collective' (Mirowski, 2013; Mirowski and Plehwe, 2009), and the power of persuasion and

---

[3] Readers will recognize this as the title of Britzman's 2009 book on psychoanalysis and education.

ideas (Burgin, 2012; Warren, Webb, Franklin and Bowers-Brown, 2012), are given a prominent place in the narrative. Chapter 4 examines the manifestations of the dominance of neo-liberal politics in the realm of education policy. Reading these developments in terms of Lacan's discourse of the university, it examines how education has become enmeshed in highly controlling and punitive forms of bureaucratic governance, and how selective forms of expertise have been drawn on to legitimate particular policies as necessary and natural, in the process disavowing the inevitably political nature of education. Chapter 5 reads the unceasing criticisms of education, schools and teachers on the part of education policymakers and the media in terms of Lacan's discourse of the hysteric. It also examines the manifestation of the pillorying of education and schools as represented in the regressive resurgence of older nineteenth-century models of schooling. Chapter 6 takes the discourse of the analyst – associated with analysing and revolutionizing – as a prompt to think about the possibilities for resisting the violence and closure of contemporary education policy and instead envisioning education as a form of permanent revolution. Chapter 7 offers a brief anti-conclusion that briefly reviews the book's journey and considers the implications for policymakers and education practitioners of Lacanian psychoanalytic theory for thinking about and realizing 'the other side of education', beyond the discourses of crisis and impasse, in the twenty-first century.

2

Contexts and Concepts: Capitalism and Desire

Part of the world has resolutely turned in the direction of the service of goods, thereby rejecting everything that that has to do with the relationship of man to desire – it is what is known as the postrevolutionary perspective. The only things it be said is that people don't seem to have realized that, by formulating things in this way, one is simply perpetuating the eternal tradition of power, namely, 'Let's keep on working, and as far as desire is concerned, come back later'.

Lacan, 1992, p. 318

Introduction

As noted in the previous chapter, this book provides a critical analysis, informed by Lacanian psychoanalytic theory, of recent and contemporary education policy. Specifically, I draw on Lacan's discourse theory and his theory of the four discourses – Lacan's attempt to explore the mutations of power and authority in society and their influence on subjectivity (Schuster, 2016, p. 170) – to explore the assumptions and assertions about the world, about human relations and about the sorts of people we are and can become that are embedded in education policy and politics. As part of this analysis, I look at the ways education policy limits and constrains, yet also shapes and moulds, what we – policymakers, parents, teachers, students, the media and the wider public – think education is and what its purposes are. In recent times, the possibilities for imagining what education, and hence education policy, might be have been particularly influenced by the politico-economic settlement, known as neo-liberalism – a term with a complex history and a contested literature (Cahill and Konings, 2017). Critically for my argument, neo-liberal capitalism has thrived by taking advantage of our psychic 'economies' and, in particular, the restless, unstaunchable and insatiable character of desire.

Recognizing desire

We usually think of desire in terms of our desire for this object or for that person. At the same time, we are all familiar with the experience of attaining the object of our desire, only to discover that this item or person on which we had pinned our hopes for finding satisfaction, and which we had invested with a certain aura, is just an ordinary material object like all our others or just an ordinary person like us. This also occurs in matters like school choice, when the institutions in which parents invest significant emotional and financial resources fail to meet their elevated expectations (Campbell, Proctor and Sherrington, 2009). For Lacan, this is because desire is constitutive of who and what we are and cannot be eliminated or satisfied. Desire in this Lacanian reading is secondary in the sense of being the desire, not so much for this or that object or person, but the desire for more desire – 'desire is produced not as a striving for something but only as a striving for something else or something more' (Copjec, 1994, p. 55). The secondary nature of desire arises from its genesis in our constitution as subjects of language and of the signifier. For the signifier is always the signifier of an absence, serving as a stand-in for the object and reliant on further signifiers for its explication. Crucially, this ceaseless sliding of signification means that language can never say everything, that there is no final word and thus that meaning is always open to further refinement, elaboration, clarification and contradiction. To the extent that it is linked to the shifting sands of the social order of language and the symbolic – which is one reading of Lacan's oft-cited aphorism that desire is always the desire of the other (Lacan, 1981, p. 235) – and given the absence of any firm foundation for the symbolic order of language, one consequence is that desire is essentially empty. In other words, 'desire has no content – it is for nothing – because language can deliver to us no incontrovertible truth, no positive goal' (Copjec, 1994, p. 55).

This emptiness renders desire vulnerable to colonization by the seductions of marketing and capitalism's promises that our desires will be fully met if we follow the latest fashion, acquire the new improved model or identify with the right brand. Neo-liberalism has exploited this vulnerability and extended capitalism's reach by rendering evermore areas of life susceptible to the competitive and comparative logics of the market. Not only do we have to choose between brands of washing powder, but we are also exhorted to compare our options and make choices about the companies that provide our water and electricity, the institutions and schemes we believe will best meet our and our families' health and social care needs and the schools we send our children to.

However, the socio-symbolic orientation of the ways in which we seek satisfaction does not exhaust Lacan's thinking about desire. Although our language always carries traces of desire it does not articulate the whole truth about our desire, meaning that there is always a residue or surplus left over that exceeds the symbolic (Evans, 1996, p. 36). Put differently, by inducting us into a world of meaning, the signifier simultaneously alienates us from unmediated access to being while also arousing 'the desire for nonbeing, for an *in*determinate something that is perceived as *extra*discrusive' (Copjec, 1994, p. 56). Gaining a full sense of the significance of this extra discursive element for psychoanalytic understanding of desire requires introducing the notion of *das Ding* (the Thing), which for Lacan, as for Freud, represents a purportedly 'lost' object, offering unlimited, and unmediated satisfaction – in other words, offering access to the overwhelming experience of *jouissance*. Critically, the Thing is not an actually existing object so much as an object, the existence of which we retrospectively project as a consequence of our enculturation into the social order of the symbolic, and in pursuit of which we spend our lives in the hope that by recapturing it we will one day undo our alienation. Any complete reconnection, of course, is impossible since the lost object is a retrospective projection, consequent upon subordination to the signifier; and even were it attainable, the object's attainment would entail a return to prelinguistic, pre-subjective existence and thus the sacrifice our recognizability as social subjects (McGowan, 2013, 2016; Ruti, 2012, 2017; Shepherdson, 2008). It is for this reason that we seek objects of desire (*objets a*) that carry an echo or trace of the Thing, thereby compensating us for its inevitable absence.

Its impossible nature notwithstanding, the Thing exerts a pervasive influence on our lives – for in Lacan's words 'at the heart of man's destiny is the *Ding*' (Lacan, 1992, p. 97) – compelling us to pursue its refracted reflection in the objects, people and experiences that populate our lives. It is this aspect of desire, its capacity to connect us to the traces of the Thing, that lies behind Lacan's assertion that 'the channel in which desire is located is not simply that of the modulation of the signifying chain, but that which flows beneath it as well' and that explains his characterization of desire as 'the metonymy of our being' (Lacan, 1992, p. 321). For education we may be subjects of knowledge but for psychoanalysis we are first and foremost subjects of desire.

The centrality of desire in our lives explains Lacan's ethics of desire, captured in his proposition that 'the only thing one can be guilty of is giving ground relative to one's desire' (Lacan, 1992, p. 321). This can be taken as a formula for self-indulgence but as Mari Ruti helpfully points out, desire is among other things relational, connecting us to the worlds of other people, social experiences and external objects that lie beyond ourselves and, in this sense, in asking us to remain faithful to our desire, Lacan is asking us to take responsibility for the consequences of our desire, and the actions undertaken in the name of our desire, for others (Ruti, 2017, pp. 80–1). In other words, Lacan's ethics of desire asks us to take responsibility for our assumption of subjectivity as subjects of desire in the absence of any final or ultimate ethical ground (Neill, 2011).

Desire is thus a double-edged sword. On the one hand, our relentless quest for satisfaction renders us vulnerable to the seductions and predations of an insatiable capitalist machinery as it 'drives us to move restlessly from one object of desire to the next in pursuit of the perfect object that would finally bring our desire to an end by offering us complete satisfaction' (Ruti, 2017, p. 222). On the other hand, our fidelity to the stubborn singularity of our desire can be a source of resistance to coercion and conformity, particularly when it insists on persons, objects or values that resonate to the frequency of the Thing, thereby enabling us to approach the Thing's sublime aura obliquely and providing us with the possibility of drawing upon its uniquely enlivening energies (Ruti, 2017, pp. 72–8).

Recognizing desire thus helps us to understand the possibilities as well as the difficulties of resisting the machinery of capitalism with its promises of satisfaction. This is particularly the case when, as under neo-liberalism, it extends its temptations and exhortations into ever-wider domains of life and ever-deeper recesses of our psyches; when its promises and its lures are accessible to us at any time and in any place via digital technology; and when it elicits our complicity by entangling our personal and professional lives in the anxious logics of quantification, measurement and metrics (Beer, 2016; Muller, 2018). But exhortations and temptations to neglect our deepest desires – the ones that carry the echo of the Thing – in order to devote ourselves to what Lacan refers to above as 'the service of goods' are nothing new. In order to consider some of these ideas further, the following discussion explores them in relation to Billy Wilder's 1960 film, *The Apartment*.

'Be a mensch!'

Despite its surface humour, *The Apartment* offers a searing critique of a world in which lives are dedicated to the deities of money and status and in which those in positions of power and authority exploit and prey upon others for their own advantage. In Lacanian terms, the film highlights how our dedication to 'the service of goods' leads us to compromise on the ethics of our desire. The banality of this world is signalled in the opening voice-over as we are told by the main character, insurance clerk C. C. 'Bud' Baxter (Jack Lemmon), that if the entire population of New York was laid head to toe they would extend all the way from Times Square to Karachi, Pakistan – pointless information that highlights the rationalization of human intercourse and the vacuousness of the system, while also subtly suggesting the laying-low of humanity that the film critiques (Armstrong, 2000).

Early in the film, Bud gets promoted as a consequence of loaning his apartment to executives in his firm as a venue for their extramarital affairs. However, focused on attaining promotion above all else, Bud is too busy enjoying the perks that come with it, including a key to the executive washroom and the ability to upgrade his attire, to think about the moral dimensions of his actions. Symbolically, he exchanges the key to the apartment, as a token of his personal integrity, for the executive washroom key, representing dedication to career advancement. But Bud is not entirely without romantic feelings and invites Fran Kubelik (Shirley MacLaine), the quirky elevator operator, to join him at a show, *The Music Man*, with tickets given him by the Personnel Director, Sheldrake, in exchange for the use of the apartment. Unbeknownst to Bud, Fran has been in an affair with Sheldrake and, on reconciling with him on the evening of the show, she stands Baxter up. Later, at the office Christmas party, Fran hands a cracked compact mirror to Bud to reassure him that he looks fine in his new executive attire. In a powerful moment, Bud recognizes the mirror as the one he found in the apartment the night after Sheldrake and his mistress had used it and as he gazes into its cracked surface, his face registers the sudden descent from buoyant gaiety to devastated dismay as he puts two and two together. The fragmented image of his face represents the divided nature of his subjectivity, split between pimp and dupe, while his desire is similarly split between unthinking professional ambition and romantic love, with Fran representing the knot linking these two incompatible worlds. In Lacanian terms, mirrors are associated with illusions of coherence, and in this sense, the broken mirror represents recognition of the enduring tragedy of human life and the non-coincidence between social and psychic reality, between external appearances and inner experience:

Fran: What's the matter?
Bud: The mirror, it's broken.
Fran: Yes, I know, I like it that way. Makes me look the way I feel.

Later that evening we see Sheldrake and Fran in the apartment. The atmosphere is as dark as the lighting, as Sheldrake back tracks on earlier commitments to initiate a divorce from his wife. A despondent Fran hands him a Christmas gift and he, clearly having not thought about a gift for her, opens his wallet and gives her a one-hundred-dollar bill before he departs, laden with a pile of wrapped gifts for his family. Recognizing his duplicity, Fran takes half a bottle of sleeping pills in a suicide attempt, only to be saved when Bud returns and, finding her lying in his bed, rushes to fetch the doctor who lives in the neighbouring apartment. With Fran out of danger, the doctor gives Bud – who he takes to be a playboy on the basis of the stream of empty liquor bottles and carnal sounds that emanate from the apartment – a lecture on his hedonistic lifestyle, admonishing him to grow up and 'be a mensch', a human being. A week later, at the end of the film, Bud repeats these words when he stands up to Sheldrake by refusing to give him a new key to the apartment to replace the one Sheldrake threw away in a moment of panic about the possible discovery of his affair. Bud does give Sheldrake a key but it turns out to be the wrong – or in terms of fidelity to the ethics of desire, the right – one:

Sheldrake:	Say, Baxter, you gave me the wrong key.
Bud:	No, I didn't.
Sheldrake:	But this is the key to the executive washroom.
Bud:	That's right, Mr Sheldrake, I won't be needing it because I'm all washed up around here.
Sheldrake:	What's gotten into you Baxter?
Bud:	Just following doctor's orders. I've decided to become a mensch. Know what that means? A human being.
Sheldrake:	Now hold on, Baxter . . .
Bud:	Save it. The old payola won't work anymore. Goodbye, Mr Sheldrake.

Bud thus bids farewell to his enslavement to 'the service of goods'; and, of course, this being Hollywood, finds his fidelity to the singular track of his desire rewarded as Fran slips away from Sheldrake on the stroke of midnight at a New Year's Eve party and joins Bud in his apartment to celebrate the New Year and, presumably, the start of their new life together. Bud has finally ceased compromising and assumed ethical responsibility for the singular track of his desire. Of course, this is fiction and in real life the brief happy ending would inevitably be a prelude to further trials and tribulations. The couple may be united for the requisite Hollywood ending, and Bud may have learned a powerful lesson about integrity through fidelity to the Thing, but the mirror remains now and forever broken with no final redemption beyond an uneasy reconciliation with lack-in-being. The inevitable challenges that lie ahead include general existential dilemmas, arising from the lack of 'fit' between psychic and social reality, self and other, as well as those challenges related specifically to a capitalist society characterized by an untenable relation between, as Fran puts it, the 'takers' and those they take from. But critical as it is of American capitalism, it is sobering to note that *The Apartment* was made during the heyday of Keynesianism; since that time the pervasive exhortations and temptations of capitalism have only become amplified as a consequence of the social, technological, economic and political developments comprising neo-liberalism that are discussed below.

A brief history of neo-liberalism

In ambition, depth, degree of break with the past, variety of sites being colonized, impact on common sense and everyday behaviour, restructuring of the social architecture, neo-liberalism does constitute a *hegemonic project*. (Hall, 2011, p. 728, emphasis in original)

If ever a political philosophy warranted the label hegemonic, surely it is neo-liberalism, at least insofar as the prospect of a serious political aspirant articulating a program based around central economic planning, public ownership of resources, anti-competition, anti-choice and pro big-government is well-nigh unthinkable; and even if some of these policies have been advocated by counter-hegemonic politicians like Bernie Saunders and Jeremy Corbyn, prevailing wisdom says that, were they elected, the disciplining effects of the neo-liberal establishment and the pro-neo-liberal markets will force their abandonment as happened with the 'asphyxiation' of Syriza in Greece in 2015 (Varoufakis, 2016, p. 232). As Harvey observes (2005, p. 3), neo-liberalism has become 'the common-sense way many of us interpret, live in and understand the world', while Mirowski notes 'the accretion of neoliberal attitudes, imaginaries, and practices that have come to inform everyday life in the first few decades of the new millennium' (2013, p. 90; see also Braedly and Luxton, 2010). As Saad Filho and Johnston bluntly put the matter back in 2005, 'we live in the age of neoliberalism' (2005, p. 1), something that, despite the onset of the global financial crisis in 2007 and the subsequent predictions of neo-liberalism's demise, seems just as true today (Crouch, 2011; Mirowski, 2013; Monbiot, 2017). We continue to live in a society in which 'everyone – left or right – talks about

the virtues of markets, private property, competition, and limited government'
(Peck, 2010, p. 71).

Yet paradoxically, as Peck goes on to argue (2010, p. 74), pinning down
the precise meaning of the term 'neoliberalism' is challenging. That this is so
among its architects and advocates, is not entirely surprising, in part because
the term tends to be a pejorative one employed mostly by critics, but also
possibly reflecting Hayek's original emphasis on the flexibility and adaptability
of neo-liberalism as a credo (2010, p. 274). The term's elusiveness also reflects
the ideological contradictions, between universally proclaimed inclusion
and identity-based exclusion, inhering in its classical liberal forebear (Hall,
2011; Parekh, 1995). This elusiveness may help explain why, despite neo-
liberalism's ubiquity as a concept in academic and media discourse across a
range of fields, there has been a recent tendency to question its existence as
a theoretical entity. As Ball puts it, neo-liberalism 'is one of those terms that
is used so widely and so loosely that it is in danger of becoming meaningless'
(2012, p. 3). Similarly, Mitchell Dean acknowledges the sceptical position,
noting that 'neoliberalism, it might be argued, is a rather overblown notion,
which has been used, usually by a certain sort of critic, to characterize
everything from a particular brand of free-market political philosophy to a
wide variety of innovations in public management' (2012, p. 1). However,
he goes on to advocate for an historically informed perspective on neo-
liberalism as an 'identifiable but heterogeneous' (p. 11) thought collective,
rather than a coherent ideology or form of state, and draws attention to the
risk of underestimating the influence of this thought collective in terms of
now-entrenched logics of government. This perspective informs the reading
of neo-liberalism offered here.

Drawing on the genealogical principle that 'a good account of the world
should be able to provide an account of how and why it arose' (Bevir, 2008,
p. 269), I adopt the view that 'clarification of the neoliberal program is first and
foremost a historical inquiry' (Mirowski, 2013, p. 29). As Peck notes, 'this means
tracking the project's uneven and uncertain progress, from its inauspicious
beginnings as a reactionary cult, through its moments of vanguardist advance,
to its effective mainstreaming as a restructuring ethos and as an adaptive form
of regulatory practice' (2010, p. xi) that has become part of the contemporary
cultural and political unconscious, thereby constituting, as Stuart Hall notes
above, a hegemonic project. The following discussion offers a brief history of
that project.

A brief history of neo-liberalism I: The Mont Pèlerin Society

The 'inauspicious beginnings' of the loose body of beliefs now known as neo-liberalism[1] can be traced at least as far back as the inaugural meeting of the Mont Pèlerin Society (MPS) in 1947 where, in the comparatively tranquil setting of the Swiss village of Vevey, Friedrich Hayek and his fellow Mont Pèlerin Society members – including such familiar names as Karl Popper and Milton Friedman – envisaged, and began preparing for, an ensuing battle of ideas over the coming generation (Mirowski and Plehwe, 2009). This was a battle framed by Hayek (1944) in his 'coruscating polemic' (Stedman Jones, 2012, p. 30) as one between freedom and serfdom. For Hayek, the main threat to freedom, and the individualism on which freedom, in his view, depended, was posed by collectivism and central planning, including not only by the distant, if living, reality of Soviet-style communism but much closer to home in the contemporary liberal welfare economics represented in the United States by the legacy of Roosevelt and in the UK by the agendas of Keynes and Beveridge (K. Tribe, 2009, p. 76). As he warned in the opening pages of *The Road to Serfdom*, 'we have progressively abandoned that freedom in economic affairs without which personal and political freedom has never existed in the past' (1944, p. 13).

Against this backdrop, the Mont Pèlerin Society brought together scholars and intellectuals from several groups that had been developing and exchanging ideas during the interwar years, including the London School of Economics, represented by Hayek himself, Lionel Robbins and others; the European Ordoliberals, comprising diasporic German economists as well as members of the Austrian school and led by theorists such as Wilhelm Röpke, Walter Eucken and Franz Böhm, and the first Chicago school of economics, led by economists such as Frank Knight, Jacob Viner and Milton Friedman's mentor, Henry Simons. Though these groups were united in their opposition to what they regarded as dangerous forms of collectivism in the shape of German Nazism and Roosevelt's New Deal, they also had their differences in that the ordoliberals were 'relatively moderate and pragmatic, espousing a humanist form of market economics' (Peck, 2010, p. 17), whereas the Chicago school was more theoretical in orientation and utopian in its idealization of the free market. It is worth noting

---

[1] The term 'neo-liberalism' was one that these same scholars had elected to adopt at an earlier meeting, the Colloque Walter Lipmann in Paris in 1938, in order to convey their sense of the need for a revived and reconstructed liberalism to meet the economic and political challenges of modern times (Davies, 2014; Polanyi, 1944).

that ambiguity, paradox and tension have always been core to the nature of neo-liberalism as an ideological and practical project.

The economic ideas and the political agenda formulated at this and subsequent meetings would have a profound impact in the final decades of the twentieth century across a range of fields, including education. Yet in many ways, the immediate post-war years were not an auspicious time for neo-liberal ideals of minimal government and individual responsibilization through competition. Indeed, the aftermath of the Second World War – a conflict which witnessed the triumph over Fascism, only after unprecedented destruction and at incalculable human cost, by the strategically allied but ideologically opposed forces of Soviet communism and Western liberal capitalism – saw a widespread hunger for state-led economic security and a belief in the possibility of a 'middle way' between the equally brutal and unforgiving poles of Soviet-style communism and laissez-faire capitalism.

The desire for a compromise between social democratic and free-market models of society found at least partial fulfilment. For despite a climate of austerity in the immediate post-war years – particularly in Europe and Britain – subsequent decades witnessed steady economic growth and the emergence of a political consensus around the need for the active involvement of government in the economy and some degree of protection and provision by the state, reflected in Richard Nixon's 1971 claim – ironically made on the eve of the slow unravelling of Keynesian economic policy – 'we're all Keynesians now'. In part, this consensus reflected a deep-seated and visceral reaction on the part of Western liberal societies to the dislocation and destruction of the 'Age of Catastrophe' (Hobsbawm, 1994) that unfolded between 1914 and 1945; but it also reflected an underlying assumption 'that the wholesale mobilization of the economy and society for the war effort had pointed the way to how social objectives might be achieved in peacetime' (Stedman Jones, 2012, p. 28). This was an assumption that neo-liberals, convinced as they were of the need for a mode of political economy grounded in competition and markets, vehemently rejected.

In contrast to the post-war faith in the power and potential of social collaboration, Hayek and his neo-liberal colleagues believed that rational self-interest, given free rein in arenas governed by competition, was the most truthful, powerful and reliable force in human affairs. For Hayek, liberalism as a philosophy of political economy 'is based on the conviction that where effective competition can be created it is a better way of guiding individual efforts than any other' (1944, p. 27). This did not mean, however, that there was no positive role for the state: as the above passage continues, 'it does not deny, but even emphasises, that, in order that competition should work beneficially, a carefully though-out legal framework is required' (1944, p. 27). He also acknowledged that 'where it is impossible to create the conditions necessary to make competition effective, we must resort to other methods of guiding economic activity' (1944, p. 27). In areas amenable to competition, however, anything grounded in a social rather than an individual ontology, and based on rational planning rather than trust in the competitive spirit, was counter to, and likely to be undermined by, human individuals' natural propensity to pursue their own self-interest. The likely success of any interventionist approach to policy was likely to be further hampered by the impossibility of adequate knowledge on which such interventions might be based, a problem exacerbated by the immensely complex and widely dispersed nature of social reality. This resistance to government intervention found further support in the economic fundamentalist belief 'that the market had a long-run evolutionary structure that government intervention could neither change nor predict' (Blyth, 2013, p. 118; see also Block and Somers, 2014).

In the post-war years, however, it was the followers of Keynes's ideas, not Hayek's, that were in the ascendant position. During these years of post-war boom, 'politicians and public alike believed they understood how to effectively manage capitalism using the tools of demand management developed by John Maynard Keynes and especially as expanded by the next generation of Keynesian economists' (Stedman Jones, 2012, p. 180). The prime goal of economic policy at this time, in large part under the shadow of the recollected trauma of the Great Depression, was maintaining low unemployment rates, something that seemed to call for greater collaboration rather than the competition so fundamental to the neo-liberals.

Interlude: Post-war progressivism and education policy

In education policy, the post-war years were characterized by a sense of optimism and political consensus around the potential of education to compensate for past and present injustices by providing equality of opportunity, thereby creating a more meritocratic society (Forrester and Garratt, 2017). This was a period in which teachers enjoyed relative professional autonomy and public trust in relation to curricular and pedagogic matters; in which progressive, child-centred approaches increasingly gained acceptance in primary schooling; and in which the comprehensive model of universal education made steady inroads in relation to the segregated models of that had been accepted in the past but that were now rejected by many on the basis that academic selection had often been a cipher for selection by class, race and gender (Pring, 2012).

Overall, there was a widespread belief that education was amenable to change and that it could, in turn, change society for the better. The optimism with regard to the potential of education during this time is reflected in the number of reform agendas and the policies these spawned, themselves linked to wider debates in the media, politics and society. For example, debates about how to transcend the historical burdens of class division in Europe and the UK found expression in attempts to create a 'comprehensive' system of secondary schools for all students and. In the United States, the burgeoning civil rights movement and concern over the continuing manifestation of the legacies of slavery in contemporary racism, fuelled attempts to achieve racial balance through policies such as busing students thereby attempting to achieve educational desegregation in the face of ongoing residential segregation (Sleeter, 2010). These and other attempts at reform typically fell short of the hopes of policymakers working within the limitations of the solution-led orientation to policy identified in Chapter 1. Indeed, the social, political and economic issues these policies sought to address were never going to be amenable to solution through policy since they revealed the far reaching and deep-seated contradictions, tensions and fissures at work in the supposed golden era of welfare state Keynesianism (Leitner et al., 2007; Lipman, 2011). The shortcomings of solution-oriented education policy agendas notwithstanding, and despite the growing condemnation of progressive education from right-wing academics and policy groups (e.g. Cox and Dyson, 1969a, 1969b, 1970), serious contestation of the post-Second World War social contract was contained until the mid-1970s. And when a serious challenge to the post-war settlement did emerge, it was as a result of turmoil in the economy and not from education, though education would certainly feel its effects in due course.

A brief history of neo-liberalism II: Crisis as opportunity, states of shock and psychic economies

While it is naïve to describe the post-war decades as a 'golden age', this period of *relative* optimism and economic stability began to unravel over the latter part of the 1960s and early 1970s. Key contributing factors included the instability of the international monetary system and the collapse of the Bretton Woods exchange rate regime under the combined pressure of the deficits incurred by the Vietnam War, President Johnson's Great Society agenda and the decline in American gold reserves. The breakdown of the Bretton Woods regime as a result of the unilateral suspension of dollar-gold convertibility in 1971 was the first of a series of crises that unfolded over the following decade providing the hitherto elusive climate for a sympathetic hearing for neo-liberal political and economic ideas.

> The end of the Bretton Woods international monetary system, two oil price shocks in 1973 and 1979, the Vietnam War, the Watergate break-in at the Democratic Party headquarters in Washington, D.C., at the behest of senior figures of the Nixon administration and the president's complicity in its cover-up, Britain's International Monetary Fund (IMF) loan of 1976, the virtual collapse of British industrial relations, and the failure of the prices and incomes policies that were supposed to fight inflation in both countries all created a policy vacuum into which neoliberal ideas flowed. (Stedman Jones, 2012, p. 215)

For neo-liberals, state-led attempts to manage the economy through Keynesian fiscal policy tools, such as price and wage controls, were anathema – misguided and hubristic attempts at imposing morality on the amoral market. From their perspective, the welfare state's 'do-gooding, utopian sentimentality enervated the nation's moral fibre, eroded personal responsibility and undermined the over-riding duty of the poor to work. It imposed social purposes on an economy rooted in individual greed and self-interest' (Hall, 2011, p. 707). Fortunately for neo-liberals, by the mid-1970s the failure of Keynesian approaches to remedy stagflation on both sides of the Atlantic created an environment open to new strategies and solutions. In the UK, a groundswell of neo-liberal ideas, promoted and elaborated by think tanks such as the Centre for Policy Studies, the Adam Smith Institute and the Institute for Economic Affairs, championed by conservative politicians, such as Margaret Thatcher and her mentor, Keith Joseph, and circulated by journalists such as Samuel Brittan, Peter Jay and future Chancellor of the Exchequer, Nigel Lawson, inaugurated the construction of a new anti-Keynesian, counter-hegemony, which would culminate in Thatcher's infamous catch cry, 'there is no alternative'. A similar pattern unfolded in the United States, involving think tanks such as the Heritage Foundation, the Cato Institute and the Manhattan Institute and individuals such as Charles Koch, Ed Crane, Alan Greenspan, George Schulz and Ronald Reagan. In a sense, the rest is history, not only because neo-liberalism went on to see its champions, Margaret Thatcher and Ronald Reagan, installed in office, their governments emblematic of the triumph of neo-liberal policies, nor because the biggest testament to the influence of these leaders is perhaps embodied in the continuation of their overarching market-driven agendas by their successors, regardless of political party. More fundamentally, as Stuart Hall, above, and many others have noted, neo-liberalism has gone on to transform the fabric of politics, economy and society in a range of global contexts. Indeed, the depth of its embedding into the understandings and practices of everyday life is one of the key factors explaining 'the strange non-death of neoliberalism' (Crouch, 2011), despite initial prognoses of its demise in the wake of the 2008 World Economic Crisis. As Connell observes (2013, p. 101), no region of the globe has gone untouched by neo-liberal ideas and policies:

> In the global metropole, i.e. North America and Europe, neoliberalism has gone far to dismantle the Keynesian welfare state, the system of regulated capitalism and state-supplied services that was dominant in the generation from 1945 to 1980. In the global periphery, neoliberalism thoroughly dismantled the strategy of autonomous economic development, and broke up the social alliances around it.

The capacity of neo-liberal ideas to fill the policy vacuum created by the series of crises that unfolded during the 1970s was not accidental but the fruit of disciplined, focused and persistent work over decades since the initial gathering of the Mont Pèlerin Society in 1947. Far from being the result of any natural evolution or unfolding of economic policy, '"neoliberalism" was and perhaps remains among the most militant and organized politically oriented thought collectives of the post-Second World War period' (M. Dean, 2012, p. 4). While not a 'conspiracy', there was nonetheless significant strategic intent behind this militant network and capacity building activity that sought to integrate ideology with praxis and thereby 'to produce a functional hierarchical elite of regimented political intellectuals' (Mirowski, 2013, p. 43), such as the 'virtual conveyor belt delivering Chicago Boys' to the key institutions overseeing the enforcement of neo-liberal ideas at the global level, the World Bank and the International Monetary Fund (IMF) (Klein, 2007, p. 161). Recognizing the scope and penetration of the activities undertaken by this collective is helpful in underlining the contingent nature of seemingly commonsensical neo-liberal ideals and values, such as markets and competition.

Mirowski captures its multilayered nature through the image of the 'Russian doll' approach to building what he terms 'the Neoliberal Thought Collective' (NTC) (2009, 2013). The inner layer of the Russian doll is represented by the MPS, whose organization and structure was shaped by Hayek's belief 'that ideas seeped into policy only very slowly' (Stedman Jones, 2012, p. 4); hence disciplined organization was prioritized over public profile, with the MPS seeking to avoid media attention and scrutiny in order to serve as a free-reining debating society for its members, who were initially hand-picked by Hayek himself, though this was later changed to a system of closed nominations. Within these structural limits there were further constraints in the form of any superimposed agenda or predetermined outcomes, though participants in the debate were united by a deep-seated rejection of all forms of collectivism, particularly contemporary forms such as the Soviet-style communism and Western welfare statism, in the face of which liberalism's laissez-faire past was deemed inadequate. Academic appointment was not a requirement, which would have placed an unnecessary and unhelpful limitation on the society, but many members were leading academics in the university departments, such as the economics department at the University of Chicago and the London School of Economics, which formed the next layer of the Russian doll. Over time the standing of many of these academics and their departments enhanced the credibility and acceptability of neo-liberal ideas in the eyes of policymakers and politicians (Stedman Jones, 2012, p. 5), who were likely to receive further affirmation of these ideas via the outputs and activities of the next outer layer of the doll. This consisted of special-purpose educational foundations, such as the Bradley Foundation and the Foundation for Economic Ideas, which were established for the specific purpose of promoting neo-liberal beliefs and ideas, and general-purpose 'think tanks', such as the Institute for Economic Affairs and the Hoover Institute, whose members were often of a neo-liberal persuasion.

The crucial ideological role that these think tanks and their connections played in the eventual triumph of neo-liberal ideals of markets and competition – vindicating the belief in the key role of intellectuals that underpinned Hayek's creation of the MPS – should not be forgotten, nor should the pragmatic political function served by this networking and promotional activity be underestimated, regardless of any deficit neo-liberalism may harbour in terms of the coherence and consistency of its ideas. In a very real sense, neo-liberalism has been a 'constructivist' project seeking to actively engender the market-based, competitive practices that it preaches (Brown, 2005; Seymour, 2014) with its ultimate aim being nothing short of remoulding human subjectivity along competitive, entrepreneurial and individualistic lines (Scharff, 2016).

At the same time, and mindful of the premature prognoses of neo-liberalism's demise after the financial upheavals in the last decade and their aftermath, it is important not to overstate the rational element to neo-liberalism as an ideological project (Cahill and Konings, 2017). While it clearly has identifiable signature traits, such as the use of the state to promote privatization, deregulation, marketization and the embrace of market-like rationalities of calculation, measurement and comparison (Davies, 2017), it is also important to recall that 'neoliberalism has often thrived on confusion and political disarray and that we would be naïve to think that its future requires an active embrace of its formal ideological tenets' (Cahill and Konings, 2017, p. 146). Critically, as noted in the introduction to this chapter, neo-liberal capitalism has thrived by tapping into, mimicking and exploiting the mobile, restless and insatiable nature of desire (McGowan, 2016).

Neo-liberalism and neo-liberal education policy: A contradictory nexus

Given the world (re)making ambitions of neo-liberalism, it would be surprising if education – a key arena for the shaping of souls – were to have been left untouched by its core tenets and preferred practices. As it was, until the 1980s, schools and teachers enjoyed public and political support in a period of relative autonomy, in which curriculum, pedagogy and assessment were largely determined at the local level. This is, of course, not to imply or pretend that everything was perfect and that teaching and learning were occurring in all contexts for all students – far from it – and, in the UK context, despite the shift towards more student-centred approaches and the growth of comprehensive schooling, segregation, discrimination and neglect characterized the encounter with education of far too many young people and families. Yet, despite these failings many educators maintained deeply held beliefs about the potential of education to contribute to increased degrees of equity and social justice.

With the election in 1979 and 1980 of political leaders in the UK and the United States sympathetic to neo-liberal ideas and ideals, it was only a matter of time before education policy in these and other contexts where neo-liberalism gained ascendancy, including Chile, China, New Zealand, South Africa and Sweden, was cleansed of any lingering collectivist orientation. Neo-liberal policies have also been imposed on a host of 'developing' countries via the 'arms free imperialism' represented by the structural adjustment programs of the World Bank and International Monetary Fund (Grant, 2008, p. xiii). The overall thrust of neo-liberal education policies reflects the emphases on marketization, deregulation and competition characteristic of the neo-liberal economic worldview. This is not surprising, for as Fisher observes, 'education, far from being in some ivory tower safely inured from the real world, is the engine room of the reproduction of social reality, directly confronting the inconsistencies of the capitalist social field' (Fisher, 2009, p. 26). Thus, although the particular mix of policies pursued varies between contexts, influenced by different traditions and competing ideologies, a number of overarching trends characterizing global neo-liberal education policy can be identified. This suggests the need to be alert to these global patterns, for 'critical policy analysis in an era of globalization requires that we recognize the *relationality* and *interconnectivity* of policy developments' (Rizvi and Lingard, 2010, p. 69, emphasis in original; see also Ball, 2012; Hirtt, 2008). However, as one might expect, these policy developments do not comprise a cohesive package and include a number of contradictory tendencies.

On the one hand, neo-liberal education policy has prioritized the deregulation and decentralization of education provision and the development of new categories of school, operating with varying degrees of managerial autonomy within and alongside the state-run sector and frequently catering for groups of students differentiated by academic selection and/or along class, ethnic or gender lines. These developments are typically justified in the name of notions like 'diversity', 'choice' and 'responsiveness' and reflect the reconfiguration of education as a marketplace, within which schools are required to vie for 'customers' or 'clients' (students and their families) through various forms of marketing, including touting their performance in examinations and inspections.

At the same time, and in direct tension with deregulation and increased flexibility, there has been an increase in state control of curriculum and teaching. This is evident in a number of developments, including the identification of 'core knowledge' that all students must learn, the mandating of outcomes-based curricula monitored via high-stakes testing and other forms of accountability, the development of ideologically driven subjects such as citizenship, and the promulgation of teacher professional standards linked to compulsory annual performance reviews and, in many contexts such as the United States, performance-based pay. The neo-liberal education policy environment has also been characterized by a renewed instrumental vocationalism. This trend is manifested in the development of school–industry partnerships and reflected in curricular emphases on core or basic knowledge and skills that are deemed fundamental to individual and societal economic welfare, such as literacy and numeracy, at the expense of more esoteric or aesthetic forms of learning, in order to prepare future workers for the challenges of competing in the global economy.

Overall, across the various developments comprising the globalized neo-liberal education policyscape, it is possible to identify a number of commonalities. Thus, for example, we can focus on key overarching policy *themes* – accountability, competition and privatization (Rancière, 2010b) – on core policy *technologies* – the market, managerialism and peformativity (Ball, 2003) – or on fundamental underlying policy *logics* – competition, instrumentalism and atomization (Clarke, 2012b) – that drive the development of new policies and practices. However, tempting as it may be to read these themes, technologies and logics as evidence of a global neo-liberal conspiracy, they are probably be more accurately considered aposteori features, identified in critical policy analysis, rather than comprising a set of ideals explicitly subscribed to and promoted by policymakers.

Indeed, just as recognizing its contradictions is core to understanding neo-liberalism as a political and economic philosophy, so too neo-liberal education policy is riven by tensions and contradictions. For instance, as is the case with neo-liberal politics generally, neo-liberal education policy's preferred scale is the individual and it is reluctant to recognize the significance of the group or community, but it relies on the societal organs of government in order to prosecute its individualizing agenda. When it does recognize society, its methodological individualist epistemology sees this entity as constituted by the aggregation of individuals, but it remains reluctant to acknowledge any reciprocal influence of society on the individual. It advocates democratic qualities of accountability and transparency, but its technologies of governance are unidirectional and, in education as in other fields, 'institutions, agencies and individual citizens are expected to make their activities visible to centers of calculation, but these centers are less required (much less enticed or persuaded) to make their activities transparent to neoliberal subjects' (Leitner et al., 2007, p. 4). A similar blind spot or moment of disavowal is conflict between, on the one hand, the promulgation of professional standards for teachers and, on the other hand, espousal of need for greater teacher professionalism, which arguably includes the autonomy such standards both question and undermine (Sachs, 2001). Likewise, emphases on tighter control of curriculum are at odds with the promotion of market values of choice, just as the latter, which pits school against school and positions parents as competitors, sits uneasily beside the communitarian values embodied in curricular emphases on citizenship and values. There are additional tensions between moves to promote aspiration more widely and the increasing inequality characteristic of recent decades, just as there are between 'the push to massify schooling, and the push to produce elite knowledges and credentials' (Thompson and Holdsworth, 2003, p. 387). Underlying many of these tensions runs the doomed fantasmatic attempt to square the circle, through conflation or colonization, by reconciling notions of quality, or excellence, defined in competitive and performative terms, with equity, fairness and justice (Clarke, 2014b; Gillies, 2008; Savage, 2011).

Tension and contradiction are also at the heart of psychoanalysis, as will have been evident in the discussion of desire earlier in this chapter, which is why it is particularly well suited to analysing the contradiction-riddled manifestations of capitalism (Harvey, 2014; McGowan, 2016) of which neo-liberalism may be seen as an intensified version. Indeed, the enduring challenge of psychoanalysis is 'to examine the fraught connection between language and the body, the symbolic constitution of human reality, with all the equivocations and paradoxes and slippages that belong to the "illogical logic" of the signifier, on the one hand, and the strangeness or perversity of an animal whose enjoyment is far from being always or unequivocally "enjoyable," on the other' (Schuster, 2016, p. 44). It is to the challenge of explaining some of the key conceptual – and often paradoxical – tools of Lacanian psychoanalysis that the discussion now turns.

Lacanian discourse theory

Lacan's theory of discourse can be considered both a summary and the summit of his contribution to psychoanalytic theory (Verhaeghe, 1995). As this suggests, Lacan's conception of discourse is about more than just communication since, for Lacan, discourse is central to human life in that it 'fabricates the context of the imaginary and symbolic world of the subjects, the borders of which are engraved and constantly defied by death, trauma, violence, anxiety, sexual acts and the like' (Vadolas, 2009, p. 135). Putting this another way, we might say that Lacanian discourse theory is about more than just speech and the exchange of ideas and information but engages at a deeper level with 'the structure of the speech exchange that accounts for the complexity of such an exchange more broadly conceived' (Hook, 2018, p. 99). This notion of discourse, therefore, transcends meaning and content in the form of the semantic intent of the subject of discourse, for the subject's meanings are always dependent upon the views, purposes and interpretations of others, which in turn rely on a background of shared social norms, values and assumptions. In other words, Lacan's discourse theory represents an attempt 'to circumvent the psychological ("imaginary") concerns of subjective sense-making and meaning by looking for an *underlying grid of interlinked symbolic positions*' (Hook, 2018, p. 99, emphasis in original).

Lacanian discourse theory may be about more than the communication of information and ideas; but the abstraction that results from the effort to transcend subjective meanings results in a level of abstraction that is initially off-putting to many readers: complex, technical and rarefied, it seems to comprise what look like exercises from an mathematics textbook with its formulas and symbols. Compared to the rich, evocative imaginary world of Freudian myths, Lacan's algebraic structures look decidedly uninviting. Nonetheless, there are at least three distinct advantages to this approach (Verhaeghe, 1995, p. 79). First, the minimalism of Lacan's model, reflecting its high level of abstraction, lends it a degree of transferability to different subject matter and contexts that is harder to achieve when a theory carries more narrative and cultural baggage. Second, and relatedly, this abstraction makes the model less prone to psychologizing – as Verhaeghe observes, Lacan's notion of a master signifier, for example, is less likely to become overlaid with pre-existing images and stereotypes than Freud's primeval father. Third, awareness of the character of each discourse and the relationships between its constitutive elements – between master signifiers and the split subject, for example – makes it possible to gauge what the potential consequences of its deployment are likely to be.

Lacan's approach to discourse also differs from that of Foucault, with which readers are more likely to be familiar. The key difference is that Foucault's focus is on the concrete materiality of discourse – on, for example, the way the modern subject of education is formed through the micro practices and technologies, including the endless grids, charts, lists, rows, tables, columns, levels, sets, streams, examinations and reports that comprise the discourse of modern schooling while 'Lacan on the contrary works beyond the content and places the accent on the formal relationships that each discourse draws through the act of speaking' (Verhaeghe, 1995, p. 81). This formality, however, does not entail that Lacan's theory of discourse is unsuited to grappling with the rough and tumble of politics and the political.

Lacan's four discourses

Much of Lacan's oeuvre can be read as an extended meditation on the nature of knowledge – clearly a practical consideration as well as a theoretical issue for a practising psychoanalyst – and in this regard, the four discourses suggest a number of ways in which knowledge can be organized (Frosh, 2012, p. 182). Specifically, Lacan highlighted how all claims to knowledge – at least in any final, absolute or complete sense and including, of course, mine and Lacan's as well as those of education policy – are undone by the unconscious, desire and the intimate alterity of otherness. This does not necessarily mean that we lapse into nihilism, but it does involve 'affirming human reality as a montage of the imaginary and the symbolic, as a rich tapestry of ambiguous and conflicted fictions – suspended over the void' (Thomas, 2013, p. 86). Such a refusal of the comforts of fixed or absolute knowledge clearly has relevance for education, the stock in trade of which *is* knowledge. It also suggests an *other side*, a subversive and subverting inverse, to the technocratic perspective of much education policy that seeks to govern and regulate education through reified notions of knowledge.

But in addition to suggesting how ideas of the other, otherness and the irreducible difference inhering in the subject and in knowledge might have for thinking about education and education policy, the book's subtitle involves a more specific reference to the title of Lacan's seventeenth seminar, *The Other Side of Psychoanalysis* (2007). In this seminar, Lacan elaborates his theory of four discourses – the discourse of the master, the university, the hysteric and the analyst – that together comprise his 'thoroughgoing critique of the quest for the One (truth, system or revolution) – arguably the most salient contemporary manifestation of an impulse to totalizing knowledge that he saw as characteristic of the political as such' (Starr, 2001, p. 34). Despite the misleading promotion of notions of choice in education today – notions which despite suggesting an open system embracing difference, catering to diversity and opposed to uniformity, are actually as much about allowing the privileged and mobile to choose not to have their children educated with their social 'inferiors' (Reay, 2017; Reay and Lucey, 2003) – recent education policy might well be characterized in terms of the 'the quest for the One' as evident in moves to centralize curriculum, standardize pedagogy and regiment assessment, legitimated by the pseudo-scientific claims of 'evidence-based' policy and practice discourse ('what works') (Hammersley, 2013).

For Lacan, discourse is a 'social link founded on language' (Lacan, 2000, p. 17). We might say that discourse forms a social bond woven by words. But though language is clearly central to the four discourses, Lacan's notion of discourse is not the same as that of linguistics or semiotics and is not reducible to grammar, phonemes or semantics. Lacan's discourse starts from the simple premise that every

relation of impossibility

agent   →   other

↑   _____   _____   ↓

truth   //   product

relation of inability

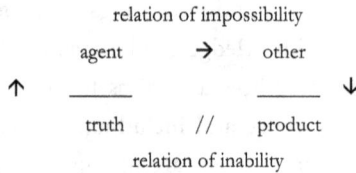

Figure 2.1 The four positions in Lacan's discourse theory (after Verhaeghe, 1995)

communicative act involves an agent who communicates something to an other. Furthermore, such an act of communication will be grounded in certain axioms and assumptions about the social and material world, taken to be truths. It will also result in some effect, or product, since for Lacan language is performative, a mode of acting on the world, rather than merely descriptive. So we now have four positions: a *truth* that drives an *agent* who speaks to an *other* which results in a consequent *product*. The four positions can be represented diagrammatically as shown in Figure 2.1.

The relative location of the positions within the diagram is significant. On the one hand, the left-hand side designates the productive factors in the discourse, while the right-hand side designates the receptive factors. On the other hand, the upper position on each side represents the conscious or explicit aspects of discourse, while the lower position represents the unconscious or implicit factors. Critically, in contrast to classic communication theory, with its ideal of perfect communication envisaged as analogous to the transmission of binary code between two computers (Schirato and Yell, 1996), for Lacan communication always fails to some degree, as indicated by the relation of impossibility in Figure 2.1 above. This is due in part to the disjunction between conscious and unconscious, represented by the horizontal bar on each side of the diagram, which means that the truth underlying the discourse can never be fully put into words.[2] In Lacan's words, 'this is the other face of the function of truth, not the visible face, but the dimension of it which is necessitated by something hidden' (Lacan, 2007, p. 187). This in turn means that perfect communication with the other can never be achieved which entails 'as a consequence the endless compulsion to repeat, as a never-ending attempt to verbalize the non-verbal' (Verhaeghe, 1995, p. 84). In similar fashion, the product of communication

[2] As Verhaeghe and others point out, in Lacanian theory there is no such thing as a truth that can be put fully into words. The best we can hope to achieve is a half-speaking of truth, 'le me-dire de la vérité'. But as Vighi reminds us (2010, p. 46), this 'does not imply that beyond this half there is some unreachable hidden substance. We should not transcendentalize Lacan's notion of truth. Rather, he suggests that beyond this half there is, literally, nothing – a nothing, however, which is given to experience as *plus-de-jouir*' or surplus jouissance.

resulting from the effect of the discourse on the other, bears no necessary relation to the agent's truth. As Verhaeghe puts it, 'once one speaks, one does not succeed in verbalizing the truth of the matter with, as consequence, the impossibility of realizing one's desire at the place of the other … resulting in the inability of the convergence between product and truth' (1995, p. 86). This relationship of impossibility is represented by the two diagonal bars separating the two sides in the lower portion of the diagram.

In addition to these four *positions* – or, as Verhaeghe describes them, four 'bags' into which we can place things – Lacan's theory comprises four *elements* that rotate through these four positions. These four elements always remain in the same relationship, or order, with respect to each other, so that *each* element occupies *each* of the possible positions over the four discourses. These elements are derived from Lacanian theory in relation to the structure of language and of the unconscious (Verhaeghe, 1995, p. 87).

It is in relation to language that we derive the first two elements: the master signifier, S1, representing the primeval cut of language into the an otherwise inchoate, semiotically speaking, existence and representing nothing but itself, yet fulfilling the necessary role of temporarily arresting the shifting flux of signifiers; and S2, representing web of signifiers comprising the wider network of knowledge. The other two elements are both effects of the signifier (Verhaeghe, 1995, p. 88).

The third element is the split subject, $, simultaneously constituted and alienated through its entry into language and divided between conscious and unconscious. This contrasts with the everyday, common-sense view of the individual subject as the originator of speech – 'the subject as it appears to itself and to the other (for example, as someone who believes herself to be a diligent student)' (Van Haute, 2002, pp. 39–40). This notion of the subject as the originator of speech, the producing subject of the statement or utterance, relates to the conscious self of the imaginary. This subject of the statement is distinct from the unconscious subject of the enunciation who is produced in communication and who emerges through the stream of signifiers and who always says more, as well as less, than s/he thinks. What Lacan is suggesting here is that rather than language merely involving a single unitary subject who uses words to convey a meaning or a sentiment, there is also a subject who is revealed in the flow of language, a subject exposed in the very words or signifiers themselves, who is not equivalent to the subject speaking as 'I' – which, after all, is what linguists refer to as a 'shifter', occupied by innumerable different people in different contexts. So the subject is split in various senses: between conscious and unconscious; between the subject of the statement and the subject of the enunciation; and between the three registers of the Lacanian psyche, real, symbolic and imaginary.

The fourth element, the object a, is probably the most abstract and elusive, representing an excess or surplus – a remnant of the real that 'functions as an internal limit to the symbolic's quest for closure' (Ruti, 2017, p. 115) and thus cannot be captured or articulated in the symbolic or imaginary registers. One way to explain this surplus is with reference to our *subject*ification through entry into language. This becoming-a-subject entails separation from a primary condition – we can call it 'nature' – condemning the subject to an endless yet futile quest to recuperate this condition and grasp some elusive Thing, as we saw in Recognizing desire section above, beyond language. As Verhaeghe explains, 'this object represents the final term of desire itself... In that sense it constitutes the motor which keeps us going for ever' (1995, p. 88). If lack, or loss, is the non-place, the void of emptiness, indifference and disorder, from which the subject desires, then it is via *objet a* that this void takes on a corporeal dimension (Schuster, 2016, p. 174).

We are now in a position to briefly outline the four discourses: the discourse of the master, the discourse of the university, the discourse of the hysteric and the discourse of the analyst. Each of the four discourses reflects a different possibility for the structuring of social relations yet 'all of the discourses, the elements of which appear in a fixed order set by the Master's discourse, represent, at one level, unconscious internal relations to the Other, Imaginary relations on which social bonds are formed and which exist to deny the underlying split (inconsistency, self-division, non-self-coincidence) of the subject – and the law' (Rothenberg, 2015, p. 43). In other words, just as the signifier gives the illusion of autonomy and agency, so discourse creates a sense of social cohesion and coherence, enabling us to forget and encouraging us to ignore the alienation and alterity, fragility and fallibility, denials and divisions that constitute both the subject and society.

As its name suggests, the master's discourse relates to mastering or the establishment of a hegemony in the social order; the university discourse refers to educating or interpellating subjects within a particular social order underpinned by expertise; the hysteric's discourse concerns protesting or resisting against a particular given order though it also involves an impossible quest for unquestioned mastery; while the analyst's discourse relates to revolutionizing or bringing about change in the social order. Furthermore, as suggested by the French title of Lacan's seventeenth seminar, *L'envers de la psychanalyse*, each of the four discourses is the inverse of another in the schema. Lacan's title is also a veiled reference to the pervasive and continuing presence of discourses of mastery, and specifically the discourse of the master, which represents the antithesis of the discourse of the most open of the four discourses, that of the analyst. My own title plays on this, in that 'the other side of education' refers, among other things, to the dominance of neo-liberal policy agendas, which represent an antithesis of key aspects of what I argue education could potentially entail, such as notions of openness and becoming, while also referring to a vision of education that offers an alternative – an other side – an 'anti-education' in relation to the version of education offered by the neo-liberal imaginary, one characterized by openness to notions of the 'other' and 'otherness' that are inextricable elements of the complex Lacanian subject.

Indeed, to say that the Lacanian subject is characterized by complexity, however, is something of an understatement. It is not merely complex but a creature of paradox, juxtaposing individuating identity and dividing plurality, intentional agency and structural necessity, identificatory sameness and alienating otherness, enunciation *of* discourse and deprivation *by* discourse (Pavón-Cuéllar, 2011, p. 235). We can think about this complexity in more detail by recognizing a number of ways in which the subject is not a unified, seamless, self-sufficient or hermetic entity but is divided from itself by a series of disjunctions involving language, by desire and the unconscious. In other words, a series of unbridgeable gaps exist: between self as subject and as object of discourse; between the subject as agent of signification and the Other of discourse; between the individuating circumscription and closure of the master signifiers with which the subject identifies and the endless, open-ended slippage in the wider network of signifiers comprising language; and between the positivity of the act of identification and the negativity of the constitutive outside upon which such acts of identification inevitably rely.

A number of enigmas surround the four discourses. We might well ask, for instance, why four (and *only* four) and why *these* four (K. Campbell, 2004, p. 57)? There is no satisfactory answer to these questions, though it is worth noting that Lacan himself later identified a fifth discourse, a mutation of the discourse of the master that he referred to as the discourse of the capitalist (Lacan, 1990), while Levi Bryant (2016), by violating the strict order of the elements in Lacan's original four discourses, has outlined what he refers to as four universes of discourse, each comprising four discourses, and thus identifies twenty-four possible discourses. We might also ask how, given the origins of the discourses in Lacan's psychoanalytic practice, valid is the move to mobilize them in social and political critique? In relation to this last point it is worth noting that Lacan himself clearly related the discourses to political patterns, both historical and contemporary, linking, for example, the university discourse to Stalinism (Lacan, 2007, p. 206), a potential that Žižek (e.g. 1996a), in particular, has built on and extended. Thus, my reason for using Lacan's theory is not because it can claim any status as a meta-theory in relation to other theories of discourse, 'but because it allows us to understand the functioning of different discourses in a unique way' (Fink, 1995, p. 129). In particular, it provides unique insights into the interrelationships between knowledge, truth, subjectivity and otherness, and how particular configurations among these elements are produced by different discourses. In the context of the predominant discourse in contemporary education policy, that is, neo-liberalism, Lacan's discourse theory helps us in grasping – and hence potentially resisting – the nature and dynamics of its hegemonic influence.

Lacan's theory thus offers a dynamic perspective on the relationship between knowledge, power, subjectivity and desire in social practices involving the formation and transformation of social relations – key concerns, I suggest, of both psychoanalysis and education. Critically for this book, Lacanian discourse theory, and in particular the two discourses of mastery, the discourse of the master and the discourse of the university, provide powerful insights into contemporary globalized neo-liberal policy discourses and how they have reshaped the meaning of both knowledge and education. Dominated by 'thought stopping' master signifiers (Gunder, 2004, p. 301), the discourses of mastery have a tendency to repress the more tentative and open discourses of the hysteric and the analyst. Neo-liberal education policies, characterized as I have argued by modernist proclivities for certainty, systematicity and the recurring blank slate, and dominated by master signifiers such as 'choice', 'competition', 'standards' and 'quality', can be read as classic instances of such discourses of mastery.

Yet as noted above, each discourse has its inverse. In contrast to these discourses of mastery, the other two of Lacan's four discourses, which we might describe as discourses of critique or discourses of thinking otherwise, offer potential signposts to the other side of education – to an education policy-world not subordinated to the totalizing master signifiers of quality, standards and reform and guided by principles other than those of competition, instrumentalism and atomization. These other two discourses are the discourse of the hysteric, associated with resistance and protest, and particularly the discourse of the analyst, associated with analysis and critique.

The following four chapters draw on the four discourses to structure its analysis and critique of neo-liberal education policy. Specifically, Chapter 1 provides a deeper exploration of neo-liberal politics through the lens of the discourse of the master. Chapter 2 examines neo-liberal education policy through the lens of the discourse of the university. Chapter 3 employs the discourse of the hysteric to think about the challenges facing teachers and teaching in the neo-liberal era. Chapter 4 draws on the discourse of the analyst to explore the location of students and learning in the era of neo-liberal education policy. Chapter 5 draws the threads of the arguments presented in the earlier chapters together in order to consider the implications of looking at education policy through the lens of Lacan's four discourses and reflect on the possibilities and the challenges inhering in the other side of education.

3

The Discourse of the Master and Neo-liberal Political Economy: Keep On Working

Getting people to work is even more tiring, if one really has to do it, than working oneself. The master never does it. He gives a sign, the master signifier, and everybody jumps.

Lacan, 2007, p. 174

Introduction

This chapter examines the dominant form of political economy in recent decades, neo-liberalism, and considers its implications for education and education policy. The chapter provides a reading of neo-liberal politics in terms of Lacan's authoritarian discourse of the master, whose main modus operandi involves 'governing/brainwashing' and whose quintessential realm is that of politics (Bracher, 1994, p. 109). With reference to the master's discourse, Lacan, speaking in 1970, noted: 'in our day it so happens that it can be uncovered in a sort of purity – and this, through something we experience directly, and at the level of politics. What I mean by this is that it [the discourse of the master] embraces everything, even what thinks of itself as revolutionary' (2007, p. 87). In other words, the discourse of the master is an ever-present threat, promising the impossible, in terms of its claims to remedy, or fix, the incompleteness and instability of the social field (Rothenberg, 2010). But beyond the pervasive presence of the master's discourse in social, political and organizational life, it is particularly important to examine issues of political economy in a book on education policy for a number of reasons.

For one thing, education, and hence education policy, is inescapably political (e.g. Apple, 2003; Saltman, 2014b; Youdell, 2011). Education and politics 'are inextricably interwoven with each other' (Kelly, 2009, p. 187), which helps explain why many political philosophers have also been major theorists of education – think of Plato, Rousseau, Dewey – whose interest in education stemmed in part from their recognition of its powerful potential for realizing their political ideals for wider society. Among the many reasons why education is not be able to compensate for society (Bernstein, 1970; see also Gorard, 2010) is that education does not sit outside society, influencing it from beyond. Education is coextensive with society, in the sense that the overall make-up of the education system reflects the norms, values, rationalities and organizational structures of wider society.

> There is no school outside of a *polis*, a *civitas*, a republic, and in these societies no form of life is protected from incivility without school. School is as such political: it constitutes the matrix of a process of psychic and collective individuation founding a civility itself founded on and through a specific formation and training of attention. (Stiegler, 2015, p. 214)

In addition, education is constituted by, and in turn (re)constitutes, a particular vision of society, in relation to knowledge, or qualification, interpersonal relations, or socialization, and intrapersonal identities, or subjectification (Biesta, 2015).[1] That is to say, any education system will necessarily comprise particular, contingent (rather than universal) views with regard to: what knowledge should be prioritized as central and what knowledge ought, by contrast, to be seen as more marginal; what attitudes should govern social relationships, including, for example, whether these are seen predominantly in terms of competition or collaboration and; what sort of individuals should education be 'producing' in relation to qualities such as obedience, initiative and responsibility. Thus, for example, a decision to focus education on the 'basics', such as literacy and numeracy, and exclude any discussion of any issues deemed to be political is in itself a political decision, just as a decision to foreground critical issues of race, gender and sexuality is also a political one. In this sense, an education system's politics will be reflected in its predominant practices in relation to curriculum, pedagogy and assessment – the 'core' message systems of education – as well as in its policies in relation to more explicitly political issues such as justice, equity and diversity. Finally, it is important to note that the possibilities and promise of education, as with other areas of life affecting the well-being of individuals and

---

[1] Here I would briefly note that Biesta's three domains of educational purpose align with Fairclough's (1992) three constitutive domains of discourse, social reality, interpersonal relations and intrapersonal identities, which in turn reflect Foucault's (1997) argument that the subject is forged in the simultaneous interplay of games of truth, power and ethics.

groups, such as health provision, are shaped and constrained by the distribution of resources within a society (Dorling, 2011; Means, 2013; Wilkinson and Pickett, 2009); this includes the resources dedicated to education as a proportion of national wealth *and* the allocation of resources within education across different sectors and institutions. These too, of course, are political decisions.

A further reason for considering politics and the political in relation to education – and one that follows from the above points – is that both politics and education have undergone a radical shift in recent decades as a consequence of what we might describe as 'the long march of the Neo-liberal Revolution' (Hall, 2011, p. 705) and the concomitant decline in the power and recognition of ideals and aspirations for social justice and change (Couldry, 2010; Fielding and Moss, 2011; Power and Frandji, 2010). My contention is that, in order to grasp the nature and scope of the myriad and daunting challenges facing those of us who would wish to revisit aspirations for a radical or alternative vision of education policy to that currently holding sway, it is critical to gain some insights into the contours of the neo-liberal politics that has so effectively captured the contemporary state – an institution that, despite increasing levels of private provision of education, still retains overall responsibility for the education system within its borders – in a range of global contexts. As a result – and mindful of the way 'the authority of the neoliberal state is heavily dependent upon the authority of economics (and economists) to dictate legitimate courses of action' (Davies, 2014, pp. 6–7) – this chapter embarks on an excursus into the history of neo-liberalism as 'the pursuit of the disenchantment of politics by economics' (2014, p. 4) in the latter half of the twentieth century. The chapter also considers how, and with what consequences, neo-liberalism has retained its hegemonic grip in the twenty-first century, the 2008 global financial crisis notwithstanding (Callinicos, 2010; Gamble, 2009). The chapter argues that the latter event foregrounded neo-liberalism's reliance on cruder forms of authority, alongside its basis in expert knowledge,[2] which is underpinned by a tacit reliance on assumptions of bioeconomic naturalism in relation to competition as a governing norm in both individual and collective life – what Dardot and Laval

---

[2] Modern political economy is usually read in terms of the discourse of the university, which involves educating, instructing and managing people from a position of expertise (Dean, 2006), albeit an expertise underpinned by the assumed 'truth' of particular authoritative master signifiers. While recognizing the value of and insights offered by such readings, I am supplementing this with a reading of neo-liberal political economy in terms of the discourse of the master to highlight its reliance on authority and, when necessary, violence.

(2013, p. 35) refer to as 'social competitivism' – that has roots in the nineteenth-century 'survival of the fittest' ideology of Herbert Spencer.

But there is a further rationale for a chapter on neo-liberal politics in a book on education, involving recognition that neo-liberalism is more than just a theory of economics or model of political power; it is also a form of public pedagogy connecting knowledge and desire in sites as diverse as television and entertainment networks, online social media, advertising spaces, shopping malls, churches, sports arenas and, of course, schools. Neo-liberalism thus

> constitutes the conditions for a radically reconfigured cultural politics. That is, it provides, to use Raymond Williams' term, a new mode of 'permanent education' in which dominant sites of pedagogy engage in diverse forms of pedagogical address to put into play a limited range of identities, ideologies and subject positions that both reinforce neoliberal social relations and undermine the possibility for democratic governance. (Giroux, 2004, p. 107)

In other words, the growth and spread of neo-liberalism involves a 'stealth revolution' that is 'undoing the demos' (Brown, 2015), while at the same time educating us across a range of sites to accept its norms and practices as the inevitable way of the world (Dardot and Laval, 2013). Neo-liberalism as a dominant form of public pedagogy thereby illustrates Lacan's (2007, p. 31) insight regarding 'the same problem that confronts us all, namely the persistence of a master's discourse', that is, an authoritative discourse in which knowledge, addressed by master signifiers that are themselves driven by particular 'truths', occupies the passive place of the Other, who is thereby dispossessed of agency in relation to this knowledge, just as workers are dispossessed of their labour in capitalist economies (Nobus and Quinn, 2005, p. 134). It is to the master's discourse that the discussion now turns.

The discourse of the master

The master's discourse is primal among the four discourses for a number of reasons. Lacan (2007, p. 20) argues that it is historically prior to the other discourses but it is also primary in the sense that it founds the symbolic order and embodies the coming into being of the subject through the alienating function of the signifier (Fink, 1995; Verhaeghe, 1995). It thus forms a sort of 'fundamental discursive unconscious configuration that precedes and underlies any other kind of discourse' (Pavón-Cuéllar, 2011, p. 233). In this chapter the

$$S1 \quad \rightarrow \quad S2$$

$$\uparrow \quad \underline{\quad\quad} \qquad\qquad \underline{\quad\quad} \quad \downarrow$$

$$\$ \quad // \quad a$$

Figure 3.1 The discourse of the master

master's discourse is read as a template to make sense of the remarkable, and remarkably resilient, dominance of neo-liberal political economy, including the economic rationalization of the state and the encroachment of markets and monetary evaluation into hitherto separate spheres of social activity, not least, of course, education. I believe this reading offers particular insights in the wake of the 2008 global financial crisis; for like the master's discourse, which, as we shall see, relies on authority rather than expertise, neo-liberal political economy 'has now become a ritual to be repeated, not a judgement to be believed' (Davies, 2014, p. 185). The discourse of the master is represented diagrammatically as shown in Figure 3.1.

In the schema of the master's discourse, the master signifier(s) addresses the field of knowledge, demanding that it be organized in accordance with the master signifier. This demand is made, not on the basis of any expertise but, because the master is the one who must be obeyed. Indeed, the master's weakness is his/her ignorance of the underlying reasons for the assertion of the master signifiers – as Lacan observes in the citation serving as one of this chapter's epigraphs, the master 'does not know what he [*sic*] wants'. This is partly because the master signifier occupying the position of agency is *in itself* empty, relying on a network of connections to other signifiers for its meaning (Laclau, 1996, 2005), but it also reflects the hidden truth of the master's discourse is the subject constituted by the signifier and divided between consciousness and the unconscious (Gunder and Hillier, 2009, p. 104). Moreover, the master's assertion of totality – reflected in the upper, explicit part of this discourse where there are only signifiers, that is, knowledge organized in accordance with the master signifiers – is achieved at the expense of expelling or repressing some extra-discursive object, the object of desire, *a*. The master's discourse thus embodies a fundamental issue characterizing human being, that is our inability to manage, and hence our compulsion to expel, the libidinal surplus within our social lives as subjects of the signifier[3] (Vighi, 2010, p. 12) – another reason why it can be seen as primal among the four discourses.

---

[3] Indeed, as Vighi argues, one way of thinking of Lacan's four discourses is as a representation of different attempts to locate the position and function of this surplus.

The master's discourse can be seen in the behaviour of particular individuals in a range of contexts; for example, in the authoritarian teacher who demands subservience from her pupils in education or in the charismatic, power-intoxicated leader who craves unremitting and unconditional adulation from his supporters in politics. However, my main focus in this chapter is not so much on particular individuals but on the rise of neo-liberal political economy as an intellectual and practical movement. In particular, the journey from a somewhat discredited and marginal movement to its current status as the default template for social organization – dominated by markets and driven by naturalized, and hence unchallengeable, assumptions about the naturalness of competition – from which few spheres of life remain immune. As I hope will become clear, the master's discourse provides valuable insights into the nature, including the weaknesses, of this powerful and seemingly irrepressible phenomenon.

Neo-liberalism as a discourse of the master

Not only has neo-liberalism had dramatic consequences for systems and structures, it has also wrought significant changes in modes of subjectivity. Crucially, 'the neo-liberal imagination collapses the epistemological distinction between economy and society', in the process 'reconfiguring roles and identities (employees, welfare recipients, managers, civil servants, citizens, consumers and so on) so as to mobilize designated actors actively to undertake and perform self-governing tasks' (Shamir, 2008, pp. 6, 8). In essence, the market becomes the overriding master signifier organizing and articulating various previously disparate fields of knowledge in line with its logics and with institutions and individuals all required to serve the needs of the master market or suffer the harsh consequences.

The aftermath of the 2008 economic crisis, when the combination of state-sponsored bailouts and state-imposed austerity served to foreclose any serious challenges (Seymour, 2014), and when the reliance of neo-liberalism on the violence and sovereign authority of the state was hence increasingly exposed (Tansel, 2016), is central to this reading of neo-liberalism as an enactment of the discourse of the master. It is important to note, however, that neo-liberal political economy can also be read, with different emphases, in terms of the discourse of the university (e.g. J. Dean, 2006).

In my reading of neo-liberal political economy as the discourse of the master, the market can be seen as the master signifier, S1, which addresses and organizes the field of discourse, or knowledge, in the neo-liberal world according to calculating, measuring and evaluating norms of neo-liberal performativity. However, it is important to note that the agent is not an omniscient master: 'the agent is not necessarily someone who does but someone who is caused to act' (Lacan, 2007, p. 169). What causes the agent to act is the underlying 'truth' located in the lower left-hand quadrant of the schema. Hence, underneath this master signifier, representing the 'truth' that it speaks, lies the split subject, $. This subject is divided, as we shall see, by the contradictions between ideals of competition and the realities of the power of corporations, as well as by the contradictions inhering in the very notion of competition, in turn reflecting the fundamental split in the subject, instituted by the operation of the signifier, between conscious and unconscious. The product of the imposition of this competitively driven, market regime, with its relentless will to impose matrices of measurement, calculation and evaluation on all walks of life, can be seen, on the one hand, in the creation of an elite whose lives are increasingly removed from the majority, even as they impact upon them in areas like house prices (Dorling, 2014a, 2014b); and, on the other hand, in the exclusion and elimination of those individuals and groups who do not fit the regime's requirements and who are thus rendered as an invisible or disposable surplus (Blacker, 2013; Stiegler, 2015). The following sections expand on these rather abstract assertions, taking the reader around each of the four positions to develop a reading of neo-liberalism as a master discourse that has reshaped our education systems as much as, if not more than, any other walk of life. I begin with the position of the addressee in the upper right-hand quadrant, representing the place where neo-liberal political economy has 'positioned' the field of education.

Education policy addressed as other

The upper right-hand quadrant in Lacan's schema of the four discourses is occupied by the other addressed by a master signifier. In my reading of neo-liberal political economy as a discourse of the master, the addressee is the field of discourse, or knowledge, specifically in relation to Education. In the neo-liberal era, this field is organized by the requirements of the market as a master signifier that demands of education that it aligns itself with the calculating, measuring and evaluating norms of managerialist performativity.

The following chapter will examine various aspects of neo-liberal performativity as an active undertaking in education in more detail, including policies such as the introduction of mandated curricula, high-stakes testing regimes and professional teaching standards, particularly in relation to how they have positioned and shaped the subjectivities of educational practitioners, but here it is important to recognize the passive positioning of education as in need of reform according to the superior logics of competitively driven market logics that have increasingly predominated since the 1970s. Between then and the end of the Second World War, education and schools were seen as key vehicles for bringing about the changes desired in wider society by so many after the traumatic crises of 1914–45. When economic crisis struck again in the late 1960s and 1970s, education came increasingly under fire for not delivering on the promises of social transformation and economic success that had been projected onto it and hence it became subject to levels of suspicion and scrutiny. In the US context, the sense of crisis was reflected in, and further stoked by, a series of reports, beginning with *A Nation at Risk* (National Commission on Excellence in Education, 1983) and continuing with *America 2000* (1991), *Goals 2000* (1993), *No Child Left Behind* (2001) and, most recently, *Race to the Top* (2009). This policy series traces a trajectory wherein economic concerns come increasingly to dominate public conversations about an education system that is persistently positioned as both the problem and the solution – not least by introducing a greater degree of market-style competition into education – in relation to these concerns.

Meanwhile, as mentioned briefly in the previous chapter, in the UK beginning in the late 1960s a series of reports known collectively 'Black Papers' (Cox and Boyson, 1975, 1977; Cox and Dyson, 1969a, 1969b, 1970) criticized progressive education methods and egalitarian developments, such as comprehensive education, pathologizing these developments as being at least partially responsible for the social upheavals of the late 1960s and arguing, in the last paper, for the introduction of greater choice, competition and increased parental control in education as the only way out of the morass. Seeming to capture this mood of impatience with education, British Prime Minister James Callaghan's 1976 speech at Ruskin College called for a national debate about the nature and purpose of education. Since then, successive governments in England have positioned education as in need of reform with a deluge of policy initiatives beginning with the landmark Education Reform Act (1988) aimed at rectifying its purported deficiencies though steadily increasing levels of prescriptiveness and accountability requirements. As in the United States, across these reforms, and within related commentary in the media, a familiar underlying pattern is visible of blaming education, schools and, in particular, ineffective teachers, for economic decline and social fragmentation. At the same time, these targets of blame have been tasked with rectifying the problems for which they are held responsible. This has been achieved through the coerced embrace by schools of the corporate cultures and managerial mechanisms crystallized in the pervasive metaphor of the market.

Neo-liberal master signifiers: The market

S1

The position of the agent in Lacan's discourse of the master is occupied by the master signifier, which organizes and quilts the field of knowledge. In this section I discuss the market as the master signifier dominating the field of knowledge in relation to neo-liberal political economy. Of course, discussions of neo-liberalism are copious, extending across a range of disciplines, but perhaps the most familiar and widely cited definition is that provided by Harvey (2005, p. 2), who argues that 'neoliberalism is in the first instance a theory of political economic practices that proposes that human well-being can best be advanced by liberating individual entrepreneurial freedoms and skills within an institutional framework characterized by strong private property rights, free markets and free trade'. A similar emphasis on the centrality of markets is found in the characterization of neo-liberalism as a phenomenon that 'promotes the virtue of a free-market economy as a more effective mechanism for the distribution of social resources, competition, privatization and individual liberty' (Forrester and Garratt, 2017, pp. 9–10), while Jodi Dean writes, 'redefining social and ethical life in accordance with economic criteria and expectations, neoliberalism holds that human freedom is best achieved through the operation of markets' (2009, p. 51). As implied by this emphasis on markets and free trade, neo-liberalism is less a complete political ideology than it is 'a theory of political economic practices' (2005, p. 2). As a result, and as Harvey notes, neo-liberalism is compatible with a range of political models with varying degrees of commitment to free democratic exchanges of ideas (Harvey, 2005; Thorsen, 2010).

Markets are also emphasized by Davies, for whom '*neoliberalism might therefore be defined as the elevation of market-based principles and techniques of evaluation to the level of state-endorsed norms*' (Davies, 2013, p. 37; 2014, p. 6, emphasis in originals). However, Davies goes on to make the point that it is not such markets per se, so much as 'particular market-based (or market-derived) forms of economization, calculation, measurement and valuation' (2014, p. 21), that render hitherto unmarketized areas of life amenable and subject to market-like behaviour, that are what is distinctive about neo-liberalism in contrast to nineteenth-century laissez-faire or classical liberalism. He also argues that what connects the various strands of neo-liberal thought (e.g. Hayekian and Friedmanite), while simultaneously providing *both* its links to classic liberalism *and* the basis of neo-liberalism's claims to authority in relation to its market-promoting behaviours, is the core ethic of competition – hence in the reading offered here, competition comprises a fundamental component of the 'truth' of the master discourse of neo-liberalism, as we shall see below.

Markets and their creation have been a fundamental thrust of neo-liberal education policy in a range of contexts (Apple, 2006; Ball, 2013; Exley and Ball, 2011; Marginson, 1997), as will be discussed in more detail in the following chapter. The marketization agenda has included promoting the privatization of schooling, as well as the diversification of school types, with 'free schools', 'academies', and 'charter schools' among the new breed of schools coming on stream, typically justified in the name of parental choice. The privatization and the diversification agendas are mutually supportive. As the marketing brochure of a UK corporate finance and investment advising company noted in 2014, employing the mixture of predatory and euphemistic language typical of the sector (something it shares with the military sector), there are rich opportunities awaiting exploitation by business investors:

> The UK education support services market is estimated to be worth £16 billion per annum. The Coalition's abolition of procurement 'quangos', Local Authority (LA) budget cuts and the erosion of their control over school decision making have all influenced how businesses now approach selling to schools. The potential customer base is now much larger and more fragmented – there

are now 3,400 autonomous academy schools in England. This has attracted new strategic players with significant scale and the distribution channels to successfully exploit this opportunity.[4]

Here we see education positioned as a vibrant business opportunity awaiting exploitation, thanks to the combined loosening of structures, regulations and procedures, compounded by the squeezing of public funding for the sector. Specific market opportunities are subsequently listed in the brochure, including the consumables market ('Budget pressures and academy schools leaving LA control means many LAs are looking to outsource functions from their education departments and share services across county boundaries. This is creating new opportunities for established Government Business Process Outsourcing (BPO) providers'), the tutoring market ('Over the next five years, the global private tutoring market is forecast to be worth over \$100 billion led by demand in Asia'), the market for English model international schools ('Growing prosperity in emerging markets, lack of quality local education institutions and increasing demand for schooling in English is leading to significant growth in the number of international schools') and the e-learning market ('The e-learning sector is the fastest growing market in education. Worth an estimated \$91 billion globally, it is forecast to grow at a CAGR of 23 per cent up to 2017 compared to 7.4 per cent for education expenditure. Evidence that the use of technology can enhance the learning process and improve outcomes is creating increasing demand'), among others.

A notable feature of this discussion is the use of the passive voice, existential verbs ('is') and organic metaphors, in order to mask human agency and create the impression of a world subject to natural forces and populated by impersonal actors, such as the growth of the e-learning sector, evidence of the benefits of using technology and 'growing prosperity in emerging markets'. Such fatalism and occlusion of responsible actors that serves to obviate analysis or critique has been key to neo-liberalism's story of success (see Fairclough, 2000). Yet, a key point to bear in mind is that 'we are talking here, then, about a long-term tendency and not about a teleological destination' (Hall, 2011, p. 708). Keeping alternative possibilities in purview is important in resisting a retrospective reading of neo-liberalism's history as the predestined unfolding of an inevitable drama or as the inexorable progression of economic, technological and social knowledge towards ever-greater levels of sophistication and development. A key

---

[4] http://www.catalystcf.co.uk/uploads/Education_Training_Sector_Report-Spring_2014.pdf.

factor in resisting such narratives and hence grasping the complex, contingent, ambiguous and opportunistic, nature of neo-liberalism is recognizing the key function played by a relatively new form of political organization, the think tank, and the role of intellectual networks in building the critical capacity of neo-liberalism to bring ideas to bear on events when the opportunity arose.

The processes of obfuscation of agency and the consequent acceptance of the forces of change that have been fundamental to neo-liberalism can be explained in Lacanian terms by the point, noted earlier, that in the discourse of the master, although the agent, that is, the master signifier, is authoritative, it is also empty, ignorant and, in a sense, 'mute'. That is, we accept the dictates of globalization or the requirements of market disciplines because they are authoritative and because this authority is grounded in the presumed naturalness of competition as a norm governing individual and collective life and hence, as Margaret Thatcher (in)famously asserted, there is no alternative. In similar fashion, the agents 'speaking' in the master discourse of neo-liberal political economy – markets and the processes associated with them, such as growth and emergence – are likewise ignorant and speechless – necessarily so, as they are abstractions – that 'exercise' power through attributions of rationality and voice. This argument, however, as stated here, is rather dense and requires further unpacking.

The mysterious movements of the market

The fact that abstractions like markets are attributed with voice and agency is not necessarily problematic since our lives necessarily involve a complex interplay between the concrete and the abstract, the material and the symbolic. Indeed, Lacan's four discourses and, of course, my work in this book, attribute agency to abstractions, including discourses and signifiers such as 'neo-liberalism', as part of an analysis of socio-material worlds. The key point for critical analysis is to move beyond mere dismissal of prosopopoeia as delusional and to ask instead what it is that motivates such attributions, for 'the delusion, as with a dream or fantasy, is a sign or marker of desire' (Jones, 2013, p. 18). Indeed, the attribution of speech tells us something significant about an era insofar as only certain things are personified and deemed capable of speaking. So the interesting question becomes what things are attributed with the capacity to speak and why, as well as what sort of subject, capable of what sort of things, is the speaking entity deemed to be?

For Hayek, the market represented a hyper-efficient information processing mechanism whose capacity to take account of an immense amount of information from a vast array of sources enabled it to avoid the inevitable errors that resulted from deliberate planning as a consequence of the unavoidable shortcomings in human knowledge (Stedman Jones, 2012). This notion of the market as a speaker of truth persists today: 'The market is hypostasized: it "thinks" this, "does" that, "feels" the other, "gets panicky", "loses confidence", "believes"' (Hall, 2011, p. 722) and, in oracular fashion, for true believers it offers genuine insight: 'When the market speaks to you, listen carefully and you might hear the truth.'[5]

However, in recent years, particularly as a result of the incomprehensible scale, sublime speed and byzantine complexity of financial trading, the market has increasingly become a speaker whose utterances can only be deciphered by a select few with the requisite decoding skills, 'which are usually conferred legitimacy by a combination of tradition and the assertion of expert command over the material at hand' (Jones, 2013, p. 41). This expertise is essential, for the truth of the market lies not on the surface but at the deeper level of intention. This notion provides a perfect foil that has enabled advocates of neo-liberalism and austerity to argue that despite all the signs to the contrary – the financial crash of 2008 being the obvious one to point to – the wisdom of the market remains intact, as 'market perfection is still retained, not at the level of speech but at the level of intentionality' (Jones, 2013, p. 43). Such assertions, however, are less convincing than they once were, as questions are increasingly raised regarding the legitimacy of the wealth accruing to the financial sector and the exclusion of dissenting voices from conversations about the nature of the economy, its relationship with society[6] and the appropriate basis for political decision-making.

> One of the critical questions, on which neoliberalism stands or falls, is why *economics* should be a better analytical basis for government than other political or scientific forms of authority. Further questions follow, including *which tradition* of economics, and which conventions of calculations are to be applied to different spheres of government. At a certain point, neoliberal discourse encounters moral questions which, at least in its more positivist manifestations, it is unable to understand or to answer. (Davies, 2014, pp. 8–9)

Hayek himself seems to have understood this when he wrote, 'the attempt to direct all economic activity according to a single plan would raise innumerable questions to which the answer could be provided only by a moral rule, but to

---

[5] This quote comes from the US River Realty website: http://www.riverrealty.net/selling-onthemarket.htm.
[6] It is important to note that the discursive divide between 'economy', 'society' and 'state' is an artifact of nineteenth-century liberalism; neo-liberalism, by contrast, collapses the distinction between these spheres (Dean, 2009; Sharpe and Boucher, 2010).

which existing morals have no answer and where there exists no agreed view on what ought to be done' (1944, p. 43). In the face of this uncertainty, Hayek's project was nonetheless a constructivist one, 'committed to the idea that it can and must provoke the change that it wants to see in the world' (Cahill and Konings, 2017, p. 139). More recent generations of neo-liberal economists have not even posed such questions but have treated neo-liberalism as a form of secular faith (Duggan, 2003). Indeed, neo-liberal capitalism seems to have achieved 'the status of being *a new transcendency – a new master*' with politics merely serving as its handmaiden (Han, 2017, p. 7, emphasis in original). In other words, the authoritarian nature of neo-liberal political economy as a form of 'market fundamentalism' that demands obedience, regardless of the absence or otherwise of any empirical evidence (Block and Somers, 2014) – that is, its status as a manifestation of the discourse of the master who must be obeyed because of who they are rather than what they say – is increasingly obvious. As Fisher (2013) notes, the 2008 crisis may have deprived neo-liberalism of its legitimacy but subsequent events have only gone on to show that it can now proceed without the need for legitimacy. Yet those within the elite, charmed circles of neo-liberal politics, disavow this lack of legitimacy by insisting that the technical and the measurable can encompass the moral and the normative, resulting in their encounter with moral questions they are thus 'unable to understand or to answer', to cite Davies above again. In this sense, post-2008 neo-liberal politics, riddled as it is with contradictions without the integrity of a coherent social project, represents a form of what Poulantzas referred to as 'blind piloting' (2008, p. 322).

Neo-liberal 'truths'

In Lacan's schema of the four discourses, the agent (in the upper left-hand quadrant) is driven by a truth (in the lower left-hand quadrant) that underpins and supports its assumption of the right to speak and addresses the other (in the upper right hand quadrant). In the following sections, I discuss how competition, choice and crisis, in different ways, fulfil this role of the 'truth' in relation to neo-liberal political economy as a discourse of the master. However, it is important to retain a sense of 'truth' in quote marks here and resist reading it in terms of some ultimate foundation. Beyond that which we are able to identify and articulate as 'truth', there is always a remainder that is irreducible to explanation and that cannot be fully accounted for (Butler, 2005; Frosh, 2013). In this sense, as we will see, to talk of truth always entails something of an enigma.

The enigmas of competition

As we have seen, neo-liberalism is not, as is sometimes asserted, mainly about the removal or reduction of the state, the anti-state rhetoric of some of its adherents notwithstanding: 'it is more accurately defined as a certain type of interventionism intended politically to fashion economic and social relations governed by competition' (Dardot and Laval, 2013, p. 46). In order to promote the governance of society and regulation of social relations by the market, the state 'has to intervene in society so that competitive mechanisms can play a regulatory role at every moment and in every point in society' (Foucault, 2008, p. 145). Indeed, it the presence of competition that differentiates markets from trade per se, which can occur on a non-competitive basis (Aspers, 2011). But though it is frequently conceived in elemental terms, it is important to remember that, like the markets through which it operates in neo-liberalized economies, competition – think here of the rules and rituals framing competition in sport, along with the specialized coaches, trainers, judges and umpires – is always already legally, institutionally and socially embedded. That is to say, we are always talking about organized rather than 'natural' forms of competition.

Herein lies one source of the fundamental enigma of competition as conceived in neo-liberalism – even more so than in classic liberalism, since it is much more actively promoted in the former than the latter – insofar as competition is viewed as at once a natural, emergent behaviour, reflecting the psychological makeup of individuals and society confronting an unpredictable and constantly changing environment; yet is also seen as something that needs to be managed, governed, nurtured and protected, by rules, regulations and structures, as well as promoted by gurus, strategists and other experts (see Davies, 2014, pp. 28–30, for a fuller discussion).

In this sense, competition can be seen as a technology for achieving inequality, intentionally creating winners and losers, such that a vote for competition is a vote for inequality (Davies, 2014, p. 30). Indeed, it can be argued that the contemporary competition-drive world of neo-liberal capitalism celebrates inequality (Crouch, 2017). Yet, competition involves a paradoxical mix of equality *and* inequality, in that competitors must be formally equal at the outset, in order for the competition to be deemed fair and for unequal outcomes to emerge at the end. 'It is meaningless to speak of "competition" unless there is not only some sense of equivalence amongst those deemed to be the competitors, but also some outlet for contingent differences to be represented. The very notion of "inequality" as an outcome assumes that there must be *something* equal about those whose difference is being measured, proven, justified or criticised' (Davies, 2014, p. 54). Indeed, one of the ways to read the shift from the old style Democrat and Labour parties in the United States and the UK to their New Democrat and New Labour versions, respectively, is in terms of a shift from a concern with trying to ensure more equal outcomes towards a tolerance for significantly different outcomes, including exponentially rising rewards for those in the upper reaches of the remuneration scale, so long as the conditions at the outset were deemed to be fair and meritocratic (Davies, 2014; Hutton, 2015). Competition requires not only the presence of equality and inequality but also a state of balance involving the maintenance of tension between these two poles. Too much *equality* and we slide towards peaceful cooperation; too much *inequality* and we end up in a situation of domination.

Competition is also typically governed by rules and norms, which is one of the ways in which fairness and equality are established, as well as a feature distinguishing competition from anarchy or unprovoked attack. Indeed, one of the reasons we describe the latter as 'senseless' is that such incidents don't seem to fit within recognized rules or respectable norms. Again, however, competition requires that there be a tension between the adherence to rules in the name of fairness and their subversion or abandonment in the search for competitive advantage. Too much adherence to the rules and we end up with polite interchange; too much abandonment and we find ourselves in situations of mortal combat.

Rules thus have a function in preserving competition, in that they must prohibit 'anti-competitive' cooperation or collusion, but, on the other hand, they also need to establish boundaries and limits to acceptable competitive behaviour (Davies, 2014). In contrast to the Hayekian perspective, which saw competition as inherently desirable in itself, and hence in need of protection against misguided intentions of central planning *and* the predation of monopoly (Stedman Jones, 2012), recent neo-liberal policies and practices have been critiqued on the grounds that 'market competition means a process whereby the most successful firms either acquire their less successful rivals or drive them out of business. In other words the end point of the competitive process is the abolition of competition' (Crouch, 2013, p. 224; see also Sennett, 2012, p. 211). In this sense, contemporary neo-liberalism might be described as a form of 'thanato-politics', whereby a social organism's self-preservation strategies stifle, and eventually suffocate, the very vitality and values they were intended to sustain (Santner, 2011, p. 7).

Indeed, Crouch (2011) argues that to talk of neo-liberalism in terms of markets characterized by purportedly free competition ignores the massive economic and political power of large corporations. In response, he urges us 'to confront honestly the fact that the political power of corporations constitutes a widely accepted but highly undemocratic feature of our de facto constitutions' (2011, p. 137). Such political power is exercised in a range of ways, including intensive lobbying, financial donations to individual politicians and political parties, the practice of appointing retiring politicians to lucrative corporate positions and the relationship with government established by corporations holding large contracts for public services, as well as the significant political influence accruing from media control. In this sense, any simple opposition between 'state' and 'market', politics and economics, is fatally undermined. Hence my reading of the 'truth' of neo-liberal political economy not only involves the ethic of competition but also the split represented by our disavowal as a society and as individual (neo-liberal) subjects of the contradictions between *ideals* of free-market competition as the essence of the market and the *reality* of the political influence/dominance of the corporation.

The intensification of the competitive ethic that has occurred as part of the neo-liberalization of society may not have had the impact at the level of the firm and its senior management that the media and politicians would have us believe, but it has 'percolated' down to influence and shape the practices and conditions of institutions in all walks of life, including schools, affecting ordinary wage earners and employees, including, of course, teachers. This has partly been achieved via the discipline of short-term contracts, job insecurity and potential unemployment, justified in terms of globalization and competitive pressures for excellence and continual quality improvement, but also modelled on the great social theatre of competitive sport, which 'has diffused to the masses a normativity centred on generalized competition' and which 'establishes competition as the general norm of individual and collective existence, of national and international life alike' (Dardot and Laval, 2013, pp. 35, 281). For schools this great social theatre has involved the spectacle of league tables and the creation of a competitive climate in which failure to achieve sufficiently strong results, and hence to attract and retain pupils, entails the risk of being branded as inadequate and facing closure.

Competition, empowerment and eliminationism in education

As noted above, education and schools have not been immune to these trends. Symptomatic of the assertion of free market ideologies of competition as a new form of common sense in education is the following from the UK government's National College for Teaching and Leadership online[7] material for their Advanced Diploma in School Business[8] Management (ADSBM) qualification:

> Most entrepreneurial governments promote competition between service providers. They empower citizens by pushing control out of bureaucracy, into the community. They measure the performance of their agencies, focusing not on inputs but on outcomes. They are driven by their goals – their missions – not by their rules and regulations. They redefine their clients as customers and offer them choices. They prevent problems before they emerge ... They put their energies into earning money, not simply spending it. They decentralize authority, embracing participatory mechanisms. And they focus not simply on providing public services, but on catalysing all sectors – public private and voluntary – into action to solve their community's problems. (Osborne and Gaebler, 1992, pp. 19–20)

This ideologically saturated set of assertions, drawn from a 'key text' that has achieved 'cult status' among policymakers and practitioners (Mautner, 2010, p. 55), catalogues a now-familiar series of significant shifts that successive governments have imposed in education and other public services. The National College of Teaching and Leadership website, in citing this material, adopts the same strategy noted above in the discussion of the brochure from Catalyst Corporate Finance, of presenting these shifts as merely naturally occurring changes that have occurred as part of progress. Yet, this is achieved by discursively constructing a set of binary oppositions: bureaucracy versus community; inputs versus outcomes; rules and regulations versus goals and missions; (implied) absence of options versus choice; spending versus earning; centralized versus participatory authority and; simply providing services versus solving problems. The overall effect is to create a world in which all that is

---

[7] https://www.nationalcollege.org.uk/transfer/open/adsbm-phase-4-module-3-transforming-organisations/adsbm-p4m3s2/adsbm-p4m3s2t4.html.
[8] Note the conflation of schools with businesses in the title of the program.

undesirable is linked to old-school bureaucratic public service, against which new model of entrepreneurial government offers a positive contrast.

To be fair, the ADSBM online material, while advocating a 'focus on the benefits of school diversity in terms of synergy and responsiveness', recognizes that 'this is not to suggest that issues of equity and fairness in the operation of quasi-markets have gone away'. But in an educational equivalent of trickle-down economics, promoting competition is currently being given priority over social justice-driven concerns with equity and fairness. Yet, whereas the justice is universal, to the extent that all citizens are (in theory) equal before the law, competition is situated and hence limited, pertaining only to a selection of individuals, considered equals before the relevant measure, be this profitability in business or points in tennis. In Laclau and Mouffe's (2001) terms, it might be argued that justice reflects a logic of difference, seeking to abolish or overcome contingent differences, whereas competition veers towards the logic of equivalence, involving the simplification and reduction of the nuances and complexities of social reality and the consequent organization of the latter into two opposing antagonistic chains, whose meaning is determined, not by the relations among elements within each chain, but purely on the basis of their constructed difference from, and hostility to, the oppositional chain. The consequence for schools is the division of the landscape into mutually exclusive categories, such as succeeding and failing, outstanding and inadequate, innovative and in need of reform – winning and losing.

In addition, justice rests on moral criteria, whereas competition may involve empirical or aesthetic, but never moral, criteria (Davies, 2014, p. 61). This distance from morality and ethics helps explain the links between competition and gaming behaviour, which seeks to exploit loopholes within the rules, pushing hard against, and sometimes transgressing, their limits (Preston, 2015). Indeed, in its pursuit of inequality, competition expresses an ethos of pure antagonism – an eliminationist logic – with no normative rationale or explanation beyond the will to triumph over one's opponents (Davies, 2014, p. 65). For education, this has meant that its purposes 'are no longer addressed as a philosophical or sociological issue (e.g. what is "education?" what is "equity?"); they are a question of winning the global competition, of situating educational achievement as a mimetic of global capitalist competition' (Stronach, 2010, p. 19).

The eliminationist dimension of neo-liberal competition goes back at least to the nineteenth century and the 'extreme naturalism' of Herbert Spencer, whose name is associated with Social Darwinism, though it was Spencer and not Darwin who coined the infamous expression 'survival of the fittest' (Dardot and Laval, 2013). In its Spencerian incarnation, 'we are no longer dealing with a logic of general promotion, but a process of selective elimination … competition is regarded not as a condition of the smooth operation of exchange in the market, but as the pitiless law of life and the mechanism of progress via elimination of the weakest' (Dardot and Laval, 2013, p. 34). This eliminationist logic is identifiable in such policy developments in education as the saddling of university students with crippling levels of debt. It can also be seen in the moves, in contexts such as England, Sweden and the United States, to replace universal public schooling with diverse forms of school provision competing in an education marketplace (Blacker, 2013; Ravitch, 2009), in which the losers face public shaming, disciplinary measures (e.g. OFSTED's 'special measures' in England) and ultimately, institutional closure.

In its eliminationist drive, competition contains something of the fierce rivalry and zero-sum logic characteristic of the Lacanian imaginary, in which the existence of the mirror image serves as a source of threat to one's own status. Latent within these antagonistic, rivalrous relations is, of course, the threat of violence if necessity requires its use. If the rules of competition represent the structuring role of the symbolic and antagonism reflects the rivalries of the imaginary, we might say that this threat of violence is symptomatic of the trauma of the real. Wavering as it does between the justice and equality represented by the rules, and the void of violence and destruction latent within antagonism, competition thus represents the split subject whose spectral truth (in the sense of not being fully or openly admitted to) underpins the master signifier of the market in the master's discourse of neo-liberalism.

Excluded desire as product

a

The attempt to organize the social field of knowledge can never be entirely successful. Inevitably, some excess or product is generated that evades the attempt to capture the social within the symbolic. In the discourse of the master, the place of this excess or surplus product is inhabited by the *petit objet a*, the object-cause of desire representing the suppressed or rejected elements which can have no substantive place in the master's system of knowledge and belief. In education, we might think here of educational purposes such as aesthetic value, the gaining of wisdom or friendship (May, 2012) that sit uncomfortably alongside the instrumentalism of neo-liberalism's competitive market logic. These surplus phenomena can only make sense within the master's competitive terms, never in and for themselves. They are only recognizable to the extent that they contribute to the competitive standing of players – individuals, schools, sectors, nations – in the education market. So, 'in a context where even imagination is appropriated by neoliberalism' (Kontopodis, 2012, p. 4), aesthetic cultivation becomes part of the marketing strategy of elite education providers, while being excluded from curricula of ordinary schools in favour of increased attention to 'basic' skills like literacy and numeracy or marketable areas of knowledge, such as technology and science, that align with the vision of homo economicus that dominates the neo-liberal educational imaginary (Brown, 2015; Fielding and Moss, 2011; Kulz, 2017; Stronach, 2010).

But neo-liberal capitalism doesn't only exclude desires for aesthetic values; it also rejects ethical and political values such as justice and equality that are incompatible with its winners versus losers logic – or to be more precise, it rejects 'equality of outcomes' in favour of 'equality of opportunity' (Cahill and Konings, 2017, p. 79). Embedded within the neo-liberal logic of competition is a deep-seated belief that economic success and the possession of wealth are functions of spiritual worth, while those who suffer misfortune are in some way deemed responsible for their fate. Within this worldview, empathy is short-circuited by callous demands to 'get over it' or 'snap out of it', as austerity, involving toughness in relation to both self and others, is advocated as the road to redemption (Konings, 2015, pp. 111–12). Likewise, freedom and choice are celebrated but only to the degree that we can be held responsible for our failures and certainly not to the degree where we might seriously envision genuine social change (Kotsko, 2018).

In education, an overriding emphasis on competition and the erosion of empathy have gone hand in hand with standardization, reductionism and compartmentalization (Fielding and Moss, 2011; Taubman, 2009). The overall consequences of these developments include, not only the loss of a shared vision, however flawed and utopian it might have been, of the common school as a site for forging democratic equality (Giroux, 2012), but also 'the elimination of public education as we have known it, an educational eliminationism that now sets its sights on the set of vestigial commitments represented in the very idea of universal education, one of modernity's core utopian promises' (Blacker, 2013, p. 204). What this means is the escalation of an already visible trend towards increasing disparity between the elite education provided to those with the requisite social, cultural and economic capital to mark them as destined for leadership and management roles and that afforded those destined to populate the precariat, whose education is more and more typified by 'repressive approaches to teaching and learning with a heavy emphasis on bodily control, eyes on the teacher, feet flat on the floor, and punishments for deviations from the norm' (Saltman, 2014b, p. 54). Such punitive, authoritarian approaches have been characteristic of US charter school networks, such as the Knowledge is Power Program (KIPP), that target 'disadvantaged' groups (Clarke, 2014a; Lack, 2009), as well as the UK free schools and academies that have embraced the 'no excuses', 'tough love' ethic as their model (Kulz, 2017). Indeed, in the UK the Coalition and subsequent Conservative governments endorsed such approaches as a necessary response to the symptoms of what is seen, particularly after the 2011 riots, as growing social indiscipline and lawlessness (Stevenson, 2015). Since then, such approaches have only grown in popularity among policymakers and the media in the UK, the United States and Australia (Johnson and Sullivan, 2016; MacAllister, 2016), though it has also been argued that the high media profile of particular schools adopting such policies, such as Michaela School, discussed in Chapter 5, exaggerates the reality on the ground (Curran, 2017). In a cruel irony representing the extension of neo-liberal capitalism's competitive logic, the schools catering to those deemed in need of such policies are being reframed as investment opportunities for those with surplus capital. In a further irony of the times, the authoritarian school regimes that extend the power of the state and/or corporations over education are frequently framed in discourses associated with the left, involving narratives of freedom and liberation from the misguided egalitarian policies deemed to have held disadvantaged students back (Fekete, 2018; Stevenson, 2015), just as in Australia the imposition on schools of tight managerialist-style accountability by the federal government was ironically framed as a 'revolution' (M. Clarke, 2012b). In each case, just as 'the re-masculinised state seeks to distance itself from the role of caring for the bodies of the vulnerable by developing a more punitive and penalizing legal system … [whose] … aim is to push poor citizens into low paid and insecure jobs by threatening to terminate benefits, while using the prison system as the ultimate sanction for those who do not conform' (Stevenson, 2015, p. 5), so the resurgence of authoritarian approaches in education employs threats against potential recalcitrants: expulsion for students and closure for schools. The choice is one between compliance or relegation to neo-liberal education's surplus.

Conclusion

This chapter has examined neo-liberalism as the dominant form of political economy in recent decades and considered its implications for education and education policy. The chapter framed this reading of neo-liberal politics in terms of Lacan's authoritarian and ubiquitous discourse of the master. Within this reading, the chapter argued that neo-liberal political economy positions education as the other to be repeatedly criticized for failing to produce sufficiently productive subjects in response to its demands that the field of knowledge be organized in accordance with its master signifier of the market. The chapter considered how the master signifier of the market is underpinned by a 'truth' divided between the power of the corporation and the ideal of competition, itself split between, on the one hand, compliance with formal rules and, on the other, a violent and destructive will to victory at any price. The consequence of this discourse is that, at the same time as it organizes the field of knowledge in education around the logic of the market, the discourse generates a surplus or excess in the form of desires and subjects that cannot be accommodated and hence must be suppressed, rejected or eliminated.

4

The Discourse of the University and Neo-liberal Education Policy: The Utopia of Rules

The university has an extremely precise function, in effect, one that at every moment is related to the state we are in with respect to the master's discourse – namely, its elucidation. As a matter of fact, this discourse has been a masked discourse for a very long time.

Lacan, 2007, p. 148

The discourse of the university is therefore a safeguard, a 'castling' manoeuvre; the master signifier is stowed away in the knapsack of the soldier/bureaucrat who rationalizes the exercise of power.

Nobus and Quinn, 2005, p. 133

Whether motivated by a faith in 'rationality' or a fear of arbitrary power, the end result of this bureaucratized notion of freedom is to move towards the dream of a world where play has been limited entirely – or, at best, boxed away in some remote location far from any serious, consequential human endeavor – while every aspect of life is reduced to some elaborate, rule-bound game … a kind of utopia of rules.

Graeber, 2015, pp. 204, 191

Introduction

The world of the twenty-first century is one in which people are expected to dedicate themselves tirelessly to economic self-advancement and the accumulation of capital in its various forms, in pursuit of what Lacan refers to, as we saw in Chapter 2, as 'the service of goods'. This is a world in which technical information and expertise are ready at hand to address any attendant anxieties, seeking to sooth and sedate disquiet with the reassuring confidence of objective knowledge. It is a world that corresponds with remarkable uncanniness to the social dynamic Lacan associates with the discourse of the university. It is important to note at the outset that this discourse is not limited to the institution of the university but describes the workings of any social regime or institutional domain that is characterized by claims to expertise, particularly when this expertise finds expression in various forms of guidelines and policy. In other words, the university discourse is the discourse of modern bureaucracy.

Thus, whereas the previous chapter examined neo-liberal political economy, providing a reading of the latter as a manifestation of Lacan's discourse of the master that operates through processes of governing and/or brainwashing, the current chapter draws on the discourse of the university – a discourse of expertise which operates through processes of educating and/or indoctrinating (Bracher, 1994) – in order to explore the field of neo-liberal education policy as one manifestation of the neo-liberal politics discussed in the previous chapter. The analysis and discussion offered here has strong links to that of the previous chapter, not least because the master and the university are both discourses of impersonal control and authority, represented in the occupation of the dominant position of agency by the master signifier, S1, in the discourse of the master and by impersonal knowledge, S2, in the discourse of the university.

The chapter begins with a brief outline of Lacan's discourse of the university as a discourse of expertise that is reluctant to examine the underlying assumptions underpinning its presumed expertise. Indeed, the discourse of the university, as manifested in neo-liberal education policy, deploys a defensive strategy, involving a strange sort of 'anti-politics' that, while steeped in ideology, nonetheless disavows its own political nature. Instead, it entertains fantasies of economic triumph, alongside threats of economic decline, linking these directly to issues of (narrowly conceived) education performance. This strategy enables neo-liberal education policy to discredit its opponents as politically or ideologically driven, while at the same time allowing it to deny its own politics, which are passed off as mere common sense. This is achieved through the operation of what I describe as a discursive duopoly, consisting of a projected consensus clustering around an instrumental vision of education, the primary justification of which resides in its capacity to service the needs of the economy – Lacan's 'service of goods'.

The discourse of the university

One way of reading the discourse of the university is in terms of the substitution of technical expertise for normative politics, enabling decisions to be made on the basis of supposedly neutral evidence and logical argument, rather than on the basis of interest and passion. Such aspirations were reflected in the search for a 'third way', that would enable government to move 'beyond left or right' by embracing 'the various myths of the *totally* reconciled society – which invariably presuppose the absence of leadership, that is, the withering away of the political' (Laclau, 2005, p. 63, emphasis in original). This denial of the political and its replacement by a regime of expertise is characteristic of Lacan's discourse of the university.

As noted above, the discourse of the university, like the discourse of the master, is an authoritarian discourse. Indeed, Lacan viewed the university discourse as the historical successor to the discourse of the master, though it is perhaps more accurate to describe it as the latter's steward, preserving and prolonging its power (Schroeder, 2008, p. 54), or perhaps its avatar (Bracher, 1994, p. 117). Regardless of the precise relationship, the two are closely related. In addition to the points already noted above, a further link between the two discourses can be seen in the way that, whereas the master's discourse expelled the object-cause of desire, *a*, as its product or surplus, the university discourse addresses this remainder of the real in the position of the other, attempting to incorporate it within a totalized field of knowledge. In this sense, both discourses are conservative, preserving existing power relations and defending the status quo by seeking to exclude or to colonize desire, rather than to allow or encourage it the freedom to assume a position of truth or agency as occurs in the discourses of the hysteric and the analyst respectively – as we will see in Chapters 5 and 6.

The emergence of the discourse of the university as a powerful social link is connected to the rise of modernity, which, for Lacan, involves an increasing importance placed upon the production and circulation of expert knowledge. This, in turn, entails the gradual displacement of politics by bureaucracy and of sovereign rule over people by the management and administration of processes (Boucher, 2006; Foucault, 1977). These shifts are reflected in movement of knowledge from the position of addressed other in the discourse of the master to the position of agency in the discourse of the university. The university's discourse involves educating and interpellating subjects, promising them direct access to satisfaction through knowledge. Yet the university's discourse simultaneously depends on the support of a 'master' whose covert authority underpins the supposed agency of knowledge. The discourse of the university is represented diagrammatically in Figure 4.1.

Unlike the discourse of the master, whose utterances flow from the position of arbitrary authority, the discourse of the university involves the pursuit of knowledge 'for its own sake' and hence purports to speak from a position of disinterested expertise. Attempting to project a neutral but comprehensive

$$S2 \quad \rightarrow \quad a$$

$$\uparrow \quad \overline{} \qquad \overline{} \quad \downarrow$$

$$S1 \quad // \quad \$$$

Figure 4.1 The discourse of the university

and systemic form of knowledge, the agent, S2, addresses the remainder of
the real in the subject's desire, *a*, seeking to incorporate this desire within the
web of discourse. However, such attempts at discursive colonization, involving
a characteristic and familiar mixture of coercion and seduction (Bracher,
2006, p. 93), inevitably fail, with the object-cause of desire, *a*, representing the
unassimilable remainder of the Lacanian real, which resists co-option into
the symbolic system and around which the latter wraps itself. The resulting
by-product is the alienated and split-subject, $. Driving the process from the
position of 'truth' is the master signifier, S1, unacknowledged and disavowed
yet all the more powerful as a result.

At first glance, the university discourse's mode of governance on the basis of
expertise seems like an improvement in comparison with the naked authority
exercised by the discourse of the master. The turn to the discourse of the university
represents the replacement of the feudal lord by 'the bookkeeper, the bureaucrat,
the statistician, and today perhaps the performance reviewer' (Wright, 2015,
p. 138). It suggests a movement from a form of rule that is based on arbitrary
authority and unthinking deference to one grounded in reason and rationality.
Yet the institution of bureaucratic rules and practices does not eliminate arbitrary
personal power and influence: 'such reforms may aim to eliminate arbitrary
personal authority, but of course they never actually do. Personal authority just
jumps up a level, and becomes the ability to set the rules aside in specific cases (a
sort of miniature version of sovereign power again)' (Graeber, 2015, p. 197). In
other words, the displacement of the master's discourse by that of the university
should not lead us into thinking that power has been replaced by knowledge, as
suggested in dominant neo-liberal narratives.

> What Lacan recognizes in the university discourse is a new and reformed
> discourse of the master. In its elementary form, it is a discourse that is pronounced
> from the place of supposedly neutral knowledge, the truth of which (hidden
> below the bar) is Power, that is, the master signifier. The constitutive lie of this
> discourse is that it disavows its performative dimension; it always presents, for
> example, that which leads to a political decision, founded on power, as a simple
> insight into the state of things (or public polls, objective reports, and so on).
> (Zupančič, 2006, p. 168)

The valorization of expertise is fundamental to the operation of neo-liberal education policy, which relies on supposedly neutral notions such as 'evidence-based policy' and the displacement of normative rationales involving ethical and political judgment by the technicist pursuit of 'what works' (Biesta, 2007, 2010). However, the apparent disinterestedness of this expert knowledge is misleading, in that it denies and disguises the mutual implications and interests characterizing the relationship between policy and politics (Dale, 1989; Ball, 1990). These connections reflect a shared etymology. As Codd argues, 'Fundamentally, policy is about the exercise of political power and the language that is used to legitimate that process' (1988, p. 235). Politics and policy are each normative, rather than merely technical domains, in that both are concerned with values – their formulation, institution, reproduction and contestation; whereas policy can be read in terms of the authoritative allocation of values (Easton, 1953), politics concerns the process of prioritizing those values (Stråth, 2005).

In education, the inseparability of policy and politics has long been recognized (e.g. Bourdieu, 1977; Bourdieu and Passeron, 1977; Bowles and Gintis, 1976). Their co-implication stems from the social and economic value attaching to education in society as a positional, and not just an inherent, good, and the inevitable requirement, given finite resources, to make decisions regarding the allocation of this good. Yet contemporary neo-liberal education policy discourses, for example those around issues of curriculum, pedagogy and assessment considered below, are often presented by politicians and policymakers as matters of technical efficiency rather than normative choices, just as neo-liberal austerity is typically presented as a matter of economic necessity rather than a policy choice; as a consequence, their political nature, including their deep implication with issues of socio-political power and privilege, is liable to being overlooked.

In what follows in this chapter I take up the issues of the technicization and attendant depoliticization of education by examining certain developments in education policy through the lens of the discourse of the university. A key point, however, is that bureaucratic institutions – for example, government departments and education policymakers – do not put forward policies for the sake of doing so or merely because it is expected of them: they do so with a purpose, typically framed in terms of a problem for which policy will provide a solution. In Lacanian terms, we might say that policymakers simultaneously identify a 'lack' and the course of action that will address, and presumably plug, or fill, this lack. Critically, however, both the identification of the problem/lack and of the solution/plugging are two sides of a coin. In other words, they are mutually constitutive activities in that the construction a problem is an integral step in justifying the policy moves that will serve as its remedy (Bacchi, 2012; Webb, 2014). As we will see, the justification of policy through claims to expertise in relation to problems that co-constituted along with their purported solution is a key aspect of the discourse of the university.

It is also important to highlight that, as noted above by Zupančič, the university discourse is closely linked to the master's discourse in a number of ways. Perhaps most obviously, as noted above, both are authoritative, rather than resistant, discourses, but since the university discourse is derived from the master's discourse by an anticlockwise quarter rotation of the elements in the mathemic diagram, we arrive at a situation where knowledge (S2), rather than power (S1), is in the seat of agency, with 'the university discourse providing a sort of legitimation or rationalization of the master's will' (Fink, 1995, p. 132). In other words, whereas the discourse of the master *demands* obedience, 'the university insists that it *deserves* to be obeyed', making it in some ways more insidious and hence dangerous (Schroeder, 2008, p. 55). Lulled by its reassurances that things are irremediably complex and hence best left to the experts (here we might recall the events leading up to the 2008 banking crisis), and disheartened by the demands of engagement, we tend to push difficult issues, including questions about how society functions and the consequences of decisions made on our behalf, out of sight and out of mind. As Robert Musil (1880–1942) wrote in his sprawling and unfinished novel, *The Man Without Qualities*,

> There is always something ghostly about living in a well-ordered state. You cannot step into the street or drink a glass of water or get on a streetcar without touching the balanced levers of a gigantic apparatus of laws and interrelations, setting them in motion or letting them maintain you in your peaceful existence; one hardly knows anything of these levers, which reach deep into the inner workings and, coming out the other side, lose themselves in a network whose structure has never yet been unraveled by anyone. So one denies their existence, just as the average citizen denies the air, maintaining that it is empty space. (1995 [1940], pp. 165–6)

In similar fashion, the pervasive power of the discourse of the university in modern life is such that we typically fail to register its enveloping presence. Yet, like Musil's 'balanced levers of a gigantic apparatus of laws and interrelations', it touches and shapes almost every aspect of our existence, from cradle to grave and beyond. This chapter considers neo-liberalism's recasting of education policy, the 'levers' of which 'reach deep into the inner workings' of education and schools and penetrate the lives of teachers and students, in this light.

Expert knowledge as agent in the discourse of the university

As befits a discourse that is characterized by claims to expertise and ambitions towards discursive assimilation, the position of the agent in the discourse of the university is occupied by S2, the field of knowledge. In contrast to the obviously biased perspective of the master signifier, here agency is exercised by the wider field of knowledge – by 'all signifiers and their unbiased wisdom, the reasonableness of *a* language (S2) whose neutral symbolic system seems to surround and grasp the real being (*a*)' (Pavón-Cuéllar, 2011, p. 266). It is from this all-encompassing position of neutral expertise, reflected in seemingly reasonable expressions like 'evidence-based' and 'best practice', that education policy as agent seeks to encircle and envelope the very existence of the institutions and individual subjects that form the object of its address.

In other words, because it suppresses its reliance on the power of its master signifiers, S1, that remain 'hidden' from view beneath the bar in the position of 'truth', the discourse of the university has a tendency to pretensions of neutral, yet all-embracing, all-inclusive expertise in relation to knowledge, or S2. Thus, in the discourse of the university, it is as if policy artefacts like national curricula were the real stuff of knowledge – authentic, comprehensive, genuine, legitimate, neutral, substantive, necessary and sufficient – not partial and situated, contingent and contestable. Therefore, on the basis of this purported neutrality and expertise, policy can be deemed necessary and sufficient for *all* schools, *all* teachers and *all* students.

The discourse of the university's pretension to neutral knowledge is reflected in the way fields like education policy articulate 'objective', for example 'evidence-based', policy goals, designed to address the collective interests and aspirations of society as a whole. In doing so, the discourse of the university seeks to integrate individual and social desire, the individual and collective *a*, within its webs and chains of signification. Consequently, 'no provision is made for individual subjects and their desires and idiosyncrasies' that do not fit within the predetermined limits of the system (Bracher, 1994, p. 115). In other words, in its mode of address to subjects, the discourse of the university is only able to conceive of them as unformed (object-*a*) – that is, as 'blank slates', 'empty vessels' – ready and waiting to be transformed through knowledge into subjects characterized by objective and object-like qualities: as transmitters or receivers of predetermined curricula, for example, or as policy subjects who are amenable to 'steering at a distance' in order to ensure correct conduct and who follow directions, rather than as agents of their own purposes with a legitimate capacity to express their own critical views on policy or to negotiate what is taught, and how, in dialogue others based on their own experience, values and beliefs.

Education as other in the discourse of the university

a

A recurring theme in this book is the fantasmatic positioning of education, and hence by extension those working within the sector and the young people they care for and educate, as the guarantors of the economy and saviours of (an ageing) society. This responsibility is being placed upon social subjects at an ever-earlier age. For example, the 2004 English government policy document *Choice for Parents* asserts the following:

> It is in everyone's interests that children are given the opportunity to fulfil their potential. This is all the more important in the context of an ageing society, where current generations will depend more heavily on those who follow ... Investment in children to ensure that they have opportunities and capabilities to contribute in positive ways throughout their lives is money well spent and it will reduce the costs of social failure. (HM Treasury, Department for Education and Skills, Department for Work and Pensions and Department for Trade and Inudustry, 2004, p. 7)

Nearly a decade later, and from a different government, the same theme about early childhood education and care as an investment in the economy is repeated in the policy document *More Great Childcare*:

> We are in a challenging global environment where we must use the best of everyone's talents. We need to support our children to be able to succeed in a world that is fast-changing, and where the skills and knowledge of a nation's population are the best guarantee of their economic security and prosperity. (Truss, 2013)

The concerns about economic competitiveness evident in these statements are compounded by anxieties as to whether the current workforce is capable of meeting the challenge and whether parents are exercising appropriate levels of forethought and responsibility. Hence, the deficit discourses of workforce as lacking go hand in hand with discourses of accountability that frame professionals as in need of regulation and inspection. For instance, the 2004 document notes that 'the quality of the workforce and the qualifications on offer at the moment are not good enough. Staff are on low pay and in too many cases lack basic skills' (p. 6) and argues for the need for a 'high quality workforce to raise the standards of provision and act as a guarantor of consistent quality' (p. 25). The document then outlines a number of strategies explaining how this is to be achieved:

> Regulation and inspection which together ensure that minimum standards of provision are met, and that quality is objectively observed and assessed, and reported transparently; and the influence of parents. First, where parents have good information and a choice between providers they can use their market power to increase quality. Second, parents can influence quality more directly where their views are incorporated into the planning and delivery of services in a systematic way. (HM Treasury et al., 2004, p. 25)

The message here is that a high-quality workforce is the key but is only to be trusted insofar as it is monitored by regular inspections and rendered visible to the gaze of parents and government. In the process, alternatives to these neo-liberal themes of audit, accountability, individuation, responsibilization and choice – including other possible values such as empowerment, autonomy and trust and alternative discourses of collaboration and relational concern – are ignored, delegitimized and hence silenced.

In some ways, these extensions of anxiety about appropriate socialization into dominant discourses to early childhood education and parenting are not surprising; for in the world of modernity, as soon as we are born – and even before – we are the object of others' readings of us, including their hopes, dreams, expectations and aspirations that shape who we can and will become. The discourse of the university, as the discourse of neutral knowledge and expertise reflects the role of government in modern societies in ensuring that we develop as competitive, entrepreneurial subjects. In order to achieve this, government shifts from sovereign rule to a mode of governance that entails its entanglement in all aspects of life:

> Government must not form a counterpoint or a screen, as it were, between society and economic processes. It has to intervene on society as such, in its

fabric and depth. Basically, it has to intervene on society so that competitive mechanisms can play a regulatory role at every moment and every point in society and by intervening in this way its objective will become possible, that is to say, a general regulation of society by the market. (Foucault, 2008, p. 145)

In order to achieve this 'general regulation', the discourse of the university's evidence-based and expert-informed policy formulations articulate suitable aims for society, and on this basis prescribe appropriate aspirations to shape the conduct and behaviour of individuals through the provision of targeted incentives and disincentives. Yet, the control sought by governance is never fully achieved but engenders resistance, in turn providing the rationale for further rounds and intensified forms of governance.

Translating this again into Lacanian psychoanalytic terms, we might say that from our earliest days, 'we occupy the position of the receiver of speech, and we do so in the form of the *a*, the as-yet unassimilated piece of the real that is the object of the desire of those around us' (Bracher, 1994, p. 115). To the extent that education is about being shaped and formed in particular ways, our education thus begins early and it is in this sense that we might understand Arendt's statement that 'the essence of education is natality, the fact that human beings are *born* into the world' (1954, p. 174). But as Foucault suggests above, the process of assimilation into would-be totalizing systems of knowledge is characteristic of the discourse of the university and is not limited to infancy or childhood. It is also characteristic of bureaucratic processes involving knowledge, of which formal, institutionalized health and education systems offer quintessential examples. In each case, objective knowledge, presumed to be all knowing, addresses a subject it constitutes as desubjectivized (Žižek, 1998, p. 78) – for example, a patient reduced to an impersonal object of diagnosis and treatment or a learner reduced to a generic object of standardized curriculum, pedagogy, assessment and evaluation.

Yet at the same time, there is also a compulsive obsession with the other in the discourse of the university. The other intrigues and fascinates in and of itself, but it is thus all the more important that it be fully incorporated and assimilated into the system. In this sense, there is a crucial ambiguity attached the other in the discourse of the university – and there is an interesting parallel to the ambiguity of Lyotard's notion of performativity (Ball, 2003) as creative regeneration *and* destructive terror (Singh, 2015) – in that 'to be other as objet petit a is to be accorded the status of something crucial to the process of knowledge production at the very same moment as one is reduced to an object' (Parker, 2001b, p. 38).

Students, for example, are sought by education institutions for their distinctive abilities as well as representing a source of making up the numbers; they are expected to offer something new and distinctive and at the same time subordinate themselves to the values and mission of the university (Parker, 2001b, p. 39).

Given that, as we saw in the previous chapter, the governing value of the master's discourse of neo-liberal political economy is that of the market, and given that the university discourse rationalizes and legitimates the master's purposes, it is not surprising that the contemporary subject of education is addressed primarily in terms of an investor in its own human capital or, in Foucault's (2008) terms, as an 'entrepreneur of the self' seeking to maximize its position and standing in accordance with the competitive logic of the market. Thus schools are incited to compete with each other for positions in league tables, as well as for student enrolments, on the basis of their performance in mandated tests. Meanwhile students compete within this same arena of examinations for limited university places and jobs by memorizing and regurgitating '"dead knowledge", furiously exchanged in a competitive rat race whose real purpose is to make sure that nothing ever changes' (Vighi, 2010, p. 47). Behaviour that does not conform to the pursuit of the objectively determined goals of the university discourse is dismissed as irresponsible or irrational and those advocating or perpetrating it risk being labelled, and possibly execrated, as trouble makers or marginalized as eccentrics or aberrations.

Despite all the furious exchange of information and frenetic, anxiety-ridden activity exhorted and exacted by the discourse of the university, the results achieved by students are never satisfactory, the levels of performance attained by schools never quite good enough. Indeed, as Lacan noted, 'the desire to know is not what leads to knowledge' (2007, p. 23), for borne along by the signifying chain, at the heart of this desire for knowledge lies an inevitable 'encounter with an unconscious knowledge in which we are concerned but which does not concern us' (Nobus and Quinn, 2005, p. 111). Put another way, we might say that for Lacan, knowledge can never be reduced to or equated with mere conceptual knowledge but is always entwined with, and enveloped within, unconscious knowledge – something we can see embodied in the product of the discourse of the university, that is, the split subject, $ (Nobus and Quinn, 2005, p. 127; Verhaeghe, 1995, p. 95). In other words, knowledge is 'a plus that, as it were, coincides with a minus … a surplus which is always-already lost' (Vighi, 2010, p. 45), entailing for the subject of knowledge a 'dialectic of frustration' (Lacan, 2007, p. 19) and fuelling a cycle of relentless, if ultimately futile, pursuit – a dynamic we can recognize in repeated exhortations to engage in lifelong learning or in the relentless quest for continuous quality improvement.

Indeed, life within the discourse of the university often feels like being on a treadmill – one on which someone keeps ratcheting up the speed, increment by increment, so that no matter how hard one runs one can never quite keep up, let alone get ahead of the curve. As McGowan (2013, p. 172) notes, 'whereas the old master remained at a distance, the expert is always in the subject's face … never allowing the subject room to breathe'. There is always more to be achieved, always room for further improvements. Whatever we have accomplished so far is never enough, for in this performative world one is either moving forwards or backwards, up or down, but never standing still,[1] in relation to the competitors against whose performance our own is constantly being compared. For students, relief at the conclusion of the exam also marks the beginning of the countdown to the next, initiating a new cycle of rising anxiety. For teachers, just as one lesson is taught, the next inevitably comes into view. For schools, the conclusion of one OFSTED inspection marks the time to begin preparing for the next, for one never knows when – how *soon* – will be the next time an inspector calls. For academics, completion of one key task only means that others immediately assume its place in one's consciousness as, for example, the acceptance of one journal article triggers anxieties about when and where the next will be written, submitted and accepted. The moment when promotion is achieved is also the time to begin building the case for the next step up the institutional ladder. To quote McGowan again, 'instead of emancipating the subject, knowledge traumatizes and plays a central role in the subjection of subject to the social order of regulation' (McGowan, 2013, p. 172).

The relentlessness of the quest for knowledge in the discourse of the university and the impossibility of this quest ever being satisfied reflects the 'disjunction of impossibility' that prevents perfect or complete communication between addressing agent and addressed other in Lacan's model of discourse (Verhaeghe, 1995, p. 84). Indeed, the existence of the disjunction of impossibility ensures that the cycle continues to repeat itself: in the specific case of the discourse of the university, the disjunction between the performative demands ensuing from the field of objectified knowledge, S2, and the object-cause of unstaunchable desire,

---

[1] The logic of continual quality improvement is endemic in today's neo-liberalized institutions, as reflected, e.g., in the logo of the University of New South Wales, Australia, 'home to those who never stand still'. See: http://neverstandstill.unsw.edu.au/.

a, which occupies the position of the addressed other, only spurs the compulsive repetition of the quest for discursive colonization.

The consequence of this relentless pursuit of objectively measurable, comparable and improvable performance, so characteristic of the discourse of the university, is that, although links are made between vast quantities of supposedly neutral 'data' about individual and collective performance, the singularity of the individual – whether understood through such everyday expressions, such as personality or, in education, in terms of teachers' and students' idiosyncratic interests and passions – is exiled or relegated from consideration. Underlying this exile is the operation of language as discourse, which operates via a binary logic – inclusions and exclusions, absences and presences, surplus and loss – that takes no account of the individual. Thus, for example, neo-liberal policy promotes notions such as 'quality', 'standards' and 'effectiveness'; the 'good' school, the 'successful' student and the 'professional' teacher. What is crucial to note here is that the dominant operative opposition to these terms is not some other version of quality, the good student or the professional teacher but the absence of quality, the bad student or the unprofessional teacher. In other words, neo-liberal policy is constituted though a series of inclusions and exclusions, which establish a structure of relations that organizes how we think about education. The links between dominant signifiers, such as quality, and particular signifieds, such as exam results, is arbitrary, insofar as the signifier (e.g. 'quality') could be attached to other signifieds (e.g. engagement) or combinations of signifieds (engagement and creativity); what is critical is the networks and relationships that are established between various signifiers – such as quality, standards and effectiveness – in order to constitute a particular discourse or to establish harmony among discourses which may or may not be commensurate.

The arbitrary and contingent, yet also political and ideological, nature of the signifiers deployed in policy is evident in the policy agenda of the 'self-improving school-led system' in England in the past decade (Greany and Higham, 2018). This agenda has incorporated a range of themes (2018, p. 23), including: the promotion of de-regulation and decentralization as schools were encouraged to become academies and 'free' themselves from local government control; the promotion of 'choice' and competition within a marketized school landscape characterized by enhanced incentives and access for new 'providers'; the championing of business-derived operational practices and governance models; and school-led capacity building and knowledge transfer in order to 'spread best practice' (Department for Education (DfE), 2016, p. 75) – all of which were intended to enhance the autonomy, agility and responsiveness of schools and which were counter-posed to the bureaucratic sclerosis that was deemed to characterize education under local education authorities. Yet, these policies have unfolded in a constantly shifting policy environment that also included de facto re-regulation and centralization in relation to the curriculum and the imposition of hierarchical governance and punitive accountability requirements, including the capacity of eight Regional Schools Commissioners to intervene in situations where schools have been deemed to be 'underperforming' or 'coasting'. The consequences of this agenda have included – ironically, for an agenda that was initially intended to enhance school autonomy – the strengthening of multi-academy trusts at the expense of schools, the replication of the unwieldy bureaucratic structures for which local education authorities were critiqued, only without any democratic mandate or accountability (Greany and Higham, 2018; Wilkins, 2017). The consequences of this agenda have also included the undermining of local teacher professionalism within a de facto environment of 'coercive autonomy' and the creation of significant practical and moral challenges for schools and school leaders 'as they seek to balance the needs of pupils with the institutional self-interest of the school in the context of local and national landscapes that are frequently incoherent and increasingly unequal' (Greany and Higham, 2018, pp. 95, 98). In Lacanian terms, what this account highlights is the inability of the symbolic to adequately map onto that kernel of the real that escapes any attempt at symbolization and the capacity of ideological agendas that refuse this impossibility, and that insist on bending the world to their ideals, to lead in Orwellian fashion to situations that are the very opposite of what they purport to promote.

As a result, discourses – and here I am using the term in its more widely recognized Foucauldian sense, rather than in the more specific Lacanian sense – which are partial and contingent, and may well also be inconsistent and incoherent, are established as dominant, not because of any inherent superiority in terms of content but as a result of the discursive work on the part of policymakers, politicians and the media. This same process can also achieve a perception of harmony among different discourses that are incommensurable, as for example, the repeated refrain on the part of policymakers to make 'every school a great school', which overlooks the tensions between discourses of quality, based on logics of competition which require winners and losers, and discourses of equality, grounded in notions of justice and fairness (Clarke, 2012b; Gillies, 2008). This absence of integrity and coherence in much of the language that circulates and dominates in society at any given time prompted Lacan to ask after the basis of meaning and to link this to the binary calculus of presence and absence that governs language:

> What is the meaning of meaning? Meaning is the fact that the human being isn't master of this primordial, primitive language. He has been thrown into it, committed, caught up in its gears ... Man [*sic*] isn't master in his own house. There is something into which he integrates himself, which through its combinations already governs ... Man is engaged with all his being in the procession of numbers, in a primitive symbolism which is distinct from imaginary representations. (1991, p. 307)

This act of repression, associated with the remainder of the real that escapes symbolic closure, is represented in the mathemic representation of the discourse of the university, in the location of the split subject, $, occupying the position of product or surplus.

The alienated split subject as product of the university discourse

As we have seen, the totalizing domination of every aspect of the *a*, representing the un-integrated remainder of the real that is also the object-cause of desire – including the desiring being of teachers, students and parents – by S2, representing the field of educational knowledge, is fundamentally impossible. Knowledge is haunted by its others, ignorance and stupidity, which constitute the necessary absence enabling its presence. However much knowledge one has is always overshadowed by how much one does not know and insofar as the learning other simultaneously learns how much it does not know, 'the discourse of the university produces in those it addresses a sense of insufficiency or lack' (Parker, 2001b, p. 39). As a consequence, the product of the discourse of the university, located in the bottom right-hand side of the diagrammatic representation, is the alienated split subject, $, at once representing both product and loss, including the division between those parts of subjects' identities that are called into being by the enunciations of the discourse and those that are excluded, or repressed, escaping conscious control and hence remaining below the bar. The other can seek to remedy this situation by gaining more knowledge yet this will only produce more loss as the inevitable consequence of the attempt to grasp knowledge fully.

Here it is possible to relate Lacan's ideas to concepts and ideas from kindred poststructural theories. In Foucauldian terms, we can think about how any discourse always entails, and even engenders, resistance to the meanings, practices and subjectivities it produces. In the terms of Laclau and Mouffe's discourse theory, we can think in terms of the impossibility of any discourse, or constellation of meaning, capturing and mapping the whole of the field of discursivity. In other words, it is impossible for any discourse to represent all potential meanings, since some 'elements', or building blocks of possible meaning, which comprise the discourse, will resist incorporation into the necessarily partial and contingent semiotic web spun by any particular discourse.

Returning to the terms of Lacanian psychoanalytic theory, the object *a* addressed by the signifying chain, S2, in the discourse of the university is precisely that element which lies beyond the reach of the signifier and the repeated attempts of the signifying chain to bring about this incorporation can only lead to further alienation/repression of desire and the division of the subject between endlessly proliferating signifiers (Verhaeghe, 1995). In other words, 'the fatal flaw of the discourse of the university is that its product, $, the (absent) subject of the unconscious merely reveals the vanity of the project to rationalize and streamline the production of human resources' (Nobus and Quinn, 2005, p. 135). The implication of this insight for education, located as it is within the discourse of the university, is that efforts to promote standards in order to achieve 'excellence' and 'quality', whether through exhortation and command, or through rational persuasion and expert evidence, can never fulfil their own expectations and consequently will only produce further alienation, division and demoralization in teachers, students and schools.

Certainly in the case of teachers and teacher educators, particularly in contexts like England and the United States, the determination on the part of policymakers to reform teaching and teacher education by imposing top-down systematization and standardization, based on the specious and simplistic notion that these groups are collectively responsible for their societies' economic underperformance, but also to 'ensure discredited ideas unsupported by firm evidence are not promoted to new teachers' (Department for Education (DfE), 2016, p. 12), has been a significant contributing factor to professional alienation and demoralization (Clarke and Phelan, 2017; Gilroy, 2014). In relation to teaching, for example, the argument has been made that the discourse of standards and accountability have led to the pedagogical equivalent of painting by numbers, whereby teachers' critical and creative agency is effectively undermined (e.g. Taubman, 2009). Yet such tight, hierarchical accountability, a reflection of neo-liberalism's deep distrust of professionals, fails to recognize how fundamental elements of good teaching are implicit, idiosyncratic and contingent. As a result, the codified knowledge in documents like teacher professional standards reduces teaching to a series of mere statements of the obvious – such as 'know how students learn'.

In the case of students, the imposition of standardized curriculum and high-stakes assessment regimes has likewise produced anxiety and alienation accompanied by high levels of stress and depression. This in turn manifests itself in destructive behaviour patterns, with symptoms ranging from drug and alcohol abuse to suicide identified as consequences of the pressure to succeed in high stakes environments in a range of contexts (e.g. Banks and Smyth, 2015; Feld and Shusterman, 2015; Shang, Li, Li, Wang and Siegrist, 2014; Wyn, Turnbull and Grimshaw, 2014). Meanwhile, all participants in education – schools, teachers, students and parents, are alienated by being positioned as responsible for the outcomes of their efforts and their choices in a policy context that is continually shifting and where structural factors like class and race are disavowed in favour of universalizing yet individualizing discourses of aspiration and ability (Kulz, 2017; Reay, 2017).

But aside from these more dramatic consequences, reflecting the production of alienation on the part of neo-liberal education policy operating as an instance of the discourse of the university, there are additional costs of bureaucratic standardization and economic instrumentalism in terms of lost opportunities to think and practice education differently. In relation to learning, the mapping of knowledge into pre-packaged curricula that each and every student is required to master positions students as passive receivers of knowledge that emanates from elsewhere and occludes possibilities for oblique, subversive, critical or creative learning. It also masks the political dimensions of education and promotes a false and cruelly optimistic ontology of potentiality that sacrifices our *im*potential in the sense of our capacity to decide *not* to be this or that within the current dominant order (T. E. Lewis, 2011). And in relation to education systems more generally, emphases on standardized knowledge and achievement, coupled with the promotion of deregulation and competition, have undermined schools' roles as sites for the promotion of justice, equality and democratic citizenship (Coffield and Williamson, 2011; Fielding and Moss, 2011; Hyslop-Margison and Sears, 2006; Kontopodis, 2012; Ravitch, 2009). In each instance, that is, in relation to teaching, learning and education more broadly, what commentators and critics are highlighting is that teaching, learning and education cannot be rendered fully knowable, captured and itemized without the risk of rendering them trivial and hollow.

In the Lacanian terms outlined earlier, because the object-cause of desire, *a*, occupying the place of the addressee in the discourse of the university, 'is also always already a lost object' (Parker, 2001a, p. 73), the totalizing ambitions of bureaucratic knowledge, in the form of S2, to colonize its object will always remain elusive. The consequent by-product of this discourse is alienation in the form of demoralized teachers who experience a disjunction between their personal and professional identities (Ball, 2003); disengaged students who feel that school learning does not connect with their sense of self and who, even when they 'succeed' as learners according to the terms of neo-liberal education policy, are 'educated' to occupy 'politically illiterate, socially uncritical and un-self-critical subject positions' (Saltman, 2014a, p. 55); and schools that are required to compete as high performance learning organizations, thereby suppressing and marginalizing alternative models, such as schools as person-centred communities of collaborative learning and democratic fellowship (Fielding and Moss, 2011). Such losses are an inevitable consequence of the competitive logic governing neo-liberal education policy, with its production of winners and losers reflected in divisions between those students who succeed and those who fail the tests of objectified, reified knowledge; between the mythological teacher as urban saviour adulated in Hollywood films and the lazy, irresponsible and incompetent teachers demonized in the popular press; and between schools deemed outstanding and those requiring what England's inspection authority, OFSTED, refers to as 'special measures'.

The market as the truth of the discourse of the university

The various examples introduced above are symptomatic of a wider global trend, reflecting what Rizvi and Lingard (2010) describe as the 'neoliberal global imaginary'. Aligned with its purported objectivism and rationality, this neo-liberal imaginary views education as a purely rational, technical enterprise, that is, 'not as a particular set of interests and political interventions, but as a kind of non-politics – a way of being reasonable, and of promoting universally desirable forms of economic expansion and democratic government around the globe' (Duggan, 2003, p. 10). As Duggan goes on to point out, when put like this, who could be against such a proposition? Yet, in denying its connections to particular interests and its contingent and contestable rather than natural or universal character, neo-liberal education policy masks its grounding in the competition-oriented and profit-driven market as the master signifier underlying its professions of 'evidence based' neutrality and proclamations of being grounded in scientific expertise. Yet this act of depoliticization of education policy is itself highly political, even as it disavows its political nature thereby masking its idelogical agenda (Clarke, 2012a). As Fielding and Moss note, 'the political and ethical have been drained out of public discourse on education and schools: the discourse is reduced to discussion of the best technical solutions for achieving predetermined and self-evident ends at the expense, at the expense of debate about critical questions, purposes, values and understandings or concepts. But the draining of politics *is* political' (Fielding and Moss, 2011, p. 21, emphasis in original).

In order to explore these ideas, I want to pick on some of the themes in the preceding discussion and link them to a broader consideration of the notion of 'the political', including consideration of the presence/absence of politics in contemporary education policy and what this implies for the underlying 'truth' of the discourse of the university. As an initial observation, it is worth noting that neo-liberal society has been characterized by an eschatological tendency, evident in proclamations of the 'end of history' or the 'triumph of liberal democracy' and resulting in the kind of 'non- politics' referred to by Duggan and Fielding and Moss above. Yet, despite neo-liberalism's disavowal of politics – reflecting what Mouffe describes as the contemporary 'post-political zeitgeist' (2005, p. 8) and what Rancière refers to as 'postdemocracy' (1999, p. 95) – its political decisions are based in power rather than in merely rational or scientific objectivity. In other words, 'the university discourse ... functions as a master discourse that disavows itself ... [that] hides its own mastering' (Pavón-Cuéllar, 2011, p. 264). In this sense, neo-liberal claims to factual objectivity and the decrying of opponents on the left as ideological is itself the consummate ideological move (Žižek, 1989), suggesting, among other things, that 'the project of a critical theory of democracy in late capitalist societies remains as relevant as ever' (Fraser, 1997, p. 69).

The underlying dominance of market-oriented, economic values as guiding truths is clearly visible in much neo-liberal education policy, including the reframing of early years education policy in England to focus on school-readiness and future employability. And of course, England is by no means unique in the subordination of education policy to utilitarian economic concerns. Such an approach reduces education policy to the realm of the technical and ignores the *political* creation, as opposed to natural origins, of the 'market' (Chang, 2010; Monck, 2005; Polanyi, 1944) that serves as its unquestioned truth. It thus represents a retreat from politics under the mask of supposedly objective knowledge and neutral expertise. The result is a denial of the political, in the sense of the projection and promotion of (an apparent) consensus rather than recognition and encouragement of antagonistic debate between equally legitimate but genuinely distinct alternatives, contributing to the disenchantment and disengagement with politics characteristic of our times.

This consensualism can be seen in the way education policy documents repeatedly use refrains such as 'we know' to project an omniscient and inclusive first-person plural subject. For instance, *More Great Childcare* asserts, 'we know from the evidence at home and abroad that the quality of staff is crucial in delivering high quality early education' (Truss, 2013, p. 27), just one of five statements beginning with 'we know...' in the document that contribute to a sense of expertise-guided agreement. Similarly, *Educational Excellence Everywhere* employs 'we know' eight times in relation to what are often ideologically loaded assertions, such as, 'we know that when teachers have extensive ITT experience in schools, they perform better',[2] which is underpinned by an ideologically loaded and controversial view of teaching as a 'craft' that is best learned working alongside a master 'craftsperson' (Mutton, Burn and Menter, 2017). As one would expect in the bureaucratic discourse of the university, power and the political are disavowed as division and controversy are masked by the authoritative assertion of consensus. By contrast, for political philosophers like Rancière, the political properly understood is constituted by difference and division:

> A *political* community is in effect a community that is structurally divided, not between divergent interest groups and opinions, but divided in relation to itself. A political 'people' is never the same thing as the sum of a population. It

---

[2] To be fair, the document does provide a footnote listing three publications, or at least the author name and date of these publications, but this nod to evidence is undermined by the absence of a reference list in the document.

is always a form of supplementary symbolization in relation to any counting of the population and its parts. (Rancière, 2010a, pp. 188–9, emphasis in original)

To the extent that it seeks to deny, or negate, this self-difference in the name of the assumed truth of the market as its governing master signifier education policy becomes inimical to critique or thinking, instead insisting on a consensus around instrumental efficiency. Indeed, instrumentalism and consensualism operate as a form of discursive duopoly, each supporting and reinforcing the other (Clarke, 2012a), reflected in the globalized neo-liberal accord with regard to the economic purposes of education (Hyslop-Margison and Sears, 2006; Rizvi and Lingard, 2010) – an accord that finds itself repeated and reaffirmed, as governments engage in policy borrowing (Finegold, McFarland and Richardson, 1993; Lingard, 2010), as international tests like PISA increasingly shape policy in a number of countries (Sellar et al., 2017), and as pervasive performativity and accountability regimes narrow conceptualizations of what it means to teach, learn and be educated (Alexander, 2009; Wayne Au, 2011; Biesta, 2010; Hursh, 2008; Moore, 2004; Stobart, 2008; Taubman, 2009). The task of re-connecting with the political (which is not the same thing as party politics) in educational policy discourses thus assumes a degree of urgency. The following section sketches out some initial steps than might be taken in this direction.

Conclusion: Re-politicizing education policy and traversing the economic fantasy

Reflected most memorably in Tony Blair's catch cry, 'Education, Education, Education', education has moved to centre stage in the political arena in recent decades, becoming in effect the new economic policy in contexts such as the UK (Ainley, 2016, p. 21). Yet, this move has been accompanied by the transposition of education to the level of the instrumental and technical, reflected in policymaker's obsession with questions of 'what works' and their lack of engagement with fundamental questions regarding education's purpose beyond stock answers. Indeed, just as neo-liberalism is summed up by Davies (2014, p. 4) as the *pursuit of the disenchantment of politics by economics*, so the insistence within current policy on the separation between education and politics represents the disenchantment of education by mangerialism, technicism and economism. 'Evidence', 'data' and 'performance indicators' take precedence over stories, feelings and relationships.

As a result, and in common with many institutions in which the bureaucratic discourse of the university dominates, schools have been turned into factories of learning (Coffield and Williamson, 2011; Hutchings, 2016; Kulz, 2017). Hemmed in by prescriptive curriculum and standards, terrorized by high-stakes testing and inspections, and overwhelmed by a welter of perpetually shifting policy initiatives, they have become what David Graeber, with reference to aspects of life that have been colonized by bureaucracy, describes as 'dead zones of the imagination' – places that are 'inherently bureaucratic, and therefore, profoundly alienating … they are instruments through which the human imagination is smashed and shattered' (2015, p. 99).

The dominance of the bureaucratic discourse of the university, enforced by managerial technologies of performativity, has worked to align education with the imperatives of the market, thereby naturalizing a view of education as a technical, instrumental, rather than an ethical or political, enterprise. The establishment and reproduction of this instrumentalism is supported by a consensual discourse, which resists reading the educational space in terms of social or political antagonism, with the consequence that the constitutive outside of consensus, that is, dissensus in the form of being 'anti-standards' or anti-excellence', is rendered unintelligible and unthinkable. Underpinning the rule of this bureaucratic discourse are a number of fantasies – of the salvation of the harmonious and exponentially prosperous nation-state through education – which go some way to account for the affective 'grip' of the discourse of the university on education policy (Clarke, 2012b).

One line of critical work for those who would challenge the depoliticization effected by this duopoly is to name and confront the economic and political fantasies, including our own complicity as compliant subjects in sustaining them – what Žižek (1989, p. 65), following Lacan, refers to as 'traversing' the fantasy – underpinning neo-liberal education policies at any and every opportunity. This would include challenging a number of hegemonic ideas, for instance: that increased productivity should be our ultimate social and educational purpose; that an emphasis on increased productivity is a reflection of economic reality rather than a political assertion; that increased accountability, rather than increased trust, is the key to educational excellence; that educational excellence achieved through a combination of managerial accountability mechanisms and market-oriented notions of choice is compatible with equity; that increased overall wealth benefits everyone in society; that there is no tension between the interests of individuals and that these can be unproblematically aggregated into some notion of overall social well-being; and that uncompromising support for the interests of the already advantaged in society can be reconciled with equity and social justice. To confront the contemporary policy consensus around these 'truths' and instead to advocate for a properly political – that is one based on antagonistic debate between genuine alternatives – view of education is a vital step in the critical task of renovating the increasingly absent politics of education policy and challenging the hegemonic grip of the discourse of the university as manifested in neo-liberal education policy. To do so requires challenging the dominance of the master signifier, whether as agent or unspoken truth and allowing desire and the divided subject to assume greater agency and prominence; this, in turn, entails engaging with the discourses of thinking otherwise – the discourse of the hysteric, which the protests in current chapter might be seen to embody, and the discourse of the analyst, which resists all attempts at domination and mastery – that are explored in the next two chapters.

5

The Discourse of the Hysteric and Radical Reform: The Return of the Past

What I am calling the hysteria of this discourse stems precisely from the fact that the discourse eludes that the distinction would enable one to perceive the fact that if this historical machine, which is fact only the progress of the schools and nothing more, ever did culminate in absolute knowledge, it would only be to mark the annulment, the failure, the disappearance at the conclusion of the only thing that motivates the function of knowledge – its dialectic with. jouissance

Lacan, 2007, p. 35

Introduction

The discourse of the hysteric probably takes the prize for the least attractive name among Lacan's four discourses, evoking images of the strained, suffocating atmosphere we associate with the Victorian era, with young women manifesting symptoms of supposed sexual repression, including seizures, contortions, paralysis and depression. Yet, such overwrought and gendered images obscure how hysteria frequently adopts less dramatic, more subtle forms, and how it is latent in all of us (Showalter, 1998). Indeed, even to talk of hysteria as if it was an identifiable entity is problematic for, despite a history going back at least four thousand years, 'hysteria' defies definition (Gherovici, 2010). Within different historical eras, it has been variously inflected through medical, religious and psychoanalytic discourses, and read, in turn, as physical affliction, demonic possession and neurological disorder. Etymologically, the term refers to the uterus and has typically been seen as equivalent to 'woman', though it has also been viewed by commentators in different historical contexts as a transgender affliction, affecting both men and women (Gherovici, 2010). Yet, even this notion of hysteria's enduring presence across contexts and cultures turns out to be a problematic historical construction that coincided with the emergence of modernity and the birth of the modern subject: 'a model of hysteria with alleged ancient roots was constructed as Cartesian science swept through Europe … just at the time … when the categories of "male" and "female" became opposites', as opposed to variations on a common core (Gherovici, 2010, p. 60). An alternative perspective thus arises in which, to the extent that, as Lacan (2009) argued, there is no sexual relation, that is, no natural complementarity between the sexes, hysteria might be read as 'the pathologization of the nonrapport' (Gherovici, 2010, p. 49). In other words, hysteria presents itself as a symptom of the social bond rather than of individuals. Put differently, we might say that for Lacan 'hysteria is not a pathology, because it defines the essence of the speaking being divided by and coming into being in language' (Gherovici, 2017, p. 77).

Despite – or perhaps reflective of – this complex genealogy, the discourse of the hysteric is perhaps the most pervasive of the discourses. In fact, we might well equate the discourse of the hysteric with 'normal' discourse (Verhaeghe, 2008, p. 56); for who among us does not like to complain? Indeed, if we are honest, despite the 'official' dim view of complaining, there seems to be something deeply and intrinsically gratifying about complaint. We complain about the weather, our employers, our politicians, our under-performing sports teams, the offerings on TV, our neighbours, our partners, the traffic … the litany goes on. Grumbling, moaning, grouching, bitching, sniping and all the other variants of complaint seem to be built into our individual and collective psychic DNA and, like it or not, we seem to derive some strange satisfaction, some perverse pleasure from running our fellow beings, or at least their ideas, actions and accomplishments, down. In other words, not only can't we get no satisfaction, to paraphrase the Rolling Stones, but we love to tell each other that we can't get no satisfaction, thereby hinting at the intimate relationship between lack and surplus enjoyment and our desire for unsatisfied desire (Schuster, 2016).

But surely there is more to complaining than the personal venting. A key dimension of social bonding and interpersonal value-checking, complaining seems to also have a masking or camouflaging purpose – as if we are saying to each other, 'I know your life is fraught with problems but don't worry because mine is too, in fact mine might be even worse than yours'. Complaining, from this perspective, might seem to have an ethical dimension. But any claims to moral superiority on the part of the complainer are at least partially undermined by the realisation that he or she is not really interested in a response or recognition from the other, so much as in the intrinsic satisfaction provided by complaining: 'the intersubjective dialectic that seemed so important ... dissolves into quasi-autistic enjoyment, where the other becomes the "partner" in a monologue' (Schuster, 2016, p. 4).

Complaint is endemic to much of our public, as well as private, lives too, with possibilities for spread and 'contagion' greatly facilitated and expanded by digital technology and the amplificatory affordances of social media. The typical newspaper editorial or opinion piece is as often as not a diagnosis of some rot or decay that is eating away at the fabric of our shared social and political institutions or a critical commentary on some aspect of our individual and collective lives that is not working as well, not functioning as healthily, as it might or should. Oftentimes, such complaint is quite generalized and sweeping in its targets, as in Samuel Huntingdon's (1975) denouncement of the 'democratic surge of the 1960s' (p. 62) and the threat it posed 'to existing systems of authority ... [including] ... the family, the university, business, public and private associations, politics, the governmental bureaucracy, and the military services. People no longer felt the same need to obey those whom they had previously considered superior to themselves in age, rank, status, expertise, character, or talents' (Huntington, 1975, pp. 74–5, cited in Cooper 2017, pp. 217–18). Huntingdon's invective provides a classic example of how the element of complaint that comprises the core of the discourse of the hysteric goes hand in hand with a yearning for authority. Sometimes public hysteria reaches a particularly audible pitch, as evident in the ongoing debates in the UK on the toxic issue of 'Brexit', with both sides of the debate accusing each other of irrational hysteria[1] and consequently ratcheting up the level of hysteria yet further in a spiral of paranoia, fanaticism and anxiety. Indeed, the Brexit example highlights the connections between hysteria and identity insofar as hysteria in politics 'at its core, boils down to an argument about group identity – it is a way of defining *who we are* by defining *whom we are against*' (Burt, 2015, p. 11). The bitter public disputes engendered by the Trump campaign and presidency in the United States offers another instance of public hysteria linked to group identity

---

[1] https://capx.co/dont-believe-the-brexit-hysteria/.
https://www.politico.eu/article/brexit-courts-fear-return-of-enemies-of-the-people-hysteria/.
http://www.dailymail.co.uk/debate/article-5018465/STEPHEN-GLOVER-hysteria-universities-Brexit.html.
https://www.telegraph.co.uk/news/2016/07/22/the-liberal-hysteria-over-brexit-shows-exactly-why-we-need-to-le/.
https://www.neweurope.eu/article/brexit-hysteria-sides-political-divide-unnecessary-time-negotiate-deal-works-everyone/.

politics. And numerous other examples can be found, such as media and public debates around gender, 'political correctness', national security, public health, and, of course, education – think, for instance, of the fevered pitch of debates around literacy during the aptly named literacy wars.

Indeed, turning to the subject of this book, education policy frequently operates very comfortably in the register of complaint, requiring the identification of inadequacy, inefficiency or ineptitude in order to justify and legitimate its prescriptions. And even when things are working well the situation can always be improved upon through codification, audit, intensification or expansion – there really is no justification, even for mere consolidation, let alone complacency. Thus we are exhorted to never stand still! But it is not only policymakers in education who are located in the discourse of the hysteric. Academics, such as myself, who write and publish critiques of the dominant policy regime are also writing/speaking from within this discourse, as are students who resist the normalizing banalities of education as typically practised in schools and classrooms. But rather than viewing the many and various manifestations of complaint, found in education and other social and professional domains, as evidence of personal weakness or irresponsibility, it is important to recognize its role as the social expression of wider anxiety and stress (Showalter, 1998).

Psychoanalysis has always had an intimate relationship with complaint. This is hardly surprising, given that its genesis, in the late nineteenth century, lies in the need felt by middle-class members of society to voice their various complaints – about their tics and ailments, guilt and anxiety, phobias and fantasies. But what Freud discovered, and what was so revolutionary about psychoanalysis was that, despite their overt complaining, his patients remained stubbornly attached to their symptoms and were 'in ways unbeknownst to themselves, deeply complicit in their own discontent ... at a certain (unconscious) level, symptoms are very much wanted and "enjoyed"' (Schuster, 2016, p. 5). Like the addict – who is really just an extreme instance of the perfectly normal individual (Lewis, 2015) – we remain attached to our suffering. We can begin to see how complaint brings together and binds such seeming opposites as pain and pleasure, tragedy and farce, optimism and pessimism. And we begin to sense how these oxymoronic conjunctions are somehow linked to the 'misfit' nature of our existence and our characters. The consequence of this 'lack of fit' is that any yearning for wholeness, harmony and completion are perpetually undermined by an intimate alterity, a lacking surplus, a constitutive fragmentation that is as much who we are as any of our symbolic roles or imagined identities. Indeed, the more we seek to expel and eradicate that which threatens our preferred identities with what we assume to be an entirely alien presence, the more this 'grotesque' other returns to disturb and undermine our ideals and our illusions in the form of unconscious repression or compulsion (Stallybrass and White, 1986).

Lacanian psychoanalysis offers one possible explanation for the pervasive presence of complaint in our personal and professional lives, linked to our status as subjects of lack and the insatiable nature of desire that perpetually pursues the doomed task of filling in this place of unstaunchable lack. The pursuit is futile because our lack is existential rather than incidental, resulting from our alienation from direct or unmediated experience as a consequence of our becoming subjects of the signifier. We are subject to a lack that can never be satisfied with each potential candidate – each new phone, car, partner and so on – inevitably falling short and eliciting a sense of 'that's not it'. It is this failure which perpetuates our desire. In other words, in Lacanian theory, desire is second order, insofar as beyond any particular desire – for this object or that experience – lies an unspoken desire for (unsatisfied) desire itself.

The discourse of the hysteric

As we have seen the discourse of the master and the discourse of the university are both authoritative discourses in which, respectively, the master signifier and impersonal knowledge occupy the speaking position of agency. In contrast, the discourse of the hysteric and the discourse of the analyst express the fragile agency of the split subject and restless desire. If the discourse of the master and the university express the impersonalized authority of presumptive power and bureaucratic knowledge, the discourse of the hysteric and the analyst represent the attempts by subjectivity and desire to question and challenge that authority. As such, the discourse of the hysteric embodies a rejection of mastery in all its forms: 'one could say that the hysteric is allergic to mastery be it in the form of a master-signifier, of another person or of the other: the hysteric is prone to prove that any authority or any mastery is ill-founded and that the master does not really know' (Klepec, 2016, p. 126). Yet, this rejection of mastery also contains a paradoxical desire for the master to be more masterful. As Lacan (2007, p. 207) retorted to the student agitators in Paris in revolution of 1968, 'what you aspire to as revolutionaries is a master.

$$\$ \quad \rightarrow \quad S1$$

$$\uparrow \quad \overline{} \qquad\qquad \overline{} \quad \downarrow$$

$$a \qquad // \qquad S2$$

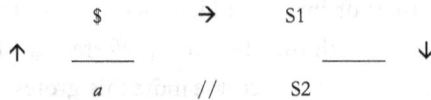

Figure 5.1 The discourse of the hysteric

You will get one.' Lacan's comment highlights the intimate connections and relationships linking each and all of the discourses. The hysteric's discourse is represented diagrammatically in Figure 5.1.

More specifically, the discourse of the hysteric represents a reversal of – literally, a 180 degree turn in relation to – the discourse of the university, challenging the latter's authoritative claims. For despite the latter's pretence of scholarly knowledge and expertise, its unacknowledged truth is the master signifier representing the status quo. By contrast, the discourse of the hysteric places the master signifier in the spotlight, or the hot seat, demanding that it justify its claims to mastery and its assumption of dominance. This is the discourse of critical inquiry on the part of the split subject – the subject of desire, the subject who does not know – representing the governed not the governor (Schroeder, 2008, p. 149). Whereas the discourse of the master declares the hegemony of the existing state of affairs, which the discourse of the university explains and the discourse of the analyst, as we shall go on the see in the following chapter, analyses and interprets, the discourse of the hysteric questions and critiques the status quo. But on what basis is this questioning made? What is its underlying justification? Underpinning the split subject, $\$$, in the lower left-hand quadrant, is *objet a* representing unstaunchable desire and as such suggesting that the split subject's questioning in the discourse of the hysteric can never receive a satisfactory response. As a result, in response to the split subject's relentless questioning, the master signifier, S1, in the position of the addressee of the discourse, can do nothing other than produce more knowledge, S2, to occupy the position of the product of the discourse. In what follows, we shall look at these positions in more detail in the context of education policy, beginning briefly with the unacknowledged desire (*a*) driving the rise of education in the modern world and then moving on to consider the split subject (\$) occupying the position of agency, the role of education as a master signifier (S1) for our time and the proliferating products (S2) in the form of the global education sector. I will then go on to look specifically at some recent products in the popular educational literature as manifestations of the discourse of the hysteric. My hope is that viewing these familiar developments through this particular Lacanian lens will provide fresh insights into the dynamics driving the seemingly unstoppable expansion of education.

The truth: Disavowed desires

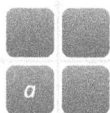

The discourse of the hysteric is underpinned by desire in the position of the underlying truth of the discourse. The entanglements of education and education policy with desire are not hard to identify. Most obviously, as we shall see below, education in the late twentieth and early twenty-first centuries has been linked to the promise of economic growth and to aspirations for individual and societal wealth. But perhaps less obviously, education and education policy are inextricably linked to our desires for individual and societal redemption, reflected in the political left's pursuit of education for emancipation and social justice and the political right's eugenically inflected attachment to the 'echoingly empty edifice of meritocracy' (Allen, 2014, p. 249). In each perspective, education is positioned as a force for good that has the potential to restore some imagined originary and/or futuristic order of rightness and goodness from which we have become detached. In a similarly fantasmatic vein, education has also come to embody associations with youth, beyond the traditional links between schooling and stage of life, with learning promoted as the key to remaining young.[2] Each of these desires – economic, ethico-political, epigenetic – can be read as a manifestation of a more fundamental desire to overcome the limits installed by our entry into the regulatory order of the symbolic realm. Painfully, if only subconsciously, aware of our finite, fragile and fragmented existence, we mobilize discourses of education and the promises it offers of growth (of wealth, wisdom and well-being) as a means of resisting and challenging the limits – spatial and temporal, psychic and social, moral and intellectual – of our being. Yet the impossibility of the transcendence and wholeness we (unconsciously) seek is not fully recognized or avowed and so the pursuit of these elusive and

---

[2] https://www.indiatvnews.com/lifestyle/news-lifelong-learning-can-reverse-ageing-378054. https://medium.com/minerva-schools/how-to-stay-young-forever-never-stop-learning-4ed5cf0b9ff8.

illusive states drives the split subject occupying the position of agency in the discourse of the hysteric.

The agent: The hysterical split subject

Given the pervasiveness of the discourse of the hysteric, it would be highly surprising if it was not prevalent in the field of education and manifested in education policy. Unsurprisingly, it is not hard to identify the adoption of complaint as mode of engagement in the education policy arena. In Chapter 3, I noted how, in the late 1960s and 1970s, when the first cracks appeared in the post-Second World War economic boom that Western societies had hitherto enjoyed, the body of knowledge comprising Education was subjected to scrutiny by discourses embodying the dominant logics of the market for not delivering on the promises of social transformation and economic success that had been projected onto it. This line of critique, embodied by the *Black Papers* in the UK and *A Nation at Risk* in the United States, has continued through the subsequent decades. And while such critique reflects aspects of the discourse of the university, in which expert knowledge, underpinned by unacknowledged hegemonic master signifiers, seeks to dominate the split subject, as described in the previous chapter, the ongoing critiques of education can also be read as a series of hysterical complaints in which outraged experts, think tanks, policymakers and media commentators rail against education for failing to provide the fullness which 'Education', when positioned as a master signifier, promises. The element of hysteria explains the shifting focus of critique, with targets including 'progressive education' (Lowe, 2007), whole language approaches to language and literacy education (Krashen, 1999), multiculturalism and the politics of recognition (Banks, 2016; Crawford, 2000), supposed cultures of 'political correctness' in education (Wilson, 1995), educational research (Tooley and Darby, 1998), policies promoting socio-economic redistribution through education (Power and Frandji, 2010) and the very concept of universal public education[3] (Blacker, 2013; Hursh, 2016; Olssen, 1996; Watkins, 2015). In each

---

[3] https://fee.org/articles/the-failure-of-american-public-education/.

case, in line with the well-established norms of 'backlash' literature, the operative assumption is that education is failing to fulfil its true potential owing to the obstacle represented by the target of critique. An example of this can be found in James Tooley's *Reclaiming Education* (2000), where he asserts that 'there are solutions to the fundamental challenges facing education. The solutions do not require much from the government other than that it leave education well alone' (2000, p. 1). Tooley, as he goes on to explain, is careful to avoid using the language of crisis, but the rhetorical formula – problem-obstacle-solution – is recognizable nonetheless. The presumed master is guilty of not being masterly enough. If for conservatives like Tooley, education is criticized for being too bureaucratic or too progressive, while for liberals it is at fault for being too traditional or insufficiently meritocratic, the common assumption is that could it but be remade (or 'reclaimed' as per the suitably conservative term used in Tooley's title) in line with the ideals of the group in question, education would be able to realize the hopes and dreams with which it is invested. Yet, for all the surface confidence and bravado of many of the public figures occupying the position of agency within the discourse of the hysteric in relation to education – and someone like former UK secretary of state for education, Michael Gove, springs readily to mind here – subjectivity relies on recognition by the other for its existence and is thus dependent upon intersubjective relations and the wider symbolic order. In Lacanian terms, desire is always desire of the other – desire to be recognized by the other, desire for what the other desires. In Žižek's words, 'the "lost object" which sets the subject's desire in motion is ultimately the subject herself, and the lack in question concerns her uncertainty as to the status of the Other's desire' (1996b, p. 164). It is this uncertainty that fuels the relentless question of the, ultimately and inevitably, inadequate master signifier.

The addressee: The inadequate master signifier – education, education, education

Previous chapters have made reference to Tony Blair and New Labour's elevation of education – embodied in the campaign catch-cry in the subtitle above – to unparalleled heights as the vehicle through which the hopes, aspirations and expectations of individuals, groups and wider society might be realized. Of course, education has long been attributed with a range of properties and powers, as the following remarks from John Roebuck during the Westminster parliamentary debate on National Education in 1833 suggests:

> Education means not merely the conferring these necessary means or instruments for the acquiring of knowledge, but it means also the so training or fashioning the intellectual and moral qualities of the individual, that he may be able and willing to acquire knowledge, and to turn it to its right use. It means the so framing the mind of the individual, that he may become a useful and virtuous member of society in the various relations of life. It means making him a good child, a good parent, a good neighbour, a good citizen, in short, a good man. All these he cannot be without knowledge, but neither will the mere acquisition of knowledge confer on him these qualities; his moral, as well as his intellectual powers, must contribute to this great end, and the true fashioning of these to this purpose is right education. Such, Sir, is the acceptation which I attribute to the term education.[4]

Yet, despite the long legacy of education being positioned as the deliverer of reason and redemption it is possible to argue that the discourse of education as a universal panacea, providing the surest path to individual success and national salvation, was given an additional boost, and was consequently taken to new heights, in the decades following the economic crises of the 1970s and the rise of global neo-liberalism. For surely it is no accident that as the same time that the state has been steadily revoking from its explicit commitments to redistributing income and reducing inequality, education has been charged with responsibility for fulfilling these aspirations. In the neo-liberal era of individualized responsibility and global anxiety, the common assumption among policymakers and media commentators is that 'education will make us more tolerant, it will dissolve our doubts about globalization and climate change, it will give us the STEM skills we need as a society to compete ... there is no social or political problem that cannot be solved with more education and job training' (Frank, 2016, p. 34). Of course, what such fantasmatic thinking about education forgets is that education is a 'positional', as well as an 'absolute', good, meaning that its value is measured in part by how much an individual has in relation to the amount possessed by others (Samuels, 2017; Wolf, 2002). So the value of a master's degree diminishes as more students complete this level

---

[4] https://api.parliament.uk/historic-hansard/commons/1833/jul/30/national-education#s3v0020p0_18330730_hoc_23.

of qualification, incentivizing those with the ambition to achieve distinction in relation to their peers to go a step further and complete a doctoral qualification. This tendency, which also lies behind the familiar phenomenon of grade inflation, has been given added impetus by the marketization of evermore areas of life.

Yet despite – or, rather, as a result of – education serving as a central master signifier of our times, its fault, like any master signifier, lies in its not being masterful enough, not being sufficiently (insert your preferred educational model) and therefore for falling short of its presumed potential as a universal panacea. It may perhaps have been a reflection of an unconscious recognition of the impossible demands being placed upon it that New Labour cited 'Education' not just once but three times in their mantra; however, no number of repetitions could have assuaged the inadequacy of education in relation to the (fantasmatic) expectations and demands placed upon it. For the underlying truth of the discourse of the hysteric is unquenchable desire.

The product: The global business of education

$$\begin{array}{|c|c|} \hline \ & \ \\ \hline \ & S2 \\ \hline \end{array}$$

Like the other discourses we have examined so far, the discourse of the hysteric involves a 'product' that is generated as a surplus, owing to the impossibility of any complete correspondence (in both the sense of a match and of communication) between the agent and the addressee of the discourse. In the discourse of the hysteric, as we have seen, the master signifier is unable to satisfy the relentless demands of the split subject for complete reassurance, cast-iron guarantee or ultimate satisfaction, and can only produce more knowledge in the form of S2. Ultimate satisfaction in our earthly existence remains not just contingently but existentially elusive.

One of the advantages of perpetual dissatisfaction is that there is always something to be done, which is incapable of getting done, and so yet more must be done. As such, the discourse of the hysteric goes hand in hand with the managerial practices of audit (grounded in mistrust that what needs to be done is actually getting done) and performativity (making sure that we are perpetually doing more in the face of the impossibility of doing what needs to be done) that have become ubiquitous features of institutional life in the neo-liberal era. But knowledge is the 'product' of the discourse of the hysteric, with its pervasive anxiety, in another sense insofar as education has become big business – a literal knowledge economy characterized by endless reorganization and frenetic reform resulting in a proliferation of programs, qualifications, schemes and awards supporting a global education industry worth over $43 trillion, with no signs of declining growth, in 2016 (Verger, Lubienski and Steiner-Khamsi, 2016). As Wolf states in the opening line of her book *Does Education Matter? Myths about Education and Economic Growth*, 'to understand modern education we need to first of all think size. For today's education sectors are huge' (2002, p. 1). Underpinned by the widespread, and largely unquestioned, belief in the economic benefits of education, the massive expansion of this sector has supported the emergence of a generation of edu-businesses and edu-preneurs (for critical readings of this trend see, for example, Ball, 2012; Rönnberg, 2017). The same conditions have facilitated the rise of popular 'edu-authors', offering diagnoses of the afflicted state of education and promoting cures that promise to restore it to health. Examples of such products abound – a select sample includes titles such as: *Creating the Schools Our Children Need: Why What We're Doing Now Won't Help Much (and What We Can Do Instead)* (Wiliam, 2018); *Cleverlands: The Secrets behind the Success of the World's Education Superpowers* (Crehan, 2018); *Education Forward: Moving Schools into the Future* (Price, 2017); *10 Mindframes for Visible Learning: Teaching for Success* (Hattie and Zierer, 2017); *The Learning Power Approach: Teaching Learners to Teach Themselves* (Claxton, 2018); *Radical: Fighting to Put Students First* (Rhee, 2013); and *Battle Hymn of the Tiger Teachers: The Michaela Way* (Birbalsingh, 2016). These books are symptomatic of a growing body of popular education titles that have great appeal to both the general public, particularly parents and teachers, but also to policymakers. In the following section I analyse the last two of the titles mentioned above, Michelle Rhee's *Radical* and Katharine Birbalsingh's *Battle Hymn of the Tiger Teachers*.

Two symptomatic case studies: Tiger teachers and radical reformer

Birbalsingh's and Rhee's books derive from different sides of the Atlantic but they have much in common in terms of their diagnoses and prescriptions for educational practice, as well in being symptomatic of the 'increasingly shrill and increasingly radical demands for "reform"' (Ravitch, 2013, p. 314) commonly heard in a range of global contexts. But as well as offering UK and US perspectives on the neo-liberal education reform movement, these books are linked in terms of their close connections to specific policy developments in the two countries. Michelle Rhee came to fame as a result of her tenure from 2007–10 as the first Chancellor of Washington, DC, public schools when the former governing body, the DC Board of Education, was stripped of its decision-making powers and reduced to the status of an advisory body. A product of the Teach for America program, she has been a relentless, if rather hypocritical,[5] champion of the neo-liberal education reform agenda, including accountability via practices such as payment by results – and failing that, firing – for teachers and principals, authoritarian disciplinary regimes for students and 'choice' for parents. Meanwhile, Katharine Birbalsingh's edited collection, whose chapters were written by the teachers at the school she leads, Michaela Free School, carries the endorsement of former UK secretary of state for education, Michael Gove (who describes the book as 'my gospel') and current – at the time of writing – UK foreign secretary Boris Johnson (who describes Michaela as 'a revolution in education'). It also boasts a recommendation from Tom Bennett, the Conservative party's go-to expert on classroom management and discipline, whose name appears a number of times in the UK government's 2016 White Paper, *Educational Excellence Everywhere* (see Clarke and Phelan, 2017, p. 109). This, then, is a book with friends in high places as far as English education policy goes. Critically, both books embody the current climate in education policy insofar as they are characterized by a pseudo-scientific gloss (with references to 'research', 'evidence' and 'best practice') that relies on the demonization of straw targets, such as 'progressive education', while masking a deeply ideological – and unscientific – set of commitments that seem more suited to the nineteenth, rather than the twenty-first, century.

When it comes to the details of these commitments, both books share a number of key themes. These include an emphasis on the memorization and recital of 'powerful' knowledge, yet with little attention to the application, analysis or critique of this knowledge, alongside an almost fetishistic attachment to the need for a rigid, 'no excuses' disciplinary regime, reflecting 'a wider turn to authoritarian methods in education' (Kulz, 2017, p. 2). Such regimes have become the hallmark of US charter school systems, such as the Knowledge is

[5] https://www.theguardian.com/money/us-money-blog/2013/apr/11/michelle-rhee-public-education-paradox.

Power Program (KIPP), that, like Michaela[6] and Rhee pursue a mission to serve/ save students from socio-economically disadvantaged backgrounds. As one would expect with the split subject in the position of agent in the discourse of the hysteric, this shared missionary zeal is at once the source of great energy and passion but also the symptom of a blind spot in relation to the limits of the master signifier – in this case, education. As with a number of recent education policy texts – here the speeches of Michael Gove or the UK 2016 white paper come to mind – the suspicion that these books are speaking from the discourse of the hysteric is further underlined by the evangelical, hectoring tone with which ideological opponents are caricatured and critiqued and ideological commitments asserted as facts.

Tiger teachers on the attack

The fighting stage of our struggle seems to have gone on forever (Birbalsingh, 2016, p. 11).

The fervent, if combative, tone that runs through *Battle Hymn of the Tiger Teachers* and is embodied in the book's title is a hallmark of the discourse of the hysteric. This fervour, but also the pugilism, is prominently on display in Katharine Birbalsingh's introduction to the collection (2016, pp. 11–15). Her subtitle *Free at Last* clearly strives to resonate with the heroic struggles of Nelson Mandela. But it also raises questions as to validity of the comparison. Mandela had been resisting an oppressive and murderous political regime and had paid the price of twenty-seven years' imprisonment. But who are the oppressors that Birbalsingh and her colleagues are fighting against? When the facts are considered it is clear that claims to victimhood are as much, if not more, about self-positioning, as they are about real circumstances and events. The founders took advantage of state funding in order to create the school, while the 2011 Education Act established the academy/free school presumption, meaning that creating a traditional local education authority community school is only possible in special circumstances. However, facts are secondary in relation to the need to project an oppressive system against which one needs to be vigilant and strong. Within this particular version of social reality, children too must be made to 'toughen up' in preparation for a hostile and merciless world, so

---

[6] Michaela have adopted the KIPP 'knowledge is power' slogan as their motto; yet for all the school's claims to radicality, it also boasts about providing a 'private school ethos', suggesting that it is driven by a traditional, conservative set of values: https://www.prospectmagazine.co.uk/politics/ michaela-free-school-tiger-teachers-burning-bright.

that 'maturation to adulthood is understood to be all about becoming through identification the aggressor rather than the victim in the drama of one's life' (Levine, 2018, p. 30). Similarly, towards the end of her introduction, Birbalsingh foregrounds the trope of victimhood as she asserts (p. 15), 'freedom from the system is the only answer', but she then goes on to add that 'freedom is there for the taking for us all and we should embrace it', suggesting that the constraints schools labour under are as much in the mind as in reality. The problem is that, in essence, the identity of the freedom fighter only makes sense so long as there are enemies to be overcome so freedom must always be kept at a distance beyond the horizon – herein lies the dilemma of the discourse of the hysteric.

Some of the contradictions, as well as the key themes, that run throughout the book are evident in the first paragraph:

> 'Where is the rigour?' was what my friend and inspiration Michaela used to shout. Michaela loved to teach from the front. She liberated herself in the classroom by closing her door so that she could get on with what worked. She did things differently, and so do we. (Birbalsingh, 2016, p. 11)

There are tensions between the critical questioning attitude of the question and the aggressive, shouted mode of its expression; between liberating and isolating oneself; between the presumption that 'rigour' equates to teaching 'from the front'; between 'rigour' and the tired cliché, 'what works', which ignores inconvenient questions of context, complexity and purpose; and between the assumption that quality and effectiveness require minority, outsider status. After several pages rehearsing the legend of the Michaela 'struggle' – a 'fighting stage' that 'seems to have gone on forever' (p. 11) – followed by a brief outline of the content of the subsequent chapters of the book, the introduction concludes with another image of imprisonment in the form of Maya Angelou's poem, 'Caged Bird'. But again, I would suggest that the bars of this cage are an issue of mind rather than matter – a case of 'mind-forged manacles', to quote Joe Kirby (and William Blake) in the following chapter (p. 27) rather than iron bars – an imaginary construction supporting a fantasy of victimhood that serves to add a frisson of enjoyment to what might otherwise appear as unglamorous hard work.

Canonical knowledge

The Michaela approach to curriculum, pedagogy and assessment is the focus of a number of the following chapters, including 'Knowledge, memory and testing' (pp. 16–27), by Joe Kirby. In the course of the discussion, the author makes some sweeping and unsupported claims, such as the following: 'English schools and their English departments still neglect facts and knowledge' (p. 16). He also argues that 'unzipping skills from knowledge fails' (p. 17) yet the chapter relies on setting up a distinction between 'engagement and skills' on the one hand, and 'knowledge and rigour' on the other (p. 16), with Michaela placed firmly in the latter camp and other schools in the former.

Kirby also quotes the statement by cognitive psychologist David Willingham that 'thinking well requires knowing facts' (p. 17). But for a school that is lauded by its policy-shaping supporters as 'a revolution in education' (Johnson), a 'trailblazer' (Bennett), the examples provided in the chapter are all of bookish, desk-based learning that is confined to the classroom. As others have noted,[7] there is no evidence of an equal emphasis on the *application* of knowledge – Willingham's 'thinking well' – beyond the acquisition and retention of information. And there is no evidence of the teachers valuing experiences beyond the school – such as visits to museums, historical sites, live events – nor of the value of cultural works beyond the Western canon beloved by arch-conservatives such as E. D. Hirsch, who is cited approvingly in the chapter. Indeed, it is clear that not any knowledge is valued in this school. It must be knowledge that has already been endowed with cultural capital by the establishment. Hence Kirby is able to make the dismissive and patronizing assertion in relation to many of Michaela's students that 'they lack families who give them knowledge' (p. 17). Questions of why some knowledges are valued more than others and who gets to make such decisions never seem to arise – yet surely such critical thinking skills are crucial in any curriculum claiming to prepare students for the rapidly changing and globalized world of the twenty-first century. As Zipin argues, particularly in relation to schools that serve students from marginalized, high-poverty contexts, 'it is vital that students, teachers, families and community stakeholders are recognised and democratically represented in deciding what curriculum work can help empower their futures' (2017, p. 88). The cultural canon-oriented and information-driven approach advocated by Michaela ignores such issues, just as it ignores how disciplinary knowledge is enriched and enhanced when put into dialectical engagement with life-based knowledge. Instead, the school foregrounds its emphasis on the ultimately less significant distinction between short- and long-term memory:

---

[7]　https://debrakidd.wordpress.com/2016/12/06/battle-hymn-of-the-tiger-teachers-a-review-part-1/.
　　https://debrakidd.wordpress.com/2016/12/09/battle-hymn-of-the-tiger-teachers-part-2/.

At Michaela, we focus on designing our curriculum, lessons and exams with long-term memory in mind. We prioritise careful sequencing and dovetailing of subject-knowledge. We ensure that every lesson and every exam week it is revisited, drilled and tested rigorously and relentlessly. In short, we aim to ensure that our pupils do not forget what they are learning for years to come, perhaps even for as long as they live. (p. 27)

Unfortunately for the students, there is no expectation that they apply what they are learning in meaningful contexts and hence have the opportunity to recognize its purpose and value, only that memorize it. Yet awareness of the limitations of such an approach is not new. Vygotsky highlighted the futility of acquiring knowledge and skills, devoid of any engagement in activity, arguing that 'a teacher who tries to do this usually accomplishes nothing but empty verbalism, a parrot like repetition of words by the child, simulating a knowledge of the corresponding concepts but actually covering up a vacuum' (1986, p. 150). The restriction of education to a desiccated 'recitation script' (Tharp and Gallimore, 1988, 1990) also precludes any expectation that students come to ask questions about why they are learning particular subject-knowledge, about what exclusions these choices entailed, or about who was and who wasn't authorized to make those choices and about what criteria provided the bases for these choices. But such issues are bypassed. Instead, we are presented with a false opposition between irresponsible 'progressive' pedagogy and the 'rigours' of drill and didactic teaching (the title of the following chapter, by Olivia Dyer, is 'Drill and didactic teaching work best'), underpinned by hysterical claims about how the former is letting children down and only the latter can offer them any hope of educational success and social redemption. Meanwhile, particular understandings of agency – or, rather, its absence – are introduced covertly as students are trained to follow the lead of adults and to restrain or repress any critical impulses they may experience lest these disrupt the smooth unfolding of the learning that the adults have planned and mapped out on behalf of the students.

The final paragraph of the chapter begins with the claim that knowledge and memory are the 'blind spot' of many English schools, while it ends with a call to arms, paraphrasing Marx and Engels, 'Teachers of England unite! You have nothing to lose but your chains'. There are multiple ironies at work here – the inability to recognize the aptness of the frequent references, here and in other chapters, to metaphors of prisons, bars, manacles and chains, in a school that chooses to see itself as a persecuted victim, committed to championing underdog minorities, while seemingly oblivious to how the uncritical compliance it promotes in its students with regard to enduring issues surrounding the politics of knowledge does them and society a disservice in the long run.

Correct comportment

The lack of agency the school and the teachers afford the students in relation to curriculum is of a piece with the hierarchical relations it insists upon and enforces in the realm of discipline and behaviour:

> At Michaela, we highly value adult authority and children's politeness and respect. All pupils are expected to follow all instructions from all adults first time, every time, without argument or protest. Whether they are interacting with the Headmistress, a Deputy Head, teacher, office staff, caterer or cleaner, the same expectations are demanded of children: respectful, polite interactions with all adults and all times. (p. 95)

The excessive enjoyment provided by this no-nonsense attitude can be gleaned from the pedantic repetitions: '*all* pupils … *all* instructions … *all* adults', 'first *time*, every *time*', '*all* adults at *all* times'. This emphatic refusal to take circumstance or context into account is all part of the 'no excuses', 'zero tolerance' approach that Michaela has embraced and that is symptomatic of the growing authoritarianism of school cultures in England and the United States. As Giroux notes, 'zero tolerance does little more than legitimate the mindless punishment of poor whites and students of colour by criminalizing behaviour as trivial as violating a dress code … under such circumstances, punishing becomes more important than educating while the practice of discriminating judgement gives way to rigid governing through [a] crime approach to schooling' (2012, pp. 14–15). Indeed, educational advocates of such 'tough love' regimes seem unaware of the origins of these approaches in the increasingly militarized prison and policing regimes in the United States (Giroux, 2004). Such 'no excuses' regimes have the superficial appeal of clarity and consistency, but life is rarely, if ever, as black and white as such regimes assume. In addition, simple and overzealously enforced rules and regulations relieve educators of the need to exercise critical judgment and deprive students of opportunities for exposure to models of careful consideration of cases that take complexity and context into consideration.

The Michaela approach to discipline is discussed in three chapters: 'No-excuses discipline changes lives', by Jonathan Porter; 'Bootcamp breaks bad habits' by Joe Kirby; and 'Authority in action' by Lucy Newman. The first of these chapters is key insofar as it outlines the School's underlying philosophy. As so often in this book, the stage is set for the argument by the construction of a straw target: 'in the decades since the Second World War we have increasingly seen adults, like Rousseau, balk at their responsibilities to correct ordinary adolescent behaviour' (p. 67). Aside from the sweeping nature of the generalization about a steady decline in behavioural standards (a form of complaint that exemplifies the discourse of the hysteric) over seventy years – an argument for which not a shred of supporting evidence is provided other than the author's assertion – the underlying assumption that 'ordinary' adolescent (and note the choice of 'adolescent', rather than the more inclusive and less suggestive 'young people') behaviours necessarily stand in need of correction (rather than guidance, comment, praise, etc.) is problematic. Potter goes on, drawing on Aristotle, to emphasize the role of habit in the cultivation of ethically desirable behaviour, but this point is valid regardless of context and does not lend special support to the sort of militarized disciplinary regime the school enacts, promotes and defends. Habit could, for instance, provide the basis for the cultivation of critical questioning and agentive inquiry about ourselves, our relations with others and the shared social reality we inhabit. Here, however, it is used to install 'our expectation [is] that pupils should be silent unless they've been asked to answer a question or work with a partner' (p. 73). These expectations include the requirement for the students to 'track' the teacher with their eyes, with failure to do so earning the students demerit points and detention,[8] even though there is no evidence that this practice has any benefits in terms of student learning and can therefore, surely, only be justified on the grounds of promoting docility and compliance.[9]

Equally problematic, alongside the sweeping claim that standards of behaviour in schools have been steadily eroded, is the assertion that behaviour is 'probably' worse in schools serving students from poorer backgrounds (p. 69) – a claim which is not backed up by any evidence but which, nonetheless, says a great deal about the assumptions and prejudices of the author. However, facts aside, the *strategic* value of this claim is to provide the justificatory basis of the school's 'no excuses' regime. As Porter puts it,

> no excuses discipline doesn't lower expectations of children from tough estates by presuming that such behaviour cannot be changed. It stands resolutely by the belief that children and young people are capable of understanding why

---

[8] https://mcsbrent.co.uk/wp-content/uploads/2018/04/Behaviour-201718.pdf.
[9] https://debrakidd.wordpress.com/2016/12/06/battle-hymn-of-the-tiger-teachers-a-review-part-1/.

> communal rules need to exist, and it contends that those pupils have the ability
> to make good choices rather than bad ones. It is a hopeful vision of all pupils
> realising their potential. (p. 78)

Here, understanding the complex factors contributing to behaviour is conflated
with fatalism about the amenability of such behaviour to change, just as children's
understanding of the need for structure is conflated with the requirement of one
particular structure. These assertions are underpinned by a belief that behaviour
is a matter of rational choice, a view that ignores the lessons of psychoanalysis
about the power of conflicting desires and unconscious processes in shaping how
we act. It is also a view that disavows the social reality of class-based privilege
and disempowerment in order to champion neo-liberal values of self-sufficiency
(Ryan, 2017). In this regard, the claim made by Michaela and similar institutions
is that the formal equality of a 'no excuses' culture mitigates the 'double
disadvantage' resulting from poverty at home compounded by low expectations
at school. According to this version of social justice it is those teachers and
school leaders who take students' backgrounds into account when setting and
modulating expectations, working in what Porter refers to as 'some excuses'
schools (p. 70), that are the true perpetrators of socioeconomic disadvantage.
Yet saying does not equal making; the social stigmas and pathologies that are
supposedly ignored – or rather, repressed – return in the guise of the 'urban
chaos' discourse that is used to justify the boot camp approach (Kulz, 2017, p. 37).
In addition, as Kulz goes on to argue, the 'no excuses' mantra 'divorces students
from their social positioning, trivialising continued hardship, institutionalised
racism and moral value judgements ... not only are disadvantaged students
further disadvantaged through formalised equality, but the heavy policing of
ethnic-minority and working-class bodies compound this disadvantage' (Kulz,
2017, p. 109). Indeed, there are clear echoes in some of the language choices in
the book of bourgeois disgust and hysteria in the face of the unruly, carnivalesque
behaviour of the classed and racialized Other: 'In shops, some of these children
have been caught shoplifting, throwing food at shopkeepers or hurling drinks at
other customers' (p. 80). Evident here is the bourgeois subject's 'disgust, fear and
desire which inform the dramatic self-representation of that culture through
the "scene of its low Other"' (Stallybrass and White, 1986, p. 202). Indeed, the
emphasis in schools like Michaela on formal equality, coupled with a rejection of
students' out-of-school subjectivities, in all their forms, not just the caricatured
version above, reveals 'the contradictory construction of bourgeois democracy'
which encodes 'in its body, bearing and taste, a subliminal élitism which was

constitutive of its historical being. Whatever the radical nature of its "universal" democratic demand, it had engraved in its subjective identity all the marks by which it felt itself to be a different, distinctive and superior class' (Stallybrass and White, 1986, p. 202). Michaela purports to hold out an invitation to its students to join this distinctive and superior class.

In other words, in making their demands upon students in the name of formal equality, democracy and 'social mobility', the classed and racialized aspects of the preferred codes and comportment are disavowed so that the students are subject to a 'double disadvantaged', only not in the sense that the school thinks, but in the sense that their lifeworld subjectivities are rejected yet they are also denied the critical resources to make sense of their own and others' place in the world. All they are offered are the neo-liberal platitudes that everyone can be a winner on the basis of hard work, discipline, aspiration and application. Returning to the final sentence of the quote above from Porter, and considering it in relation to the problematic nature of bourgeois claims to democratic equality, while few, if any, would wish to disagree with the vision of an education that enables all pupils to succeed, success for all is not possible in an education system driven by capitalist logics of competition (Lawler and Payne, 2017; Moore and Clarke, 2016). In fact, what is advocated here is the slightly different aim of all pupils realizing their 'potential', again suggesting that, for all its claims to be on the side of the underprivileged, Michaela School, like neo-liberal discourse more widely, is guided by a deeply entrenched version of social Darwinism, in which destiny, or at least its limits, are inborn.

Overshadowing this underlying deterministic perspective, however, is the official ideology – the 'Michaela magic' (p. 202) – that insists that structural limits and systemic contradictions can be overcome through individual effort – an imagined world where anyone can be a winner. Yet, for some to be winners means that others have to lose – otherwise the term ceases to have any meaning but is reduced to a platitude. Likewise, for a school that claims to be on the side of the underprivileged, Michaela adopts a decidedly elitist perspective and views the majority of the urban population with a disconcerting degree of disdain, as evident in this example of the daily 'sermon from the bench':

Top of the Pyramid people – there aren't many of us. We're special. We make the right choices. Even when it's difficult. Especially when it's difficult. We don't hang around 'Sam's Chicken'. We don't drop litter. We don't swear. We don't swarm at the bus stop. We don't pull our shirt out and take our tie off. We don't have two haircuts on one head and we don't wear trainers with our uniform. We are Michaela.

We are not normal. Make no bones about it. We are NOT normal. You know what normal kids do? They shout in the street. They push and shove at the bus stop. They never say thank you to shopkeepers. They never give up their seat for older people on the bus They don't know how to shake hands properly. They don't make eye contact or smile when they speak. I don't want you to be just normal. (p. 203)

The relentless running down of 'normal' kids reflects the discourse of the hysteric's rejection of the status quo, while the repeated attempts to define 'the Michaela subject' ('we do this ... we don't do that') betrays an underlying insecurity in relation to the positivity of the subject's being (Schroeder, 2008, p. 152) – an insecurity in relation to which the discourse of the hysteric represents the paradigmatic, rather than an exceptional, case (Schroeder, 2008, p. 153; Žižek, 1996b). In other words, the hysterical subject is perpetually asking the Other, *What is it that I lack? What is it that you want from me? What do I need to do to elicit your desire and deserve your attention?* But asking the Other what it wants is tantamount to recognizing that the Other is also lacking – a lack which forms the basis of its desire. This recognition, in turn, is likely to evoke hostility to the Other. For how dare the Other presume to tell me what I need to do in order to achieve completion when it too is incomplete? This dynamic helps explain the oscillation between subservience and hostility the hysterical subject manifests towards the established social order and which we see reflected in Michaela's celebration yet condemnation of education, schools and students.

But perhaps more troubling is the encoding within the above exhortations to correct comportment of a series of rejections of the embodied subjectivities of non-white students

Reform's radical champion

My rage returned and it felt good to articulate it. (Rhee, 2013, p. 176)

The discourse of the hysteric derives its oxygen from a sense of crisis. Whereas the message of *Battle Hymn of the Tiger Teachers* is centred around the Michaela school, Michelle Rhee's book *Radical: Fighting to Put Students First* revolves around Rhee as an individual bent on reforming and improving schooling in response to a perceived crisis at the system level. In each case crisis is key. But in contrast to Katharine Birbalsingh, whose contrived sense of embattlement is directed at her school's real and imagined detractors, Rhee's argument is reliant upon, and justified by, imagery of conflict, struggle and crisis on a grander, more epic scale.

Rhee is, in fact, quite open about the need to manipulate people and engender motivation by appealing to a sense of crisis: 'A message that says, "Hey, everything in the school system is great – come and be a cog in the wheel!" is not very compelling. Tell people they can make a difference, and they will come' (p. 75). This comment occurs in the context of Rhee's conversations with marketing staff in relation to the teacher recruitment agency, The New Teacher Project. For the most part, however, her imagery and discourse lives out the notion of crisis. Thus, for example, she describes how her decision to leave classroom teaching and seek a larger canvas for her energies was driven by her recognition that there were struggling schools, like Harlem Park, the Baltimore school she had worked in, all across the country and that 'generations of children were getting shortchanged. I could not stand for that.... I began to believe that public policy had to change: how we run schools and select our teachers, how we train them, how they relate to students – so much had to change for all the kids who look like my kids to have an equal shake in life' (p. 54). How she went about addressing these challenges made her the darling and the public face of the corporate reform movement in American education (Ravitch, 2013).

As indicated above, Rhee launched The New Teacher Project (NTP) in 1997 following three years of teaching in Harlem Park Elementary School in Baltimore. Like Teach for America, the NTP was a national agency that sought to recruit young graduates for teaching posts in hard-to-staff urban schools. It also provided Rhee with a national platform and drew the attention of national figures like Joel Klein, the lawyer who became the Chancellor of the New York City Department of Education in 2002, Don Fisher, founder of the Gap clothing chain and subsequent educational philanthropist, and Wendy Kopp, the founder of Teach for America, who, like Bill Gates and Mark Zuckerberg, dreamed up her scheme while still a student in a university dorm. Indeed, the links to corporate America are not coincidental and reflect Rhee's championing of this group's educational philosophy, including policies such as payment (or job loss) by test results for teachers and principals, opposition to established practices of tenure and collective bargaining for teachers, privatization and charter schools and the use of vouchers to enable students from poor backgrounds to attend private schools. Her pursuit of these policies was single-minded and relentless, matched by a 'brusque and unapologetic style' (Ravitch, 2013, p. 147).

In time, her high profile and connections, as well as her national involvement in teacher recruitment, brought her to the attention of Adrian Fenty, the mayoral candidate for Washington, DC – a high-poverty district that had become a byword for failing public schools in America. From 2007 until Fenty's fall from power in 2010 – in part a consequence of Rhee's alienation of voters, owing to her uncompromising and abrasive approach – she served as the first Chancellor for the Washington, DC, public school system, doggedly pursuing the above corporate education reform agenda. Following this, she launched the StudentsFirst organization. The StudentsFirst organization was nothing if not ambitious. Rhee went on the Oprah Winfrey Show to announce it and solicited funds from the likes of investment billionaire Ted Forstmann, Texan hedge fund billionaires John and Laura Arnold, and other members of the rich and famous that she met though giving presentations at events such as Forstmann's 'annual visionary conference for the smart, the wealthy, and the well connected' (p. 176). The organization worked with US state governors, city mayors and other powerful groups and individuals to undermine the system of teacher tenure in US schools and bring in pay-for-performance reforms. These powerful corporate and government figures loved Rhee's toughness, her decisiveness and the relentlessness with which she executed her reform drive. In these qualities, Rhee embodies the way the discourse of the hysteric, with its insistent and obsessive focus, can operate as a powerful tool for the production of truth (Gherovici, 2017).

As this brief discussion suggests, Rhee's solutions to the pressing political issue of education were largely individualistic[10] ones that targeted group solidarities, mobilizing the well-established neo-liberal tactics of fear and crisis to justify cuts, closures and redundancies (Klein, 2007; Phillips-Fein, 2018). This was all in the name of 'putting students first', though these same students were given no say in terms of curriculum, pedagogy or assessment. Rhee's approach was grounded in her faith in test scores as an adequate measure of educational quality and her firm belief that the problems presented by students' unequal backgrounds, that is, by poverty, racism and other forms of systemic discrimination, can be addressed 'if you have an amazing teacher in the classroom' (p. 171). Her recipe for 'fixing public education' is thus the simple – and simplistic – one advocated by programs like Teach for America: 'Recruit, select, and train the

---

[10] It is no surprise that the film, *Waiting for Superman* (Guggenheim, 2011), with its image of the teacher as a heroic individual, has provided such a powerful rallying cry for 'radical' US education reformers like Rhee. For a critical reading of such imagery, see Alex Moore's (2004) book *The Good Teacher*.

most outstanding young people in our country to spend two years teaching in some of our most troubled urban or rural public schools' (p. 59). Rhee seems untroubled by the innatist depiction of the mostly middle-class graduates she has in mind, as 'the most outstanding young people in our country', rather than, say, as the most socio-economically privileged, just as she is unperturbed by the depoliticization inherent in depicting the communities that are victims of America's systemic inequality as 'troubled'. Indeed, her language conveys a sense of blithely unawareness of these potential issues. In this respect, her crisis-laden discourse embodies the notion of crises as blind-spots that are incapable of seeing their own conditions of emergence (Roitman, 2014).

Even when, at times, Rhee's individualism is tempered by a more sober acceptance of the complex and intractable nature of education policy, as when she recognizes the impossibility 'that educators and schools can fix all of society's ills', she immediately undermines any sense of nuance with the assertion that 'the single most effective strategy for combatting generational poverty is education' (p. 209). Similarly, she reports how other education reformers advised her that 'fixing' American education would require a much broader focus on factors such as curriculum, nutrition and social services, for instance. Yet, Rhee remained determined in the target of her reforms and kept her focus 'tightly on teaching and teacher quality, all directed to improving student outcomes' (p. 190) because, as she repeatedly tells us, 'she cares about the kids' – as if only she and other advocates of 'radical', corporate reform of education, but not teachers and leaders working in schools, really care about children and their futures. Never mind that those same kids have no say in the content and method of their education. Never mind that these kids are used, cynically some might say, to justify a range of punitive and demoralizing policies that alienated educators[11] and the wider community.[12] And never mind that the consequences of her preferred corporatized, market-led brand of reforms have included 'cheating, teaching to bad tests, institutionalized fraud, dumbing down of tests, and a narrowed curriculum'.[13] In both the single-mindedness of her focus and the insatiability of her desire for her chosen model of 'reform', including her belief in the existence of a relatively simple set of solutions to overwhelmingly complex social problems, self-proclaimed 'radical' Rhee, like the tiger teachers

---

[11] 'Miss Grundy Was Fired Today – Once Deified, Now Demonized, Teachers Are under Assault' http://nymag.com/news/features/michelle-rhee-2011-3/.

[12] 'D.C. Schools Chancellor Rhee's Approval Rating in Deep Slide' http://www.washingtonpost.com/wp-dyn/content/article/2010/01/31/AR2010013102757.html??noredirect=on.

[13] https://www.thedailybeast.com/michelle-rhees-cheating-scandal-diane-ravitch-blasts-education-reform-star.

of Michaela School, represents the strengths and the weaknesses of the discourse of the hysteric.

Conclusion

The pervasive narrative about a profound crisis in education and the teachers and schools that are failing our students, while superficially seductive, is premised on a number of false assumptions and assertions. Like the split subject in the discourse of the hysteric berating the master for not being masterful enough, the crisis narrative insistently proclaims the cruelly optimistic narratives that all children matter equally (they don't), that everyone can succeed in a system built around notions of competition, averages and continuous quality improvement (they can't), and that schools can compensate for society by redressing economic inequalities (they can't). In a theme that has recurred throughout this book, education serves as a scapegoat for a society that is unable, or unwilling, to seriously grapple with the growth in wealth, poverty and inequality. Success for all may be a chimera, but the discourse of the hysteric in education policy, embodied in the rhetoric of figures like Katharine Birbalsingh, Michelle Rhee, Michael Gove or Joel Klein, will not listen to excuses and has zero tolerance failure – consequently, when not all succeed and when 'standards' fail to rise inexorably, someone must be held to account and punished. Yet, 'some students will not be proficient in standardized tests no matter how hard they try, no matter how talented their teachers or how dedicated their principal. Some students will be distracted by crises in their lives; some will lack motivation or interest; some will inevitably land in the bottom half of the bell curve because the bell curve always has a bottom half' (Ravitch, 2013, p. 315). Moreover, in a further twist of cruel optimism, those who point such inconvenient truths out and dare to challenge the fantasmatic narrative of equal access to opportunity are deemed to be the ones who are discriminate against the less advantaged, who lack faith in the ability of all children to succeed and who limit children's futures by highlighting the links between demography and destiny. In any 'race to the top', some will fall behind, for schooling 'operates as an enormous academic sieve, sorting out the educational winners from the losers in a crude and often brutal process that prioritises and rewards upper- and middle-class qualities and resources' (Reay, 2017, p. 26).

But there is another dark side to the narrative of failing education and the relentless focus on standardized test results, insofar as it serves to legitimate the neo-liberal privatization agenda, with corporate- and philanthropic-funded charter schools in the UK and academies in the UK taking over public schools as the latter are closed or restructured on the basis of their purportedly inadequate performance. This was initially justified on the basis of claims that privately run schools and a greater array of 'choice' would somehow magically raise standards, but as the evidence for this assumption has failed to materialize[14] (Tell, 2016), just as it failed to materialize in relation to claims that these new types of school would enhance social justice (Gorard, 2014), neo-liberal politicians have revealed the ideological, rather than pedagogical, basis for their policies, as when the UK government declared in its 2016 White Paper (Department for Education (DfE), 2016) that all schools would become academies by 2020 – a commitment it later backed down on following an outcry from the policy's opponents.

Unsurprisingly, the neo-liberal corporate education agenda has not gone unchallenged, with resistance coming from educators, parents, activists, community groups and the academy, and taking varied forms such as refusals to administer or take standardized tests and assessments, protest marches and online activism[15] (Au, 2016; Baldridge, 2017; Green and Castro, 2017; Hursh, 2017; Rudd and Goodson, 2017). However, it is all too easy for such resistance to be circumscribed within the discourse of the hysteric – for instance, by complaining that 'true' education needs to reassert itself and throw-off the shackles of neo-liberalism. As noted in this chapter's introduction, the danger here is that a fantasmatic belief in the transformative power of a master signifier and therefore a position of subordination in relation to this master – in this case, education – is retained. What is also needed is the production of new master signifiers, which only the discourse of the analyst can achieve.

---

[14] 'No Proof Academies Raise Standards, Say MPs' https://www.bbc.co.uk/news/education-30983081.
[15] See, for example, the following from the UK: https://reclaimingschools.org/.

6

The Discourse of the Analyst and the Other Side of Education: Subversion and Reinvention

Lacan has been the only one since Freud who has sought to refocus the question of psychoanalysis on precisely this question of the relations between the subject and truth.... Lacan tried to pose what historically is the specifically spiritual question: that of the price the subject must pay for saying the truth, and of the effect on the subject of the fact that he has said, that he can and has said the truth about himself.

Foucault, 2005, p. 30

Because the objects we endow with the Thing's nobility contain a trace of the real, they automatically challenge the notion that the Other's reality principle is all that we have got. In this sense, it is exactly the fact that reality does not fully correspond to itself – that it is always punctured by the energies of the real – that forges an opening for the reinvention of (personal or social) ideals, values, and systems of representation.

Ruti, 2012, pp. 151–2

Don't expect anything more subversive in my discourse than that I do not claim to have a solution.

Lacan, 2007, p. 70

Introduction

Sometimes saying nothing can speak volumes. Chapter eight of Vic Kelly's (2009) book *The Curriculum, Theory and Practice* is entitled 'What the Average Politician Understands about Education'. The title occupies page 213 and the unprepared reader turns to page 214 expecting to read the introduction to the chapter, only to be confronted with the title and introduction to chapter nine, 'The Flaws Endemic to Central Planning by Politicians'. It's a bold and witty way to make a point and at times I considered something similar for this chapter as I grappled with the challenges of writing about the discourse of the analyst. For the analyst's key task is to listen and to serve as a non-judgemental audience for the analysand, not to offer advice or solutions. In similar fashion, the discourse of the analyst is a space of listening rather than an invitation to preach, hold forth or offer pronouncements. It is an invitation to 'play by ear' (Johnson, 2014), to improvise rather than to perform in accordance with a predetermined or memorized script. For it is only by listening attentively to 'the specific features and idiosyncrasies of each particular case history that one avoids the imposition of an obsolete vocabulary on slippery facts' (Gherovici, 2017, p. 63). In its aversion and resistance to pre-scripted – or prescriptive – agendas, the discourse of the analyst is also, therefore, about 'the desire to begin something for the sake of the beginning and not the end' (Peters, 2017, p. 7). For a focus on ends typically entails the identification of predetermined outcomes that exclude non-dominant voices. This makes the discourse of the analyst particularly incompatible with the instrumental, goal- and outcome-oriented models of education policy and practice that are dominant today.

But all speech and all writing involve a degree of improvisation unless it is recitation in the case of the former or, in the latter case, mere copying. Our unconscious deliberations are always interrupting our conscious pronouncements; in Foucauldian terms, discourse speaks us as much as we speak discourse. But beyond this, performance and improvisation are rendered indistinguishable 'in the end', as the latter's 'false starts, the trials and errors, the moments of aesthetic judgment and misjudgment, all necessary for a work to come into being, are all erased *prior* to the work's eventual emergence as a finished work' (Peters, 2017, p. 8). Completion all too often results in the reification and naturalization of the finished product, as decisions that were taken – and just as importantly the possibilities that were declined, ignored or neglected – are rendered invisible.

At the same time, this discussion raises a serious challenge for anyone tasked with writing a chapter on the discourse of the analyst – for to the extent that the latter places restless desire in the position of agency, the question arises as to how this might be reconciled with the assertion of a seemingly complete, coherent and synoptic text? How can the mobility and vivacity of desire survive entombment within the confines of a chapter or a book? For whereas desire is infused with the unruly energies of the real, the regulatory order of language and the symbolic 'cuts *into* the smooth facade of the real, creating divisions, gaps and distinguishable entities and laying the real to rest, that is, drawing or sucking it into the symbols used to describe it, and thereby annihilating it' (Fink, 1995, p. 24, emphasis in original). Again, echoing Peters above, desire seems more attuned to the openness of the initial gesture than to the closure of completion.

For this reason, the discourse of the analyst, in which desire assumes the position of agency, 'only exists on the fly. In fact, it may never exist at all, but is rather only a goal, a hypothetical, tantalizing possibility' (Johnson, 2014, p. 199).

This challenge, moreover, is one that seems parallel to a key dilemma facing the education policymaker: how does one order and regulate a vital, dynamic and unpredictable process such as education in a way that does not undermine and destroy the vitality of the thing under one's charge? If meaningful education is a process and a space of discovery, one necessarily infused with risk, uncertainty and the possibility of failure (Biesta, 2013), then how does one square this with the prior determination of knowledge through prescribed curricular outcomes? If the professional autonomy and creativity of school leaders and managers lies at the heart of education policy reforms, 'designed to empower and extend the reach of the best leaders … bringing fresh vision, strong leadership and clear accountability' (Department for Education (DfE), 2016, pp. 40, 80), then how is this to be reconciled with critical research arguing that much school leadership today is unreflexively authoritarian, comprising 'school leaders implementing relentlessly the ideology of standards, and misrecognising the external provenance and homogeneity of this mission as contextual, personal and unique' (Courtney and Gunter, 2015, p. 413). And if neo-liberal governments in a range of global contexts would recognize and endorse the English government's commitment to 'ensuring our school system offers greater choice, innovation and competition' (2016, p. 62), what are we to make of the growing segregation in compulsory schooling that such choice policies are increasingly encouraging, as reported in research from different international contexts (Brandén and Bygren, 2018; Gorard, 2014; Kotok et al., 2017; Mayer, 2017). There are, of course, no final answers to these questions, no final solutions to the timeless dilemmas of education, which is why, for Freud, educating, like analysing and governing, is an impossible profession. The specific challenge for the discourse of the analyst is how to move beyond critical awareness of the limitations and falsehoods of today's masterful and universal discourses in education and instantiate some form of meaningful alternative practice, while resisting the temptation to reify, formalize and institutionalize these forms of resistance, thereby turning today's tentative solutions into tomorrow's systemic oppression.

The discourse of the analyst

One way of highlighting the distinction between the discourse of the hysteric and the discourse of the analyst, and between these two and the discourses of the master and the university, is by comparing the response of each discourse to such tensions and contradictions. Both the discourse of the hysteric and the discourse of the analyst speak from a position of 'radical negativity' (Schroeder, 2008, p. 107). This contrasts with the surfeit of positivity, in the sense of bodies of knowledge, institutions and structures that do not question their own foundations (Clarke and Phelan, 2017; Coole, 2000), characteristic of the discourses of the master and the university. Hence, as we saw in Chapters 3 and 4, the tendency of these discourses is to assert the dominance of the master signifier, either overtly, as in the case of the discourse of the master, or covertly, in the case of the discourse of the university.

In contrast to these discourses of mastery, the discourses of the hysteric and the discourse of the analyst may be thought of as discourses of thinking otherwise (Campbell, 2004). Yet, as we saw in the previous chapter, the discourse of the hysteric, in which the split subject occupies the place of agency, for all its vehemence and passion also speaks from a place of division, trauma and confusion, typically employing tones of outrage in its biting invective as part of its protests and complaints. However, as we also saw, in its insistence on answers, the discourse of the hysteric ends up reinstating the master as idol who must tell the subject who s/he is. Hence, as we saw in the previous chapter, for educators speaking from the discourse of the hysteric, their response to the sense that something is awry in education, and their belief that schooling is not fulfilling the expectations placed upon it, is to reassert a model of education in which knowledge and discipline are more authoritative, thereby instating a new master. In this sense, despite the undoubted passion of energy of its attacks on established authorities, the discourse of the hysteric always ultimately falls short of its aims and ambitions.

By contrast, the discourse of the analyst is more truly revolutionary insofar as it is diametrically opposed to the closure and rigidity of the discourse of the master. However, rather than mounting a full-frontal attack, the discourse of the analyst is more likely to be reflected in symptomatic readings of a policy text or practical situation, which seek to expose the blind spots and contradictions that those whose identities are entangled within the text or situation cannot see or recognize. The inherent trauma and confusion of the subject that are denied and disavowed by the discourse of the master and the university – both of which can be understood as part of an 'imperialising project, in which difference is refused' (Brown, Atkinson and England, 2006, p. 131) – and that the discourse of the hysteric seeks to overcome by insisting that the master

$$a \quad \rightarrow \quad \$$$
$$\uparrow \quad \overline{} \qquad \overline{} \quad \downarrow$$
$$S2 \quad // \quad S1$$

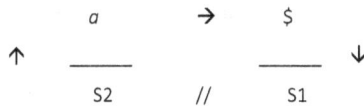

Figure 6.1 The discourse of the analyst

provides certainty, is accepted by the discourse of the analyst as the necessary starting point. The discourse of the analyst is represented diagrammatically in Figure 6.1.

Specifically, within the discourse of the analyst, desire, *a*, underpinned by unconscious knowledge, S2, in the place of truth, addresses the split subject, $, and initiates the production of a new master signifier, S1. The 'catch' this sets up for this chapter, and indeed for anyone looking to 'mobilise' the four discourses for practical purposes and perhaps looking to the discourse of the analyst as the 'answer' to the problems resulting from overly intrusive forms of authority, is that the uniqueness characterizing the production of new master signifiers that align with the singularity of the subject's desire – a singularity that reflects our idiosyncratic embodied experience and that 'persists as a nonnegotiable kernel of the real beyond all social predicates, taxonomies, generalizations, and economies of comparison' (Ruti, 2012, p. 2). The agency of this singularity in the discourse of the analyst means that there can be no blueprint or template which can be 'rolled out' or 'scaled up'. Indeed, were this roll-out to happen, the danger is that the circuit of discourse keeps turning and that the new master signifier comes to occupy the position of truth, landing us back in the discourse of the university, or assumes the position of agency, returning us to the discourse of the master. As Lacan observed, 'this is the difficulty faced by anyone whom I try to bring as close as I am able to the analyst's discourse ... because it is easy after all to spin off into the discourse of mastery' (Lacan, 2007, p. 69). For this reason, remaining in the discourse of the analyst requires an ongoing dialectic between centring and decentring, something akin to a continual twisting of the kaleidoscope so that fresh patterns and new possibilities continually come into view (Johnson, 2014, p. 199; Felman, 1978, p. 245). It requires navigating the slippery terrain of the möbius strip – the twisted sliver of paper in which one side flows seamlessly into the other side – where the boundaries separating knowledge and ignorance, truth and uncertainty, self and other, desire and death, are porous and therefore potentially generative but also always potentially perilous.

Unconscious knowledge occupies the place of truth

Among the four discourses, the discourse of the analyst clearly comes as close to an ideal as is possible within the generally anti-idealistic worldview of Lacanian psychoanalysis (Frosh, 2012, p. 183). Yet by placing knowledge below the bar, in the place of unconscious truth, the discourse of the analyst is also the only one of the four discourses that doesn't mistake itself for truth, at least not in any full or final, timeless or universal, sense: 'this truth that we are seeking in a concrete experience is not that of a superior law' (Lacan, 1992, p. 24). Instead by placing knowledge in the place of unconscious truth, the discourse of the analyst recognizes that knowledge can never be coterminous with truth, in part because truth, for Lacan, always refers to desire and in part because it is unconscious and therefore always located to some degree outside, before or beyond any discourse (Lacan, 1975; Leupin, 2004, p. 80).

Desire assumes the place of agency

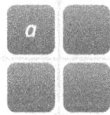

Lacan's seventeenth seminar, in which he outlined the theory of the four discourses, was conducted during the heady days of the revolutionary upheavals of 1968. Against this backdrop, it would be easy to read the location of desire in the place of agency in the discourse of the analyst as advocating a counterculture era version of the philosophy of desire, of the 'turn on, tune in, drop out' variety, and therefore as representing a naïve politicization of the vital energies of the libido (Wright, 2015). Similarly, it would be easy to confuse the agency of desire with the endless pursuit of pleasure characteristic of late capitalism. Indeed, in relation to this risk, a key insight of *Seminar XVII* is that under the conditions of late capitalism, the commodification of labour, far from merely leading to alienation, transforms work into a form of enjoyment – albeit not for *all* forms of work and albeit tinged with pain *as well as* pleasure – thereby 'rendering loss and surplus two sides of the very same coin' (Wright, 2015, p. 138). For instance, as educators, we both lose ourselves and find ourselves through our subordination to the symbolic worlds of teaching and learning, literally paying with our lives in terms of the time spent labouring for our institutional masters, while deriving enjoyment from those moments of success, when our students 'get it' or when our peers accept, cite and celebrate our work. In relation to these considerations, the point to bear in mind is not that countercultural activism or professional striving may never be worthy of occupying the place of the agent in the discourse of the analyst; but, as highlighted in the discussion of desire in Chapter 1, such striving is only likely to do so 'insofar as it seems to contain an echo of the object cause of desire (the Thing) … to embody what Lacan calls "the dignity of the Thing"' (Ruti, 2017, p. 223), thereby maintaining fidelity to the singular track of desire that (universally) marks each and every one of us.

In a similar vein, the key contribution of the analyst's discourse is not the provision of a superior metadiscourse that transcends the pitfalls and problems attendant in the others; rather it lies in that insofar as it gives priority to desire – for Lacan 'the metonymy of our being' (Lacan, 1992, p. 321) – by its positioning in the seat of agency, it attunes us to the location of desire, including attempts at its repression, colonization and subordination, in the other discourses. In other words, rather than providing a metalanguage or an Archimedean point outside or beyond discourse, the discourse of the analyst elucidates the workings and structure of discourse itself (Fink, 1995, p. 137).

The split subject in the place of the other

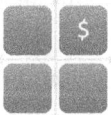

The discourse of the analyst puts the subject with all its divisions and contradictions directly in the firing line, subjecting it to the insistent questioning and probing of desire. This involves a self-questioning by the subject in relation to its desire and with regard to its alienating submission to master signifiers as manifested in hegemonic discourses, narratives and values. This self-questioning may take forms such as 'which elements of my past, which genealogical inheritances, which unacknowledged phantasy, what unknown jouissances have brought me here, to accept these situations, to console myself with these objects, to repeat these impasses?' (Koren, 2014, p. 253). This is not merely a therapeutic process but a political one in the sense of questioning the basis of the subject's subjection and opening the possibility of creating new master signifiers as the product of the discourse of the analyst.

The product: Generating new master signifiers

The discourse of the analyst is unique among the four discourses in not being dominated by the master signifier. For while the latter is the agent in the discourse of the master, the unacknowledged truth of the discourse of the university and always-inadequate other of the discourse of the hysteric, the discourse of the analyst is distinguished by its production of new master signifiers distinctive to the subject and its history. Specifically, the questioning of the split subject that occurs in the discourse of the analyst in relation to the subject's desire, and concerning its subordination to hegemonic values, beliefs and practices, prompts the production of new master signifiers; and because desire occupies the place of agency, the likelihood is that these new master signifiers will bear greater fidelity *to* the subject's desire and resonate with the echo of the singularity of the Thing as theorized by Lacan and as discussed in Chapter 2 – that unfathomably precious (non)object that we imagine having once had and subsequently lost and that serves to organize our desire through a series of substitutes (*objet a*).

The negative side to this picture, as noted above, is the risk that we misrecognize our new master signifiers as the final answer and elevate them to the status of general truths in a new iteration of the discourse of the university or attribute independent agency to them and thus establish a new discourse of the master. Put differently, the ever-present temptation is to imagine that when we finally regain the lost object it will redeem our (ontologically) lacking status and close the (unbreachable) gap between meaning and being that opens as a consequence of our subjection to the signifier, even though, as discussed in Chapter 2 and despite all our strivings, the 'reality' is that our lack as subjects, and the desire this generates, is constitutive and hence irredeemable (Ruti, 2017).

The positive edge to this potentially bleak picture is that while we may never achieve complete satisfaction or find any final answers to the perennial issues in education policy and in our wider existence, we do have the capacity to generate new master signifiers that are in some sense fundamental to us, in the sense that they echo the obstinate singularity of the unconscious truth of our desire, whilst also being accountable to and contestable by others. The remainder of this chapter explores the implications of the tensions, paradoxes and dilemmas attendant upon the discourse of the analyst, initially by approaching the discourse of the analyst obliquely via a discussion of Jaroslav Hašek's (1883–1923) twentieth-century Czech novel, *The Good Soldier Švejk*, and then through a further discussion of the relationship between desire and ethics in Mari Ruti's reading of Lacan and placing them in dialogue with notions of voice, resonance and politics drawn from the work of Italian philosopher, Adriana Cavarero.

Resistance I: Subversive irony

As highlighted in Chapter 3, and its discussion of the discourse of the university, today's education policy is dominated by the world of technical rationality, according to which rigorous scientific research provides us with incontrovertible findings that form the evidence base for policy and practice. Yet, as others have pointed out, evidence-based policy is often a matter of policy-based evidence-making (Boden and Epstein, 2006; Strassheim and Kettunen, 2014), involving politicians, policymakers and bureaucrats cherry-picking research findings that support an ideologically predetermined policy agenda. A classic example occurred in the case of synthetic phonics and literacy teaching in English education policy – a case in which evidence from a narrow disciplinary base was favoured to the exclusion of all other research, in order to impose a particular teaching method on schools, teachers and students that reflected an impoverished and inadequate view of literacy, that rode roughshod over teachers' professional expertise, and that excluded any considerations of individual and contextual difference (Davis, 2012; Ellis and Moss, 2014). As this case highlighted, knowledge is never innocent or value-free; likewise policy is always entangled with power and politics. What we need, therefore, in Stephen White's (2000) terms, is to move from a 'strong ontology' – an ontology which, underpinned by conviction and certainty, is beholden to dominant master signifiers and which purports to depict the world 'as it is' – to a 'weak ontology', underpinned by contingency and indeterminacy and offering insights that are recognized as necessarily tentative and contestable.

With this cautionary note in mind, I want to consider the implications and possibilities for educators seeking to resist the constraints of neo-liberal education policy of thinking with fictional texts. The advantages of thinking through fictional texts – and in this I include film as well as literature – include transporting us beyond the confinements of the present at a time in which it is increasingly difficult to imagine a world outside neo-liberal capitalism, thereby encouraging us to overcome the curtailment of the imagination that the neo-liberal hegemony entails. In this sense, fictional texts offer possibilities for opening up new avenues of thought, new lines of flight, rather than remaining confined within familiar circuits. Fiction offers possibilities for keeping debates open and questions in play, rather than promoting premature closure by seeking universal solutions and conclusive answers. Furthermore, literary texts can offer us insights into truths that are of a different order to the empirical and factual explanations of science and social science (Rolfe, 2002). At a deeper level it is also important to note that the line between fact and fiction is not hard and fast and that seemingly obvious facts require embedding within socially and historically constructed interpretative and narrative systems in order to make (or rather, be made to make) sense (Poovey, 1998). In other words, the lines separating fantasy and politics are porous while the psychic, emotional, aesthetic, social and political registers are intimately connected. Finally, in relation to this book's engagement with psychoanalytic theories, it can be argued that literature is the aesthetic form closest to the approach of psychoanalysis (Azari, 2008; Harari, 2002), given their common concern with language, subjectivity and desire.

Jaroslav Hašek's comic novel *The Good Soldier Švejk and His Adventures in the World War* (henceforth, *GSS*), written in 1921–2 and published unfinished in 1923 after Hašek's death from tuberculosis, is a much-loved classic of popular culture across Central Europe, if less well-known to English speaking audiences. The book tells the tale of the eponymous 'hero' and his misadventures in the Austro-Hungarian army after he enlists at the outbreak of the First World War in 1914. The ironic tenor of the novel is established at the onset in the author's preface as the humble Švejk is compared to a number of illustrious historical figures:

> Great times call for great men. There are unknown heroes who are modest, with none of the historical glamour of a Napoleon. If you analysed their character

you would find that it eclipsed even the glory of Alexander the Great. Today you can meet in the streets of Prague a shabbily dressed man who is not even himself aware of his significance in the history of the great new era. He goes modestly on his way, without bothering anyone. Nor is he bothered by journalists asking for an interview. If you asked him his name he would answer you simply and unassumingly: 'I am Švejk.'

Similarly, the key dynamics of the book, involving 'the 'little man' fighting officialdom and bureaucracy with the only weapons available to him – passive resistance, subterfuge, native wit and dumb insolence' (GSS, back cover), are established in the opening paragraphs of the novel, in which Švejk is clearly depicted as at odds with the forces of history:

> 'And so they've killed our Ferdinand,' said the charwoman to Mr Švejk, who had left military service years before, after having been finally been certified by an army medical board as an imbecile, and now lived by selling dogs – ugly, mongrel monstrosities, whose pedigrees he forged.
>
> Apart from this occupation he suffered from rheumatism and was at this very moment rubbing his knees with Elliman's embrocation.
>
> 'Which Ferdinand, Mrs Müller?' he asked, going on with the massaging. 'I know two Ferdinands. One is a messenger at Průša's the chemist's and once by mistake he drank a bottle of hair oil there. And the other is Ferdinand Kokoška who collects dog manure. Neither of them is any loss.'
>
> 'Oh no, sir, it's his Imperial highness, the Archduke Ferdinand, from Konopiště, the fat churchy one.' (GSS, 3–4)

While the events described here are the catalyst for the world war of the novel's title, their epoch-making nature is completely at odds with the offhand manner with which they are discussed, setting up a tension between, on the one hand, the forces of history and the bureaucratic apparatus of the Habsburg empire and the day to day lives and prosaic local concerns of everyday characters on the other. In this regard, Svejk's seemingly meaningless patter is in fact a meaningful defence against the meaninglessness of war (Stern, 1968). The device we see here is repeated on countless other occasions in the novel, as Švejk subtly subverts and critiques familiar narratives, in the process revealing the inability of the discourses of power from ever becoming fully totalizing (Beall, 2012; Fleming and Sewell, 2002; Kuus, 2008). As such, the novel stages a struggle between the hegemonic authority of the discourse of the master and the subversive irony of the discourse of the analyst. As Beall puts it, 'the historical forces which motivate the plot are structurally analogous to the master's discourse, while

Švejk occupies the position of the analyst, punctuating the drive of plot in order to "unwork" desire bound up in formulaic plot structures and interpellate the reader with ambivalent desire for both plot and anti-plot' (2010, p. 60). Hašek exploits the distinction, or the gap, between the words of signification and the significatory context against which those words take on meaning and in light of which language is always to some degree ambiguous and polysemic. Specifically, Švejk continually subverts the seriousness of dominant nationalist political discourses, undermining them with inappropriate local references, as in the excerpt above, or confounding them through a seemingly obtuse literalism, as in the following anecdote in which he takes his former lieutenant's metaphor at face value, thereby mocking and ridiculing it:

> But in the army you must have discipline, otherwise why would anyone bother at all? Our Lieutenant Makovec always used to say: 'There's got to be discipline, you bloody fools, otherwise you'd be climbing about on the trees like monkeys, but the army's going to make human beings of you, you god-forsaken idiots.' And isn't that true? Just imagine a park, let's say at Charles Square, and on every tree an undisciplined soldier! It's enough to give you a nightmare! (*GSS*, 8-9)

This utterance occurs in a local pub, The Chalice, to which Švejk retires following the exchange with his charwoman. Prior to Švejk's arrival, a plain clothes police office, Bretschneider, is trying to lure the bartender, Palivec, into conversation about politics and hence the possibility of making a seditious remark, by inquiring into the whereabouts of a picture of the emperor that used to hang on the wall. Sensing a possible trap, Palivec replies, 'it did hang there, but the flies used to shit on it so I put it away in the attic' (*GSS*, 8). Despite the possibility of interpreting this removal as a patriotic act intended to protect the royal portrait from defilement, Palivec finds himself arrested, as we discover a few pages later, on the basis that merely to claim that he and Bretscheider live in a world in which flies can defecate on the emperor's portrait, indeed just to link the royal personage with filth in the same utterance, is treasonous. Irony arises as a consequence of the contrast between the repressive world of the discourse of the master with its intrusive bureaucratic machinery and the ordinary world of Czech subjects like Palivec and Švejk – a world in which a banal response to a mundane question, based on the most trivial and prosaic reality, can be read as undermining the empire's ideological integrity (Beall, 2012).

Typical is the episode that occurs at the end of the first part of the book, in which a dog, Max, belonging to Colonel Kraus, a pompous Austrian officer with a penchant for subjecting his subordinates to long-winded, idiotic explanations of everyday objects such as windows and ditches, is stolen by Švejk and an accomplice as a gift for his long-suffering company commander, Lieutenant Lukáš. On spotting the lieutenant out walking the dog, the enraged colonel subsequently arranges to have Lukáš transferred to the front. On returning to his quarters, the furious lieutenant roars out: 'Švejk, you *stole* the dog!' to which Švejk calmly responds, 'Humbly report, sir, I know of no such case recently and I would like to observe, sir, that you yourself took Max this afternoon out for a walk and so I couldn't have stolen it.' After digressing into a narrative about a bag maker he once knew who kept losing dogs, Švejk admits he knew the dog was stolen. 'Švejk, Jesus Mary, Himmelherrgott, I'll have you shot, you bastard, you cattle, you oaf, you pig. Are you really such a half-wit?' This outburst elicits the predictable response from Švejk, 'Humbly report, sir, I am.' (*GSS*, 209).

As the novel progresses, it becomes clear that the targets of the relentless satire include all forms of modern bureaucratic authority, along with the labyrinthine structures and byzantine rules by which they seek to control ordinary people's lives. Švejk's strategy for resisting such forms of authority is to covertly undermine them by overly literal readings of their pronouncements that avoid the risks attendant upon more overt forms of resistance. Švejkian politics thus come to stand for resistance in modern society where power traverses the entire social body:

> In today's society, it is increasingly difficult to stand heroically on the edge of the system of power one opposes and to practice dissent in an overt, conscience-driven rejection of an official practice. Rather, we need to look at passiveness, irony, and anonymity as resources for resistance. In this context, the jolly figure of Švejk can offer invaluable insights. (Kuus, 2008)

In other words, like the discourse of the analyst, Švejk serves as a potential model for covert forms of transgression beyond overt acts of resistance conceptualized in terms of some transcendent organizing principle. Such Švejkian resistance can be considered in terms of the following four dimensions (Fleming and Sewell, 2002, pp. 866–8). *Equivocal affirmation* involves appearing to align oneself with the values of the organization but in a manner which preserves a space of distance and sense of difference. *Practice as performance* involves enacting the routines and practices in overly zealous ways that expose their meaninglessness, such as filling a suggestion box with trivial ideas and proposals or completing a staff survey in clearly exaggerated and glowing positive terms. Deploying *an ironical disposition* involves feigning ignorance so as lure the antagonist into revealing the underlying basis of their agenda and hence expose it to ridicule. Finally, *scepticism and cynicism* can be used to reveal the disavowed realities underlying the specious rhetoric of organizations, for instance, management's professions of common cause and mutual interest in relation to their workers. We see a number of these dimensions in operation in an incident in Part III of the book, in which Švejk's rambling narratives draw the ire of another company officer.

> Lieutenant Dub stared in rage at the serene face of the good soldier Švejk and asked him angrily: 'Do you know me?'
>
> 'Yes, I know you sir.'
>
> Lieutenant Dub rolled his eyes and stamped: 'I tell you, you don't know me yet.'
>
> Švejk answered once more with the serene calm of someone making a report: 'I know you, sir, humbly report. You are from our march battalion.'
>
> 'You don't know me yet,' Lieutenant Dub shouted again. 'You may perhaps know me from my good side, but wait til you know me from my bad side. I'm nasty. Don't imagine I'm not. I make everyone cry. Very well, then, do you know me or don't you know me?'
>
> 'I know you sir.'
>
> 'I tell you for the last time that you don't know me, you mule, you. Have you any brothers?'
>
> 'Humbly report, sir, I have one.'
>
> Infuriated at the sight of Švejk's calm unruffled expression, and unable to control himself any longer, Lieutenant Dub shouted out: 'And your brother must certainly be as big a bloody mule as you are. What was he?'
>
> 'A schoolmaster, sir. He was in the army too and passed the officers' exam.'
>
> Lieutenant Dub looked at Švejk as though he wanted to run him through with his sabre. Švejk bore his furious look with dignified composure, so that for the moment their whole conversation ended with the word: 'Dismiss!'
> (*GSS*, 526)

Of course, scope for deploying these strategies depends on the specific features and ambiguities characterizing practice in different institutional contexts, while they all rely, to some degree or other, on individuals' courage and capacities for feigning and dissembling. Individually or collectively they cannot provide a sure-fire path to institutional justice. Despite these caveats, 'švejkism may still represent a significant reconstitution of subjectivity in organizations, acting as an alternative to the supine or credulous acceptance of the rhetoric and practice of contemporary management' (Fleming and Sewell, 2002, p. 869).

Examples illustrating the potential of subversive irony in relation to education policy can be found in abundance in the news and on social media. For example, as I write this chapter, the school year in England is coming to a close, with all the attendant festivities and celebrations this typically entails. However, the hypercompetitive environment engendered by neo-liberal education policy with its monitoring and inspection regimes has encouraged some schools to seize the opportunity to subordinate such occasions to their accountability and performativity concerns. Specifically, there have been numerous incidences of schools holding picnics and parties to reward pupils with the highest attendance records while excluding those falling short of these targets[1] – in some cases limiting participation in the event to those with 100 per cent attendance records.[2] The schools in question have justified their actions in terms of the importance of attendance in supporting pupils' achievement but the practice has been criticized by many parents – in the words of a parent from the school rewarding only perfect attendance records, 'all they seem to care about is their Ofsted report. I'm not going to send her into school on the day to be punished for something that's not in her control.' In one case, excluded parents took matters into their own hands by organizing an alternative picnic immediately outside the school grounds,[3] thereby highlighting the injustice of the school's actions yet without engaging in direct confrontation. Examples such as this highlight the subversive potential of Švejkism as a strategy for resistance that draws attention to power and injustice through non-violent mimicry and ridicule.

On the other hand, it might be argued that Švejk – like Herman Melville's Bartleby, another literary figure held up as a model for transgressive resistance by figures like Žižek (e.g. 2006, pp. 381–5), though also one who, for others, 'is less an alternative than he is a realization, an acknowledgement of the contemporary political-economic impasse' (Dean, 2006, p. 131) – restricts our thinking in relation to resistance to subversion as opposed to more active, defiant modes of resistance. After all, although Švejk frustrates the war machine and incenses those responsible for its smooth operation, and although he, unlike Bartleby, does at least survive, he offers little by way of alternative realities. To this extent, it might be argued that Švejkism underplays the creative, imaginative scope for envisaging different possible futures, thereby colluding in what Ruti (2012, pp. 153–5) describes as 'the banalization of the world'. With this in mind,

---

[1] For example, https://www.liverpoolecho.co.uk/news/liverpool-news/children-left-floods-tears-classmates-14914117. I am grateful to Charlotte Haines Lyon for drawing these instances to my attention.

[2] http://www.kentonline.co.uk/dartford/news/parents-outrage-over-fun-day-exclusion-186603/.

[3] https://www.grimsbytelegraph.co.uk/news/local-news/live-protest-lincoln-gardens-scunthorpe-1801847.

the next section returns to the question of desire and the possibilities it might suggest for thinking further about resistance to the discourses of mastery.

Resistance II: Desiring voices in resonance

> The analyst has to keep silent, at least in principle and a great majority of the time. But here a curious reversal takes place: it is the analyst, with his or her silence, who becomes the embodiment of the voice as the object. She or he is the personification, the embodiment, of the voice, the voice incarnate, the aphonic silent voice. This is not His Master's Voice, not the voice of a command or of the superego, but, rather, the impossible voice to which one has to respond. It is the voice which does not say anything, and the voice which cannot be said. It is the silent voice of an appeal, a call, an appeal to respond, to assume one's stance as the subject. One is called upon to speak, and one would say anything that happens to come into one's mind to interrupt the silence, to silence this voice, to silence the silence; but perhaps the whole process of analysis is a way to learn how to assume this voice. It is the voice in which the linguistic, the ethical, and the political voice join forces, coinciding in what was the dimension of pure enunciation in them. (Dolar, 2006, pp. 123–4)

> An antimetaphyscial strategy, like mine, aiming to valorize an ontology of uniqueness finds in the voice a decisive – indeed obligatory – resource. The point is not simply to revocalize logos. Rather, the aim is to free logos from its visual substance, and to finally mean is as sonorous speech – in order to listen, in speech itself, for the plurality of singular voices that convoke one another in a relation that is not simply sound, but above all resonance. (Cavarero, 2005, pp. 178–9)

For Lacan, as we saw in Chapter 2, desire arises in response to the individual's emergence as a separate subject of language, entailing the loss of a primordial object, the Thing, that the subject never had, and this purportedly lost object's retroactive symbolization within the order of language. This picture may sound pessimistic, but our primordial loss and our status as lacking subjects also opens us up to possibilities for creativity. As Lacan writes with reference to the potter creating the vase around a void, 'emptiness and fullness are introduced into a world that by itself knows not of them. It is on the basis of this fabricated signifier, this vase, that emptiness and fullness as such enter the world, neither more nor less, and with the same sense' (Lacan, 1992, p. 120). Moreover, to the extent that the desire that accompanies our lacking status carries traces of the primordial Thing, it has the power to express and conjoin, not just the linguistic, but also the ethical and political register of our being, as Mladen Dolar suggests above. As such, fidelity to the singularity of desire that echoes with the resonance of the Thing opens up 'a space where the signifier and the real, word and affect, thought and eros ... come together' (Ruti, 2017, p. 168) to generate the potential reinvention of the subject and the transfiguration of its relation to knowledge.

It is also the case, admittedly, as we also saw in Chapter 2, that the mediation of desire through the socio-symbolic order of language makes it susceptible to hijacking by dominant social discourses, such as those of neo-liberal capitalism. But the signifier and the symbolic order can never completely colonize or contain desire, since an unrepresentable kernel of the real always remains as a surplus, while desire also carries traces of our idiosyncratic embodied experience and this too has libidinal consequences. As a consequence, parts of the self will always resist the banalization of the world and subsumption by its normalizing discourses. And just as the impossibility of perfect communication provides the impulse for ongoing dialogue, so too in education, 'if perfect fits were achievable between social relations and psychic reality, between self and language, our subjectivities and our societies would be closed. Completed. Finished. Dead. Nothing to do. No difference. There would be no education. No learning' (Ellsworth, 1997, p. 44).

Another way of capturing these abstract ideas is to argue that the register of the real represents a void or surplus around which the symbolic seeks to wrap itself and that thereby the real functions as an internal limit to the possibilities for achieving closure. Indeed, to the extent that the symbolic order of language is (fantasmatically) deemed to have achieved such closure – to have said the final word – it becomes detached, desiccated and deadening. This is one reason why the prescriptivism of education policy in contexts such as the UK has been such a restricting and mortifying, rather than edifying or animating, force. This is not a matter of relinquishing our anchoring in the symbolic entirely or abandoning it for the real for 'the valorization of the real as a site of political and ethical "purity" all too easily turns into a post-political pipedream that, paradoxically enough, transforms singularity into something that no longer signifies as such' (Ruti, 2012, p. 123). To be meaningful, singularity requires the social and semiotic coordinates of the symbolic, even as it sits to some degree outside them. But at the same time, this suggests that, while we cannot let go of our moorings in the symbolic realm completely, or we risk descending into psychosis, the possibility exists for the signifier to be revitalized by the energies of the real in a way that the creative work of a writer like James Joyce exemplifies (Harari, 2002; Ruti, 2012, 2017; Thurston, 2002). This creativity is what the discourse of the analyst opens up in terms of the production of new master signifiers unique to the subject.

The Lacanian notion of resisting the hegemony of the authoritative discourses of the master and the university with their normative orders of morality and subordinating regimes of knowledge by pursuing the truth of one's singular desire – a desire that takes account of its effects on the other – resonates powerfully with Foucault's (2005) concept of *epimeleia heatou* involving care of the self in conjunction with care of the other. Specifically, as Ruti argues, 'both Foucault's care of the self and Lacanian clinical practice aim at a revitalization of being: both, in short, aim at the rewriting of destiny' (2017, p. 165). In both cases a practice that is individual, yet socially situated, spiritual, yet embodied, passionate, yet reasoned, is undertaken in order to bring about the transformation of the subject, its relations with others and its world.

Of course, insofar as there can be no ultimate ground of meaning, the truth emerging from such practice is always idiosyncratic, partial and tentative, rather than timeless, universal, and certain. This means that any new master signifier is no less of a 'fiction' that those dominating the authoritative discourses of the master and the university. Crucially, however, 'it is a fiction that does not turn the subject into a dupe because he [*sic*] has created it himself, based on his particular way of jouissance' (Verhaeghe and Declerq, 2002, p. 74). Lacan's name for this new self-creation is a *sinthome* (Lacan, 1976). Importantly, the *sinthome* entwines the three registers of the real, imaginary and symbolic but it also rests on recognition of lack in the Other – the fact that there is no Other of the Other, or, in other words, that the big Other does not exist. This raises the possibility of reclaiming, re-articulating and possibly replacing key signifiers, such as 'education', 'school', 'teacher', 'student', 'teaching', 'learning', 'curriculum', 'pedagogy' and 'assessment', by infusing them with the singularity of the desire which carries the echo or trace of the Thing and thereby reworking them towards experimental and creative, rather than just regulatory and normative, possibilities. As McNulty (2014) suggests, this activity is not so much a matter of freeing ourselves from the symbolic order's perceived limits, as it is a reanimating of the symbolic in ways that allow creativity, agency, novelty and invention to emerge within processes of symbolization.

On the other hand, the other side of the inability for our alienation to ever be complete, owing to the surplus kernel of the real that, no matter how tightly it wraps itself around, the symbolic can never fully erase or subsume, is that it can never be completely redeemed either. This means that the task of working with and through our constitutive alienation, loss, lack, emptiness, negativity – each term offering different ways of capturing the same fundamental insight – can never be finalized either but must perpetually begin again – requiring repeated turns of the kaleidoscope, to return to the metaphor used earlier at the opening of this chapter.

But this also raises the question of how we might move from the individual level of the singular track of desire that caries the echo of the Thing, and the individual creation of the *sinthome*, to the intrapersonal register of the political. Here I want to build on Ruti's (2012, 2017) reading of the singular and embodied dimensions characterizing the track of desire that resonates with the echo of the Thing and thereby carries ethical force, linking these ideas to Adriana Cavarero's (2005) notions of vocality and resonance. For Cavarero 'the meaning of resonance lies first of all in the vocal relation to which singular voices are called. In other words, the resonance is musicality in relation; it is the uniqueness of the voice that gives itself in the acoustic link between one voice and another. It is a vocal exchange where the repetition of sound, and all its tonal rhythmic variants, expose uniqueness as an understanding [*un'intesa*] and a reciprocal dependence' (2005, p. 180). Underlying this is a view of voices as not merely signifying information but as a fundamental means of communicating to one another who we are (p. 197). In Žižek's Lacanian terms, we might say that voice carries something of the real, 'that traumatic "bone in the throat" that *contaminates* every ideality of the symbolic' (Butler, Laclau and Žižek, 2000, p. 310). And whereas the authoritative discourses of the master and the university seek to devocalize logos in favour of the disembodied rationality of the semantic, the discourse of the analyst, insofar as embraces the embodied singularity of voice opens that path to politics as a form of 'uniqueness-in-resonance' – a 'politics of Saying where the uniqueness of each speaker makes itself heard as a plurality of voices that are already linked to one another in resonance' (Cavarero, 2005, pp. 199, 200).

This uniqueness-in-resonance is utterly distinct from the tribal nationalism of the nation state, which requires all its subjects to sing in unison and lose themselves in the 'national anthem', and also different from the fundamentalism of the state which seeks to reconcile universality with territoriality in a single contradictory logic (2005, p. 201). By contrast, a politics of voices opens up 'a revolutionary perspective' that 'allows for an elaboration of the concept of a local without territory' (2005, p. 204). This absolute local enables a politics without borders that is not a nation or a land but 'extends as far as the interactive space that is generated by reciprocal communication. It is a relational space that happens with the event of this communication and, together with it, disappears. The place and duration are contingent and unforeseeable' (2005, pp. 204–5). Unlike the neo-liberal capitalist state that is built on the aggregation of interchangeable autonomous individualisms, this taking-place of the politics of the absolute local is founded on 'the unrepeatable uniqueness of every human being' and grounded in an 'ontology of plural uniqueness and relation' (2005, p. 205). This politics, which like psychoanalytic theory, cuts across traditional divides between 'public' and 'private' (Cavarero, 2000), is compatible with and complements a Lacanian ethics of desire, as articulated by writers like Ruti (2012, 2015, 2017) and Neill (2011), insofar as it implies a degree of intersubjective responsibility for the assumption, or taking-up, of our own of subjectivity and the vocal expression of our singularity that may be harmonious or discordant with that of others.

Conclusion

I opened the discussion in this chapter with the caveat that given that the discourse of the analyst is about listening, beginning afresh and the creation of new master signifiers unique to the analytic subject, any chapter on this discourse in a book such as this was almost doomed to fail and bound to disappoint. Yet, as also noted early on in the chapter, one thing the discourse of the analyst can be said to stand for is opposition to the discourse of the master and authoritative discourses in general. After discussing a Švejkian politics of subversive irony as one possibility for thinking about resistance to discourses of mastery the chapter has explored the opportunities afforded by what we might describe, drawing on concepts from Lacan and Cavarero, as a *sinthomatic* politics of voice, for articulating a more positive vision of a relational politics. In introducing these ideas, I have emphasized their links to embodiment and singularity but I would also stress, however, that I read this politics not as a rejection of reason, thought, ideas and signification but an attempt to rethink them along less authoritative and tyrannical lines than those of neo-liberal capitalism with its mantra of 'there is no alternative' and the contemporary nation-state with its heavily policed inclusions and exclusions. Like the *sinthome* that knots together the imaginary symbolic and real registers, this politics takes places at the intersection of imaginary reconstitution, symbolic contestation and the embodied energies of the real. Both, therefore, engage with issues of singularity, ethics and politics, potentially leading to possibilities of resistance that go beyond the ironic subversion of the authoritative normalization of today's dominant neo-liberal discourses yet without offering ready-made solutions or lapsing into the spectres of epistemological value and plenitude warned against in the chapter's opening epigraphs.

7

Looking Awry at Education Policy

In these languid and empty hours, a sadness felt by my entire being rises from my soul to my mind – a bitter awareness that everything is a sensation of mine and at the same time, something external, something not in my power to change.

Pesoa, 2001, p. 14

What is at stake in the endeavor to 'look awry' ... is not just a kind of contrived attempt to 'illustrate' high theory, to make it 'easily accessible,' and thus to spare the effort of effective thinking ... The point is rather that such an exemplification ... renders visible aspects that would otherwise remain unnoticed ... reveal[s] its otherwise hidden inconsistencies ... exhibit[s] the way its very subjective position of enunciation undermines its 'enunciated,' its positive contents.

Žižek, 1992, p. 3

The very notion of a quarter turn evokes revolution, but certainly not in the sense in which revolution is subversion. On the contrary, what turns – that is what is called revolution – is destined, by its very statement (énoncé), to evoke a return.

Lacan, 2000, p. 41

Introduction

Having revolved through all four of Lacan's discourses – the master, the university, the hysteric and the analyst – in the previous four chapters, this brief final chapter seeks to adopt a more synoptic perspective and to answer the 'so what?' question from the point of view of policy and practice. By way of a spoiler, my response to this question is partly embodied in the title of the chapter, as well as in Žižek's words quoted above, in that I argue that thinking through Lacan's four discourses, and the Lacanian psychoanalytic thought that they embody, enables us to 'look awry' at education policy and practice.

As Fernando Pesoa (1888–1935) suggests above, and as Lacanian psychoanalysis insistently reiterates, there is something out of kilter, or out of joint, something – to use Žižek's term – *awry* about our experience in, and of, the world. Foucault was arguably getting at a similar idea when he famously referred to 'man' [*sic*] as 'a strange empirico-transcendental doublet' (1970, p. 318). Indeed, much of the conceptual vocabulary we have inherited from other twentieth- and twenty-first-century social theorists, including notions such as contestation, deconstruction, deterritorialization, *différance*, hybridity, simulacrum and transgression, can similarly be read as attempts to describe 'the downfall of the humanist subject' (Ruti, 2017, p. 144), whose fully rational, autonomous, self-contained and self-transparent nature was only ever a presumption.

Given this background, it is hardly surprising that this book has not sought to follow a medical model in its analysis of education policy, a linear process reflecting a problem-solution orientation, involving the diagnosis of education policy's ills in order to prescribe a corrective course of action. But at the same time, the reader will have been very aware that I believe things are amiss – and have gone awry – with education policy in the neo-liberal era. Highlighting some of the unproductive pathways down which education policy has led the field of education – not, of course, in any comprehensive or complete manner but in ways that, I hope, resonate with readers – has been one of my key purposes in writing this book. At the same time, the book has sought to engage with the complex but rigorous framework afforded by Lacanian psychoanalytic theory for eying the pronouncements of policymakers askance, in order to approach education policy obliquely from multiple perspectives, rather than taking it at face value. In other words, the book has attempted to share a framework for looking awry at education policy, one which 'renders visible aspects that would otherwise remain unnoticed ... reveal[s] its otherwise hidden inconsistencies ... exhibit[s] the way its very subjective position of enunciation undermines its "enunciated", its positive contents', as Žižek puts it in my epigraph above. In this final chapter, my purpose is to elaborate on these points in order to consider the implications of the conceptual world introduced in the book for policy and practice in education.

Recapping Lacanian discourse theory

As individuals working in education, we are likely to have been trained to recognise the importance of language and are attuned to the often-subtle distinctions between the meanings of different words – between the words chosen and those left unsaid as well as between the meanings of the words people use and the alternative meanings spoken by their actions. We recognize the ways in which language works to position us and others in ways that may not be entirely comfortable or consensual. Such positioning is partly a function of the *content* of the discourse including the themes, narratives, arguments and assumptions that 'fill out' the discourse. But Lacanian discourse theory draws our attention to the way discursive positioning is also a function of the *structure* of the discourse, including the sets of relations, or the social links, established between participants that hold the discourse together (Hook, 2018; Verhaeghe, 1995). In emphasizing how discourse operates as a social link, Lacan's theory seeks 'to circumvent the psychological ("imaginary") contents of subjective sense-making and meaning by looking to an *underlying grid of interlinked symbolic positions*' (Hook, 2018, p. 99, emphasis in original).

We can think about this in relation to the hypothetical case of a school that has been deemed 'requires improvement' or 'inadequate', to use the language of the four-point grading scale employed by the UK's OFSTED inspection regime. Importantly, while these labels are not completely unrelated to practical and material realities in the institution, they do not make reference in any simple, direct or unproblematic way to some essential property of the school in question, so much as they locate them in relation to other possible signifiers ('good' and 'outstanding'), thereby ensnaring them in a web of signification that foreground certain aspects of socially shaped reality (e.g. attendance) while excluding others (e.g. student/staff happiness). Of course, this act of semiotic labelling will have material consequences for the school, significantly affecting practice in relation to curriculum, pedagogy, recruitment (of staff and students) and governance. But rather than seeing such labels as merely pointing to some essence, or essential property, of the school in question, it is important to recognise how labelling and categorization are also political acts that entangle individuals and institutions in the webs or chains of signification that comprise discourse as a social link. In this case, in terms of discourse as a social link, OFSTED's inspection regime is an instance of the discourse of the university, involving the deployment of purportedly neutral, technical expert bureaucratic knowledge, underpinned by the unacknowledged master signifiers of the market and its logics of competition, addressing and seeking to subsume the other's desire but instead generating the alienated split subject, torn between compliance and resistance, as a product. Looking awry at policy in this way helps us to see how the enunciated content, in the form of the judgments passed on schools, are undermined by the tensions in the position of enunciation between the supposed objectivity and expertise of the judgement and the latter's grounding in the master signifier – 'the nonsensical signifier, the signifier with no rhyme or reason' (Fink, 2017, p. 31).

In emphasizing the supra- or trans-individual aspect of the social link, Lacan is also highlighting the distinction between imaginary identification, which privileges sameness, and symbolic identification, which relies on difference. It is this complexity that accounts for how our social-symbolic roles – teacher, parent, citizen – do not map completely, congruently or synchronously with our preferred psychological-imaginary identities (Hook, 2018, pp. 103–4). But Lacan is also acknowledging the unruly reality of the real that denies all closure and prevents any comfortable complementarity between the components of any binary pair, be this man/woman, black/white, teacher/student, success/failure or knowledge/ignorance. A further consequence of these disjunctions and dislocations is the impossibility of there being any metadiscourse. As Fink (2017) notes, even when we are talking about the four discourses we are still operating within a particular discourse.

The inconsistency of the world, with its disjunctions, dislocations and failed connections, translates into the impossibility of any closure, or perfect fit, at various levels – between enunciating and enunciated subject of speech, between the word and the world, between self and other, between psychic and social reality, between conscious and unconscious and between the desiring subject and the object of its desire. This pervasive non-coincidence, or non-concurrence, is deeply unsettling as the lines from Pesoa make clear, but it also ushers in the important role of fantasy in providing a reassuring but illusory sense of consistency, reliability and attainability so as to mask the existentially precarious status of the non-self-coinciding subject, both in relation to 'itself' and in relation to its world.

The four discourses and the polyvocality of policy

As the discussion in this book has, I hope, made clear, policy does not 'speak' with a singular voice but adopts a variety of registers and modes in different contexts. It is easy to forget this, owing, in part, to the reificatory tendency of language, which encourages us to equate a word with an object in one-to-one fashion. There is value in this tendency insofar as it tames the complex and otherwise inchoate riot of social reality by pinning it down into stable terms and concepts that can be shared across time and space, but there is also a cost in terms of the simplifications, reductions, essentializations and reifications that such sedimentation of meaning entails. In this sense, and in similar fashion to the way Lacan's distinction between the subject of enunciation and the enunciated subject of speech helps us resist the seductions of a singular, self-contained and self-sufficient view of identity, distinctions such as that between policy as text and policy as discourse (Ball, 1993), between the speaking subjects *of* policy and the discourse which speaks those subject *to* policy (Ball, 2015) or between policy intentions and policy effects (Ball, Maguire and Braun, 2012) help us recognize and come to terms with the complex, dynamic and multifaceted nature of policy.

Lacan's four discourses complement such insights into the complexity of policy. Specifically, the four discourses remind us that policy can involve (at least) four social stances: commanding in the discourse of the master, rationalizing in the discourse of the university, complaining in the discourse of the hysteric, and analysing in the discourse of the analyst. Lacan's discourse theory highlights how, schematically speaking, there are four 'positions' in any policy discourse – agent, other, product and truth – and that any of these positions may be occupied by four 'elements' in the shape of dominant master signifiers (S1), the field of knowledge (S2), the split subject ($) and the object-cause of desire (*a*). Translating policy into these, albeit highly formalized, terms affords nuances of insight into the polyvocal nature of policy that are otherwise liable to remain elusive.

Beyond this, Lacan's discourses – and, indeed, Lacanian psychoanalysis more generally – remind us that policy involves inevitable tensions and discordances reflecting the non-congruence between addresser and addressed, truth and product, conscious and unconscious in any discourse. In particular, the role of unconscious desire in policy processes and its capacity to undermine conscious knowledge and reason is one of the most powerful insights offered by a psychoanalytic perspective. For instance, unconscious desires for mastery and certainty help explain how new knowledge produced in the discourse of the hysteric or new master signifiers produced in the discourse of the analyst so often evoke a return, as Lacan notes in the epigraph above, to the authoritative discourses of the master and the university. This also entails that critique of, and resistance to, policy in general, and neo-liberal policy in particular, also needs to be polyvocal, strategically employing rational argument (the discourse of the university) and polemical protest (the discourse of the hysteric), as well as reflective listening and subversive irony (the discourse of the analyst), even if it eschews the authoritarian dominance of the discourse of the master. Such critique also needs to be polyphonic in the sense of bringing multiple and disparate voices – of activists, academics, teachers, students and community members – together in order to create wide-ranging, yet focused and insistent, resistance.

Recognizing policy as fantasy

Returning to my comments above about the essential role of fantasy in providing a reassuring but illusory sense of consistency, reliability and attainability, an enduring theme in this book is that policy, in education as in other domains, serves a fantasmatic function (Clarke, 2012b) by simplifying the inchoate messiness of social reality and making it appear amenable to rational planning and management. A key element of this simplification process is the identification of a neutral notion of the common good, a desired or imagined future that purportedly represents the public interest or the public good. Yet notions of the 'public good' are inevitably fantasmatic, simplifying and glossing over intractable political contestations and social antagonisms: 'our societies are never harmonious ensembles. This is only the fantasy through which they attempt to constitute themselves. Experience shows that this fantasy can never be fully realized. No social fantasy can fill the lack around which society is always structured' (Stavrakakis, 1999, p. 74). However, despite its fantasmatic nature, policy's persistent attachment to the notion of society as a harmonious ensemble – and nationalism plays a key part here too, promoting a 'we're all in this together' ethos – is the disavowal of partiality and the masking of whose specific interests policy actually promotes. The justification of ability grouping in schools in England, despite considerable evidence of its regressive effects on social equality (Francis et al., 2015), is a classic example of this fantasmatic policy process. Underpinned by a disavowed eugenicism, this policy agenda is legitimated by an ideological attachment to discredited notions of 'meritocracy' (Littler, 2018) and underpinned by simplistic claims about the unalloyed benefits of competition.

It is important to recall, however, that fantasy is not something that is hidden deep inside policy; in fact, it typically appears 'out there' on the surface of discourse (Žižek, 1997). Take, for instance, the UK government's 2016 White Paper (Department for Education (DfE), 2016), *Educational Excellence Everywhere*. The title suggests the attainability of a harmonious and 'full' state of affairs in which failure, scarcity, privilege and disadvantage have become things of the past. However, the effectiveness of this title relies on the emptiness of education as a signifier; and tellingly, education is never defined or debated in the policy document, in terms of its aims and purposes. What we get instead are assertions about how it 'unlocks opportunity' and functions as 'the engine of social justice and economic growth' (p. 5). Similarly, the notion of excellence as a cipher, a tautological, non-referential term, so that, for example, 'the excellent University is excellent at being excellent' (Royle, 2003, p. 55). The third term, 'everywhere' exacerbates the fantasmatic logic at work in the title, not least by contradicting and undermining the comparative logic embodied in 'excellence', thereby underlining the latter's emptiness. Moreover, in this case, we can judge a book by its cover, for the empty, fantasmatic journey continues when we read beyond the title and encounter repeated references to empty notions like 'world class' education, 'great teachers', 'great leaders', all contributing to a 'dynamic', 'school-led' system offering 'gold-standard qualifications' and characterized by 'freedom' and 'autonomy'. Pursuing this line of thought further, we can think about the fantasmatic nature of education policy in relation to five (and this is not meant to be an exhaustive taxonomy) specific fantasies (Clarke, 2018b).

Fantasies of control are embodied in the assertions of agency embodied in categorical language choices, as we see in *Educational Excellence Everywhere*: 'we will step in to build capacity, raise standards and provide confidence for parents and children' (Department for Education, 2016, p. 3). In such statements, which are pervasive in this and in other education policy documents, an unproblematic link between action and consequence is presumed. *Fantasies of objectivity* are evident in the effort put into painting a picture of policy as governed by science, logic and reason. This is reflected in the penchant in current policy for claims to be grounded in 'evidence' and the preference for terms like 'rigorous' and 'firm'. *Fantasies of inclusion* can be seen in policy agendas such as Every Child Matters, when clearly in an unequal, capitalist society in which education serves a reproductive purpose in relation to established social hierarchies, some children matter more than others. Fantasies of inclusion are also, as noted above, reflected in the title of the 2016 UK government's White Paper, which disavows the selective function of education in neo-liberal society and the requirement for some students to fail in order that others can succeed. *Fantasies of productivity* are reflected in the widespread claims in education policy statements about the links between education and economic achievement at both the individual and the societal level, despite evidence to the contrary, such as the growing number of university graduates working in low paid and low skill employment. Finally, *fantasies of victimhood* are evident in the promotion of nationalist discourses in education policy, particularly in the post-9/11 world, whereby the bolstering of national identities relies on the positing of threats – externally from terrorists and internally from those lacking sufficient levels of aspiration – in contradistinction to which the asserted national identity defines itself.

The four discourses, fantasy and policy

Of course, every theory carries dangers as well as offering potential insights and this is certainly the case with Lacan's theory of the four discourses. One key risk is that the four discourses are read as a 'menu' from which a speaker can pick and choose. In particular, having recognized the authoritarian strains in the discourse of the master and the university we might be tempted to locate ourselves in the two discourses of speaking otherwise, the discourse of the hysteric and the discourse of the analyst. To assume this, however, would be to misread the theory on several key points, taking discourse as a matter of individual or dialogic speech, rather than as a social link, and seeing it as operating at the subjective and inter-subjective, rather than the trans-subjective, level. For another thing, this view overestimates the role of consciousness in the operation of discourse. Indeed, to the extent that fantasy represents a denial of the unconscious and a corresponding valorization of consciousness, the four discourses can be read as representing different relationships to fantasy: in the discourse of the master, fantasy is disavowed; in the discourse of the university, it is orchestrated; in the discourse of the hysteric, it is performed; and in the discourse of the analyst, it is problematized.

Bearing these distinctions in mind, reading a policy document such as *Educational Excellence Everywhere* – and here I am taking the 2016 White Paper as both symptomatic and emblematic of the broader thrust of neoliberal policy agendas – in terms of Lacan's four discourses helps us to engage in a nuanced yet critical assessment of its ideological strategies and to identify the various guises that fantasy takes to support these strategies. Armed with the four discourses, we can note how such policy is poly-vocal in that we can identify different discourses operating at different moments.

The deployment of the authority of the state, reflected in the official government stamp and the placing of name of the government department on the cover, in the placing of the ministerial signature at the end of the ministerial foreword and also in the bald assertions of power and use of threats ('Where local authorities are failing in this duty, the government will not hesitate to intervene', p. 73) are symptomatic of the discourse of the master. Noting this reminds us that policy involves the assertion of authority (S1), the underlying 'truth' of which is the split subject. In other words, the policy's authoritative stance belies the fact that the then minister for education, Nicky Morgan, is an ordinary human being (and now a backbench Member of Parliament having been sacked after the transition from David Cameron to Theresa May as prime minister) with no particular expertise, knowledge or experience of education as a professional field. In terms of the addressee, we can see how the master's authority (the minister of education representing the government and the crown) seeks to organize the field of knowledge insofar as the policy comprehensively addresses issues of curriculum, pedagogy, assessment, teachers, school leadership and governance, parents and pupils, but we can also note that its naked assertion of authority excludes desire which emerges as the product of the discourse of the master.

The discourse of the university comes to the fore in the 2016 White Paper in the places where it lays claim to scientific expertise. We see this, for instance, in relation to the justification of the need for core knowledge on the basis of the findings of 'cognitive science' (p. 89), or in the attacks on 'grade inflation' based on research from the Royal Society of Chemistry and the University of Durham (p. 91). However, this scientific sheen masks the policy document's promotion of an ideological agenda comprising 'choice' (reflected in the frequent references to academies and academization), competition (grade inflation means too many are succeeding) and tradition. Governed by these ideological master signifiers the policy's preferred educational knowledge, S2, attempts to colonize (our) desire, *a*, thereby producing the terrorised subject, $, split between compliance and resistance.

The discourse of the hysteric can be seen in the moments when the White Paper complains about schools (particularly those labelled as 'failing' or 'coasting'), education (too skills-focused, prone to grade inflation) and the legacy of the previous (Labour) government. ('In 2010, we inherited an education system where 1 in 3 young people left primary school unable to read, write and add up properly; where the number of young people studying core academic subjects had halved in 13 years. Far too many schools were failing, and far too many children were left out or left behind. Recent international assessments, comparing the performance of our young people in 2011/2012 with their international peers, have shown that our education standards have remained static, at best, whilst other countries have moved ahead.') In effect, the White Paper holds education responsible for the social, economic and moral state of society, and therefore insists that education be more masterful, ignoring the impossibility, that Bernstein highlighted over forty years ago, of education compensating for society. As a result, more and more education knowledge aligned with the government's ideological agenda will be produced, yet the gap between education and society, between fantasy and reality, remains open and incapable of closure.

The discourse of the analyst is conspicuous in its absence in the White Paper, as it is in policy more widely, for while policy promotes, preaches and punishes, it rarely listens. The discourse of the analyst is, in many ways, the 'hero' of the four, insofar as it encourages unconscious desire to speak and to interrogate the subject in its subjection to discourses of mastery and to go on to create new and distinctive master signifiers, but here too risk inheres in the possibility of elevating these new master signifiers to the status of transcendent universals, thus re-turning the cycle to the discourses of mastery. In order to avoid this fate, the discourse of the analyst needs to achieve 'a modest but nonetheless revolutionary vanishing act as an auto-erasing moment that generates true change precisely through quietly receding into the background' (Johnston, 2009, p. 159). Ironically, the discourse of the analyst is at once the most 'educational' of the four discourses but also the one most inimical to the world of official education policy; for its interrogation of the role of master signifiers in authoritative discourses and its insistence on the primacy of lack, desire and unconscious knowledge goes against the grain of the positivism of policy. As such, the discourse of the analyst offers us a glimpse of the other side of education.

A non-conclusion . . .

But ultimately, 'the other side of education' should not be confused with notions of individual or societal redemption, or of a promised land where the enduring tensions and traumas of education will find resolution. Such notions of reason and redemption through education have led education policy to remain fixated on fantasies, in the shape of purported education 'revolutions'. For as Lacan reminds us in the epigraph to this chapter, every revolution is also a return, and our dreams of installing *Educational Excellence Everywhere* or of creating 'the knowledge society' are likely to remain the fantasies they always already are. Indeed, 'the other side' can also be read as a lining, or the two sides of the möbius strip, in the sense that, like lack and desire, knowledge and ignorance, conscious and unconscious, thought and feeling, questions and answers, criticality and creativity, mastery and analysis, the two sides are perhaps most fruitfully conceived as partners engaged in an interminable dialectical dance – one in which sustaining movement along the porous lines of tension simultaneously separating and connecting each pair, while looking awry at any siren-like fantasies of closure or evocations of salvation, is the optimal space that education and education policy might seek to inhabit.

References

Ainley, P. (2016). *Betraying a Generation: How Education Is Failing Young People.* Bristol: Policy Press.

Alexander, R. (ed.) (2009). *Children, Their World, Their Education: Final Report and Recommendations of the Cambridge Primary Review.* London: Routledge.

Allen, A. (2014). *Benign Violence: Education in and beyond the Age of Reason.* Basingstoke: Palgrave Macmillan.

Anievas, A. (2014). *Capital, the State, and War: Class Conflict and Geopolitics in the Thirty Years' Crisis, 1914–1945.* Ann Arbor: University of Michigan Press.

Apple, M. W. (2003). *The State and the Politics of Knowledge.* New York: Routledge.

Apple, M. W. (2006). *Education the 'Right' Way: Markets, Standards, God and Inequality* (2nd edn). New York: Routledge.

Arendt, H. (1954). 'The Crisis of Education'. In *Between Past and Future: Eight Exercises in Political Thought.* New York: Penguin Books.

Armstrong, R. (2000). *Billy Wilder, American Film Realist.* Jefferson, NC: McFarland.

Aspers, P. (2011). *Markets.* Cambridge. Polity Press.

Au, W. (2011). 'Teaching under the New Taylorism: High-Stakes Testing and the Standardization of the 21st Century Curriculum'. *Journal of Curriculum Studies, 43*(1), 25–45.

Au, W. (2016). 'Social Justice and Resisting Neoliberal Education Reform in the USA'. *Forum, 58*(3), 315–24.

Azari, E. (2008). *Lacan and the Destiny of Literature: Desire, Jouissance and the Sinthome in Shakespeare, Donne, Joyce and Ashberry.* London: Continuum.

Bacchi, C. (2012). 'Why Study Problematizations? Making Politics Visible'. *Open Journal of Political Science, 2*, 1–8. Doi:10.4236/ojps.2012.21001.

Baldridge, B. J. (2017). '"It's Like This Myth of the Supernegro": Resisting Narratives of Damage and Struggle in the Neoliberal Educational Policy Context'. *Race Ethnicity and Education, 20*(6), 781–95.

Ball, S. J. (1990). *Politics and Policy Making in Education: Explorations in Policy Sociology.* Hoboken: Taylor & Francis.

Ball, S. J. (1993). 'What Is Policy? Texts, Trajectories and Toolboxes'. *Discourse: Studies in the Cultural Politics of Education, 13*(2), 10–17.

Ball, S. J. (2003). 'The Teacher's Soul and the Terrors of Performativity'. *Journal of Education Policy, 18*(2), 215–28.

Ball, S. J. (2007). *Education Plc: Understanding Private Sector Participation in Public Sector Education.* London: Routledge.

Ball, S. J. (2008). *The Education Debate*. Bristol: The Policy Press.

Ball, S. J. (2012). *Global Education Inc: New Policy Networks and the Neo-Liberal Imaginary*. London: Routledge.

Ball, S. J. (2013). *The Education Debate* (2nd edn). Bristol: The Policy Press.

Ball, S. J., Maguire, M. and Braun, A. (2012). *How Schools Do Policy: Policy Enactments in Secondary Schools*. London: Routledge.

Banks, J., and Smyth, E. (2015). '"Your Whole Life Depends on It": Academic Stress and High-Stakes Testing in Ireland'. *Journal of Youth Studies*, 18(5), 598–616.

Banks, J. A. (2016). *Cultural Diversity and Education* (6th edn). New York: Routledge.

Beall, J. P. (2010). *The Poetics of Subversion: Irony and the Central European Novel* (Doctor of Philosophy), Rutgers University-Graduate School, New Brunswick, NJ.

Beall, J. P. (2012). 'Prosaic Irony: Structure, Mode, and Subversion in *The Good Soldier Švejk*'. *Comparatist*, 36, 207–25.

Beer, D. (2016). *Metric Power*. London: Palgrave Macmillan.

Berlant, L. (2011). *Cruel Optimism*. Durham: Duke University Press.

Bernstein, B. (1970). 'Education Cannot Compensate for Society'. *New Society*, 15(387), 344–7.

Bevir, M. (2008). 'What Is Genealogy?'. *Journal of the Philosophy of History*, 2, 263–75.

Bibby, T. (2011). *Education – An 'Impossible Profession'? Psychoanalytic Explorations of Learning and Classrooms*. London: Routledge.

Biesta, G. (2007). 'Why "What Works" Won't Work: Evidence Based Practice and the Democratic Deficit in Educational Research'. *Educational Theory*, 57(1), 1–22.

Biesta, G. (2010). *Good Education in Age of Measurement: Ethics, Politics, Democracy*. Boulder: Paradigm.

Biesta, G. (2013). *The Beautiful Risk of Education*. Boulder: Paradigm.

Biesta, G. (2015). 'What Is Education For? On Good Education, Teacher Judgement, and Education Professionalism'. *European Journal of Education, Early View*, 50(1), 1–13.

Birbalsingh, K. (ed.) (2016). *Battle Hymn of the Tiger Teachers: The Michaela Way*. Woodbridge: John Catt Educational Ltd.

Blacker, D. (2013). *The Falling Rate of Learning and the Neoliberal Endgame*. Winchester: Zero Books.

Block, F., and Somers, M. R. (2014). *The Power of Market Fundamentalism: Karl Polanyi's Critique*. Cambridge: Harvard University Press.

Blyth, M. (2013). *Austerity: The History of a Dangerous Idea*. Oxford: Oxford University Press.

Boden, R., and Epstein, D. (2006). 'Managing the Research Imagination? Globalisation and Research in Higher Education'. *Globalisation, Societies and Education*, 4(2), 223–36.

Boucher, G. (2006). 'Bureaucratic Speech Acts and the University Discourse: Lacan's Theory of Modernity'. In J. Clemens and R. Grigg (eds), *Jacques Lacan and the Other Side of Psychoanalysis* (pp. 274–91). Durham: Duke University Press.

Bourdieu, P. (1977). 'Cultural Reproduction and Social Reproduction'. In J. Karabel and A. H. Halsey (eds), *Power and Ideology in Education* (pp. 487–511). New York: Oxford University Press.

Bourdieu, P., and Passeron, J. (1977). *Reproduction in Education, Society and Culture*. Beverly Hills: Sage.

Bowles, S., and Gintis, H. (1976). *Schooling in Capitalist America*. New York: Basic Books.

Bracher, M. (1994). 'On the Psychological and Social Functions of Language: Lacan's Theory of the Four Discourses'. In M. Bracher (ed.), *Lacanian Theory of Discourse: Subject, Structure and Society* (pp. 107–28). New York: New York University Press.

Bracher, M. (2006). *Radical Pedagogy: Identity, Generativity and Social Transformation*. New York: Palgrave Macmillan.

Braedly, S., and Luxton, M. (eds) (2010). *Neoliberalism and Everyday Life*. Montreal and Kingston: McGill-Queen's University Press.

Brandén, M., and Bygren, M. (2018). 'School Choice and School Segregation: Lessons from Sweden's School Voucher System'. *Institute for Analytical Sociology Working Paper Series*, (1), 1–42.

Brennan, T. (1993). *History after Lacan*. London: Routledge.

Bridges, D. (2008). 'Educationalization: On the Appropriateness of Asking Educational Institutions to Solve Social and Economic Problems'. *Educational Theory*, 58(4), 461–74.

Britzman, D. (2009). *The Very Thought of Education: Psychoanalysis and the Impossible Professions*. Albany: State University of New York Press.

Brown, T., Atkinson, D. and England, J. (2006). *Regulatory Discourses in Education: A Lacanian Perspective*. New York: Peter Lang.

Brown, W. (2005). *Edgework: Critical Essays in Knowledge and Politics*. Princeton, NJ: Princeton University Press.

Brown, W. (2015). *Undoing the Demos: Neoliberalism's Stealth Revolution*. Cambridge, MA: MIT Press.

Bryant, L. R. (2016). 'Žižek's New Universe of Discourse: Politics and the Discourse of the Capitalist'. *International Journal of Žižek Studies*, 2(4), 1–48.

Burgin, A. (2012). *The Great Persuasion: Reinventing Free Markets since the Depression*. Cambridge: Harvard University Press.

Burt, A. (2015). *American Hysteria: The Untold Story of Mass Political Extremism in the United States*. Guilford: Lyons Press.

Butler, J. (2005). *Giving an Account of Oneself*. New York: Fordham University Press.

Butler, J., Laclau, E., and Žižek, S. (2000). *Contingency, Hegemony, Universality: Contemporary Dialogues on the Left*. London: Verso.

Cahill, D., and Konings, M. (2017). *Neoliberalism*. Cambridge: Polity Press.

Callinicos, A. (2010). *Bonfire of Illusions: The Twin Crises of the Liberal World*. Cambridge: Polity.

Campbell, C., Proctor, H., and Sherrington, G. (2009). *School Choice: How Parents Negotiate the New School Market in Australia*. Crows Nest: Allen & Unwin.

Campbell, K. (2004). *Jacques Lacan and Feminist Epistemology*. London: Routledge.

Cavarero, A. (2000). *Relating Narratives: Storytelling and Selfhood* (P. Kottman, trans.). New York: Routledge.

Cavarero, A. (2005). *For More Than One Voice: Towards a Philosophy of Vocal Expression* (P. A. Kottman, trans.). Stanford: Stanford University Press.

Chang, H.-J. (2010). *23 Things They Don't Tell You about Capitalism*. London: Allen Lane.

Clarke, J., and Newman, J. (2010). 'Summoning Spectres: Crises and Their Construction'. *Journal of Education Policy*, 25(6), 709–15.

Clarke, M. (2012a). 'The (Absent) Politics of Neo-liberal Education Policy'. *Critical Studies in Education*, 53(3), 297–310.

Clarke, M. (2012b). 'Talkin' 'bout a Revolution: The Social, Political and Fantasmatic Logics of Education Policy'. *Journal of Education Policy*, 27(2), 173–91.

Clarke, M. (2014a). ' "Knowledge Is Power"? A Lacanian Entanglement with Political Ideology in Education. *Critical Studies in Education* (ahead-of-print), 1–15.

Clarke, M. (2014b). 'The Sublime Objects of Education Policy: Equity, Quality and Ideology'. *Discourse: Studies in the Cultural Politics of Education*, 35(4), 584–98.

Clarke, M. (2018a). 'Education beyond Reason and Redemption: A Detour through the Death Drive'. *Pedagogy, Culture & Society*, 1–15.

Clarke, M. (2018b). 'Eyes Wide Shut: The Fantasies and Disavowals of Education Policy'. *Journal of Education Policy*, 1–17.

Clarke, M., and Phelan, A. (2017). *Teacher Education and the Political: The Power of Negative Thinking*. London: Routledge.

Claxton, G. (2018). *The Learning Power Approach: Teaching Learners to Teach Themselves*. Carmarthen: Crown House.

Coffield, F., and Williamson, B. (2011). *From Exam Factories to Communities of Discovery*. London: Institute of Education.

Commonwealth of Australia (2008). *Quality Education: The Case for an Education Revolution in Our Schools*. Canberra: Department of Education, Employment and Workplace Relations. Retrieved from http://apo.org.au/system/files/9133/apo-nid9133-41591.pdf.

Connell, R. (2013). 'The Neoliberal Cascade and Education: An Essay on the Market Agenda and Its Consequences'. *Critical Studies in Education*, 54(2), 99–112.

Coole, D. (2000). *Negativity and Politics: Dionysus and Dialectics from Kant to Poststructuralism*. London: Routledge.

Cooper, M. (2017). *Family Values: Between Neoliberalism and the New Social Conservatism*. New York: Zone Books.

Copjec, J. (1994). *Read My Desire*. Cambridge, MA: MIT Press.

Couldry, N. (2010). *Why Voice Matters: Culture and Politics after Neoliberalism*. London: Sage.

Courtney, S. J., and Gunter, H. M. (2015). 'Get off My Bus! School Leaders, Vision Work and the Elimination of Teachers'. *International Journal of Leadership in Education*, *18*(4), 395–417.

Cox, C. B., and Boyson, R. (1975). *Black Paper 1975: The Fight for Education*. London: JM Dent.

Cox, C. B., and Boyson, R. (1977). *Black Paper 1977*. London: Temple Smith.

Cox, C. B., and Dyson, A. E. (1969a). *Black Paper 1: Fight for Education*. London: Critical Quarterly Society.

Cox, C. B., and Dyson, A. E. (1969b). *Black Paper 2: The Crisis in Education*. London: Critical Quarterly Society.

Cox, C. B., and Dyson, A. E. (1970). *Black Paper 3: Goodbye Mr Short*. London: Critical Quarterly Society.

Crawford, J. (2000). *At War with Diversity: US Language Policy in an Age of Anxiety*. Clevedon: Multilingual matters.

Crehan, L. (2018). *Cleverlands: The Secrets behind the Success of the World's Education Superpowers*. London: Unbound Books.

Crouch, C. (2011). *The Strange Non-Death of Neoliberalism*. Cambridge: Polity Press.

Crouch, C. (2013). 'From Markets versus States to Corporations versus Civil Society?'. In A. Schäfer and W. Streeck (eds), *Politics in the Age of Austerity* (pp. 219–38). Cambridge: Polity Press.

Crouch, C. (2017). *Can Neoliberalism Be Saved from Itself?* London: Social Europe Edition.

Curran, F. C. (2017). 'The Law, Policy, and Portrayal of Zero Tolerance School Discipline'. *Educational Policy*, 1–39. Doi:10.1177/0895904817691840.

Dale, R. (1989). *The State and Education Policy*. Milton Keynes: Open University Press.

Dardot, P., and Laval, C. (2013). *The New Way of the World: On Neoliberal Society* (G. Elliot, trans.). London: Verso.

Davies, W. (2013). 'When Is a Market Not a Market?: "Exemption", "Externality" and 'Exception' in the Case of European State Aid Rules'. *Theory, Culture & Society*, *30*(2), 23–59.

Davies, W. (2014). *The Limits of Neoliberalism: Authority, Sovereignty and the Logic of Competition*. London: Sage.

Davies, W. (2017). *The Limits of Neoliberalism: Authority, Sovereignty and the Logic of Competition* (revised edn). London: Sage.

Davis, A. (2012). 'A Monstrous Regimen of Synthetic Phonics: Fantasies of Research-Based Teaching "Methods" Versus Real Teaching'. *Journal of Philosophy of Education*, *46*(4), 560–73.

Dean, J. (2006). *Žižek's Politics*. New York: Routledge.

Dean, J. (2009). *Democracy and Other Neoliberal Fantasies*. Durham, NC: Duke University Press.

Dean, M. (2012). 'Rethinking Neoliberalism'. *Journal of Sociology*, 1–14. Doi:10.1177/1440783312442256.

Department for Education (DfE) (2016). *Educational Excellence Everywhere*. UK: HMSO.

Dolar, M. (2006). *A Voice and Nothing More*. Cambridge, MA: MIT Press.

Donald, J. (1992). *Sentimental Education: Schooling, Popular Culture and the Regulation of Liberty*. London: Verso.

Dorling, D. (2011). *Injustice: Why Social Inequality Persists*. Bristol: The Policy Press.

Dorling, D. (2014a). *All That Is Solid: How the Great Housing Disaster Defines Our Times, and What We Can Do about It*. Harmondsworth: Penguin.

Dorling, D. (2014b). *Inequality and the 1%*. London: Verso.

Dryzek, J. (1993). 'Policy Analysis and Planning: From Science to Argument'. In F. Fischer and J. Forester (eds), *The Argumentative Turn in Policy Analysis and Planning* (pp. 213–32). Durham, NC: Duke University Press.

Duggan, L. (2003). *The Twilight of Equality: Neoliberalism, Cultural Politics, and the Attack on Democracy*. Boston: Beacon Press.

Eagleton, T. (2001). 'Enjoy!' *Paragraph*, 24(2), 40–52.

Easton, D. (1953). *The Political System*. New York: Knopf.

Ellis, S., and Moss, G. (2014). 'Ethics, Education Policy and Research: The Phonics Question Reconsidered'. *British Educational Research Journal*, 40(2), 241–60.

Ellsworth, E. (1997). *Teaching Positions: Difference, Pedagogy and the Power or Address*. New York: Teachers College Press.

Evans, D. (1996). *An Introductory Dictionary of Lacanian Psychoanalysis*. London: Routledge.

Exley, S., and Ball, S. J. (2011). 'Something Old, Something New … Understanding Conservative Education Policy'. In H. M. Bochel (ed.), *The Conservative Party and Social Policy* (pp. 97–118). Bristol: Policy Press.

Fairclough, N. (1992). *Discourse and Social Change*. Cambridge, UK: Polity Press.

Fairclough, N. (2000). *New Labour, New Language*. London: Routledge.

Fekete, E. (2018). *Europe's Fault Lines: Racism and the Rise of the Right*. London: Verso.

Feld, L. D., and Shusterman, A. (2015). 'Into the Pressure Cooker: Student Stress in College Preparatory High Schools'. *Journal of Adolescence*, 41, 31–42.

Felman, S. (1978). *Writing and Madness* (M. N. Evans, S. Felman and B. Massumi, trans.). Stanford, CA: Stanford University Press.

Felman, S. (1987). *Jacques Lacan and the Adventure of Insight: Psychoanalysis in Contemporary Culture*. Cambridge, MA: Harvard University Press.

Fielding, M., and Moss, P. (2011). *Radical Education and the Common School: A Democratic Alternative*. London: Routledge.

Finegold, D., McFarland, L., and Richardson, W. (1993). *Something Borrowed, Something Learned? The Transatlantic Market in Education and Training Reform*. Washington, DC: The Brookings Institution.

Fink, B. (1995). *The Lacanian Subject: Between Language and Jouissance*. Princeton: Princeton University Press.

Fink, B. (2017). 'The Master Signifier and the Four Discourses'. In D. Nobus (ed.), *Key Concepts of Lacanian Psychoanalysis* (pp. 29–47). London: Karnac Books.

Fisher, M. (2009). *Capitalist Realism: Is There No Alternative?* London: Zero Books.

Fisher, M. (2013). '"A Social and Psychic Revolution of Almost Inconceivable Magnitude": Popular Culture's Interrupted Accelerationist Dreams'. *e-flux journal, #46 June 2013* (online).

Fleming, P., and Sewell, G. (2002). 'Looking for the Good Soldier, Švejk: Alternative Modalities of Resistance in the Contemporary Workplace'. *Sociology, 36*(4), 857–73.

Flyvbjerg, B. (2001). *Making Social Science Matter: Why Social Inquiry Fails and How It Can Succeed Again*. New York: Cambridge University Press.

Forrester, G., and Garratt, D. (2017). *Education Policy Unravelled* (2nd edn). London: Continuum.

Foucault, M. (1970). *The Order of Things*. New York: Random House.

Foucault, M. (1977). *Discipline and Punish: The Birth of the Prison*. London: Penguin.

Foucault, M. (1988). 'The Ethic of Care for the Self as a Practice of Freedom'. In J. Bernauer and D. Rasmussen (eds), *The Final Foucault* (pp. 1–20). Cambridge: MIT Press.

Foucault, M. (1997). *Ethics, Subjectivity and Truth: Essential Works of Foucault 1954–1984* (Vol. 1). New York: The New Press.

Foucault, M. (2005). *The Hermeneutics of the Subject: Lectures at the College de France, 1981–1982* (G. Burchell, trans.). New York: Picador.

Foucault, M. (2008). *The Birth of Biopolitics: Lectures at the Collège de France, 1978–1979* (G. Burchell, trans.). Basingstoke: Palgrave Macmillan.

Francis, B., Archer, L., Hodgen, J., Pepper, D., Taylor, B., and Travers, M.-C. (2015). 'Exploring the Relative Lack of Impact of Research on "Ability Grouping" in England: A Discourse Analytic Account'. *Cambridge Journal of Education, 47*(1), 1–17.

Frank, T. (2016). *Listen, Liberal or Whatever Happened to the Party of the People?* Brunswick, VIC: Scribe.

Fraser, N. (1997). *Justice Interruptus: Critical Reflections on the "Postsocialist" Condition*. New York: Routledge.

Freud, S. (1937). 'Analysis Terminable and Interminable'. *International Journal of Psycho-Analysis, 18*(4), 373–405.

Frosh, S. (2010). *Psychoanalysis Outside the Clinic: Interventions in Psychosocial Studies*. London: Continuum.

Frosh, S. (2012). *A Brief Introduction to Psychoanalytic Theory*. Basingstoke: Palgrave-Macmillan.

Frosh, S. (2013). *Hauntings: Psychoanalysis and Ghostly Transmissions*. Basingstoke: Palgrave Macmillan.

Gamble, A. (2009). *The Spectre at the Feast: Capitalist Crisis and the Politics of Recession*. Basingstoke: Palgrave Macmillan.

Gamble, A. (2014). *Crisis without End? The Unravelling of Western Prosperity*. London: Continuum.

Gherovici, P. (2010). *Please Select Your Gender: From the Invention of Hysteria to the Democratizing of Transgenderism*. New York: Routledge.

Gherovici, P. (2017). *Transgender Psychoanalysis: A Lacanian Perspective on Sexual Difference*. Abingdon: Routledge.

Gillies, D. (2008). 'Quality and Equality: The Mask of Discursive Conflation in Education Policy Texts'. *Journal of Education Policy, 23*(6), 685–99.

Gilroy, P. (2014). 'Policy Interventions in Teacher Education: Sharing the English Experience'. *Journal of Education for Teaching, 40*(5), 622–32.

Giroux, H. (2004). *The Terror of Neoliberalism: Authoritarianism and the Eclipse of Democracy*. Boulder, CO: Paradigm.

Giroux, H. (2012). *Education and the Crisis of Public Values: Challenging the Assault on Teachers, Students and Public Education*. New York: Peter Lang.

Glynos, J., and Howarth, D. (2007). *Logics of Critical Explanation in Social and Political Theory*. London: Routledge.

Gorard, S. (2010). 'Education Can Compensate for Society – a Bit'. *British Journal of Educational Studies, 58*(1), 47–65.

Gorard, S. (2014). 'The Link between Academies in England, Pupil Outcomes and Local Patterns of Socio-Economic Segregation between Schools'. *Research Papers in Education, 29*(3), 268–84.

Gove, M. (2012). How Are the Children? Achievement for All in the 21st Century. In Speech at the Spectator Conference: London.

Graeber, D. (2015). *The Utopia of Rules: On Technology, Stupidity and the Secret Joys of Bureaucracy*. Brooklyn: Melville House.

Grant, N. (2008). Foreword. In D. Hill and R. Kumar (eds), *Global Neoliberalism and Education and Its Consequences* (pp. vii–xvii). London: Routledge.

Greany, T., and Higham, R. (2018). *Hierarchy, Networks and Markets: Analysing the 'Self-Improving School-Led System' Agenda in England and the Implications for Schools*. London: UCL Institute of Education Press.

Green, T. L., and Castro, A. (2017). 'Doing Counterwork in the Age of a Counterfeit President: Resisting a Trump–DeVos Education Agenda'. *International Journal of Qualitative Studies in Education, 30*(10), 912–19.

Grek, S. (2009). 'Governing by Numbers: The PISA "Effect" in Europe'. *Journal of Education Policy, 24*(1), 23–37.

Guggenheim, D. (2011). *Waiting for 'Superman'*. Hollywood, CA: Paramount Pictures.

Gunder, M. (2004). 'Shaping the Planner's Ego-Ideal: A Lacanian Interpretation of Planning Education'. *Journal of Planning Education and Research, 23*(3), 299–311.

Gunder, M., and Hillier, J. (2009). *Planning in Ten Words or Less: A Lacanian Entanglement with Spatial Planning*. London: Ashgate.

Hall, S. (2011). 'The Neo-Liberal Revolution'. *Cultural Studies, 25*(6), 705–28.

Hammersley, M. (2013). *The Myth of Research-Based Policy and Practice*. London: Sage.

Han, B.-C. (2017). *Psychopolitics: Neoliberalism and New Technologies of Power* (E. Butler, trans.). London: Verso.

Harari, R. (2002). *How James Joyce Made His Name: A Reading of the Final Lacan* (L. Thurston, trans.). New York: Other Press.

Harvey, D. (2005). *A Brief History of Neoliberalism*. New York: Oxford University Press.

Harvey, D. (2014). *Seventeen Contradictions and the End of Capitalism*. London: Profile Books.

Hašek, J. (1973 [1923]). *The Good Soldier Švejk: and His Fortunes in the World War* (C. Parrott, trans.). Harmondsworth: Penguin.

Hattie, J., and Zierer, K. (2017). *10 Mindframes for Visible Learning: Teaching for Success*. London: Routledge.

Hayek, F. (1944). *The Road to Serfdom*. London: Routledge & Kegan Paul.

Hess, F. M. (2011). *Spinning Wheels: The Politics of Urban School Reform*. Washington, DC: Brookings Institution Press.

Hirtt, N. (2008). 'Markets and Education in the Era of Globalized Capitalism'. In D. Hill and R. Kumar (eds), *Global Neoliberalism and Education and Its Consequences* (pp. 208–26). London: Routledge.

HM Treasury, Department for Education and Skills, Department for Work and Pensions, and Department for Trade and Industry (2004). *Choice for Parents, the Best Start for Children: A Ten-Year Strategy for Childcare*. London: HM Stationary Office.

Hobsbawm, E. (1994). *The Age of Extremes: A History of the World, 1914–1991*. New York: Michael Joseph.

Hook, D. (2018). *Six Moments in Lacan: Communication and Identification in Psychology and Psychoanalysis*. London: Routledge.

Huntington, S. P. (1975). 'The United States'. In M. Crozier, S. P. Huntington and J. Watanuki (eds), *The Crisis of Democracy: Report on the Governability of Democracies to the Trilateral Commission* (pp. 59–118). New York: New York University Press.

Hursh, D. (2008). *High-Stakes Testing and the Decline of Teaching and Learning: The Real Crisis in Education*. Lanham, MD: Rowman & Littlefield.

Hursh, D. (2016). *The End of Public Schools: The Corporate Reform Agenda to Privatize Education*. New York: Routledge.

Hursh, D. (2017). 'The End of Public Schools? The Corporate Reform Agenda to Privatize Education'. *Policy Futures in Education*, 15(3), 389–99.

Hutchings, M. (2016). *Exam Factories? The Impact of Accountability Measures on Children and Young People*. Retrieved from https://www.teachers.org.uk/files/exam-factories.pdf.

Hutton, W. (2015). *How Good We Can Be: Ending the Mercenary Society and Building a Great Country*. London: Little Brown.

Hyslop-Margison, E., and Sears, A. (2006). *Neoliberalism, Globalization and Human Capital Learning: Reclaiming Education for Democratic Citizenship*. Dordrecht: Springer.

Irwin, J., and Motoh, H. (2014). *Žižek and His Contemporaries: On the Emergence of the Slovenian Lacan*. London: Bloomsbury.

Johnson, B., and Sullivan, A. (2016). 'Against the Tide: Enacting Respectful Student Behaviour Polices in "Zero Tolerance" Times'. In B. Johnson, A. Sullivan and B. Lucas (eds), *Challenging Dominant Views on Student Behaviour at School* (pp. 163–80). Dordrecht: Springer.

Johnson, T. R. (2014). *The Other Side of Pedagogy: Lacan's Four Discourses and the Development of the Student Writer*. Albany: State University of New York Press.

Johnston, A. (2009). *Badiou, Žižek, and Political Transformations: The Cadence of Change*. Evanston, IL: Northwestern University Press.

Jones, C. (2013). *Can the Market Speak?* Winchester: Zero Books.

Jones, T. (2013). *Understanding Education Policy: The 'Four Education Orientations' Framework*. Dordrecht: Springer.

Kamberelis, G., and Dimitriadis, G. (2005). *On Qualitative Inquiry: Approaches to Language and Literacy Research*. New York: Teachers College Press.

Kay, A. (2011). 'Evidence-Based Policy-Making: The Elusive Search for Rational Public Administration'. *Australian Journal of Public Administration*, 70(3), 236–45.

Kelly, A. (2009). *The Curriculum: Theory and Practice* (6th edn). London: Sage.

King, S. D. (2017). *Grave New World: The End of Globalization and the Return of History*. New Haven, CT: Yale University Press.

Klein, N. (2007). *The Shock Doctrine: The Rise of Disaster Capitalism*. New York: Metropolitan Books.

Klepec, P. (2016). 'On the Mastery in the Four "Discourses"'. In S. Tomšič and A. Zevnik (eds), *Jacques Lacan: Between Psychoanalysis and Politics* (pp. 115–30). London: Routledge.

Konings, M. (2015). *The Emotional Logic of Capitalism: What Progressives Have Missed*. Stanford, CA: Stanford University Press.

Kontopodis, M. (2012). *Neoliberalism, Pedagogy and Human Development: Exploring Time, Mediation and Collectivity in Contemporary Schools*. New York: Routledge.

Koren, D. (2014). 'Agonistic Discourses, Analytic Act, Subjective Event'. In I. Parker and D. Pavón-Cuéllar (eds), *Lacan, Discourse, Event: New Psychoanalytic Approaches to Textual Indeterminacy* (pp. 247–56). Hove: Routledge.

Kotok, S., Frankenberg, E., Schafft, K. A., Mann, B. A., and Fuller, E. J. (2017). 'School Choice, Racial Segregation, and Poverty Concentration: Evidence from Pennsylvania Charter School Transfers'. *Educational Policy*, 31(4), 415–47.

Kotsko, A. (2018). *Neoliberalism's Demons: On the Political Theology of Late Capitalism*. Stanford, CA: Stanford University Press.

Krashen, S. D. (1999). *Three Arguments against Whole Language & Why They Are Wrong*. Portsmouth, NH: Heinemann.

Kulz, C. (2017). *Factories for Learning: Making Race, Class and Inequality in the Neoliberal Academy*. Manchester: Manchester University Press.

Kuus, M. (2008). 'Švejkian Geopolitics: Subversive Obedience in Central Europe'. *Geopolitics*, *13*(2), 257–77.

Lacan, J. (1974). ' "*This So Called Crisis, It Does Not Exist*": Jacques Lacan on *Pyshcoanalysis in 1974/Interviewer: E. Granzotto*. https://www.versobooks. com/blogs/1668-there-can-be-no-crisis-of-psychoanalysis-jacques-lacan-interviewed-in-1974 (accessed 1 May 2018).

Lacan, J. (1975). 'Peut-être à Vincennes'. *Ornicar*, *1*(5), 3–5.

Lacan, J. (1976). ' "Le Sinthome". Seminar of March 16'. *Ornicar?*, *9*, 32–40.

Lacan, J. (1981). *The Four Fundamental Concepts of Psychoanalysis* (A. Sheridan, trans.). New York: Norton.

Lacan, J. (1990). *Television/A Challenge to the Psychoanalytic Establishment* (D. Hollier, R. Krauss and A. Michelson, trans. J. Copjec, ed.). New York: Norton.

Lacan, J. (1991). *The Seminar of Jacques Lacan, Book II: The Ego in Freud's Theory and in the Technique of Psychoanalysis, 1954–1955* (S. Tomaselli, trans.). New York: Norton.

Lacan, J. (1992). *The Seminar of Jacques Lacan, Book VII: The Ethics of Pyschoanalysis, 1959–1960* (D. Porter, trans.). New York: Norton.

Lacan, J. (2000). *The Seminar of Jacques Lacan, Book XX: On Feminine Sexuality, the Limits of Love and Knowledge, 1972–1973* (B. Fink, trans., J.-A. Miller, ed.). London: Norton.

Lacan, J. (2007). *The Seminar of Jacques Lacan, Book XVII: The Other Side of Psychoanalysis, 1969–1970* (R. Grigg, trans.). New York: Norton.

Lacan, J. (2009). 'L'Etourdit'. *The Letter: Lacanian Perspectives on Psychoanalysis*, *41*, 39–80.

Lack, B. (2009). 'No Excuses: A Critique of the Knowledge Is Power Program (KIPP) within Charter Schools in the USA'. *Journal for Critical Education Policy Studies*, *7*(2), 127–53.

Laclau, E. (1996). *Emancipation(s)*. London: Verso.

Laclau, E. (2005). *On Populist Reason*. London: Verso.

Laclau, E. (2014). *The Rhetorical Foundations of Society*. London: Verso.

Laclau, E., and Mouffe, C. (2001). *Hegemony and Socialist Strategy: Towards a Radical Democratic Politics* (2nd edn). London: Verso.

Larner, W. (2003). Neoliberalism? *Environment and Planning D: Society and Space*, *21*, 509–12.

Lasswell, H. (1951). 'The Policy Orientation'. In D. Lerner and H. Lasswell (eds), *The Policy Sciences: Recent Developments in Scope and Method* (pp. 3–15). Stanford, CA: Stanford University Press.

Lawler, S., and Payne, G. (eds) (2017). *Social Mobility for the 21st Century: Everyone a Winner?* London: Routledge.

Leitner, H., Sheppard, E. S., Sziarto, K., and Maringanti, A. (2007). 'Contesting Urban Futures: Decentering Neoliberalism'. In H. Leitner, J. Peck and E. H. Sheppard (eds), *Contesting Neoliberalism: Urban Frontiers* (pp. 1–25). New York: Guilford Press.

Leupin, A. (2004). *Lacan Today: Psychoanalysis, Science, Religion*. New York: Other Press.

Levine, D. P. (2018). *Dark Fantasy: Regressive Movements and the Search for Meaning in Politics*. London: Karnac.

Lewis, M. (2015). *The Biology of Desire: Why Addiction Is Not a Disease*. London: Scribe.

Lewis, T. E. (2011). 'Rethinking the Learning Society: Giorgio Agamben on Studying, Stupidity, and Impotence'. *Studies in Philosophy and Education*, 30(6), 585–99.

Lindblom, C. E. (1959). 'The Science of "Muddling Through"'. *Public Administration Review*, 19(2), 79–88.

Lindblom, C. E. (1979). 'Still Muddling, Not Yet through'. *Public Administration Review*, 39(6), 517–26.

Lingard, B. (2010). 'Policy Borrowing, Policy Learning: Testing Times in Australian Schooling'. *Critical Studies in Education*, 51(2), 129–47.

Lingard, B., Martino, W., and Rezai-Rashti, G. (2013). 'Testing Regimes, Accountabilities and Education Policy: Commensurate Global and National Developments'. *Journal of Education Policy*, 28(5), 539–56.

Lipman, P. (2011). *The New Political Economy of Urban Education: Neoliberalism, Race, and the Right to the City*. New York: Routledge.

Lipman, P. (2014). 'Capitalizing on Crisis: Venture Philanthropy's Colonial Project to Remake Urban Education'. *Critical Studies in Education* (ahead-of-print), 1–18.

Littler, J. (2018). *Against Meritocracy: Culture, Power and Myths of Mobility*. Abingdon: Routledge.

Lowe, R. (2007). *The Death of Progressive Education: How Teachers Lost Control of the Classroom*. Abingdon: Routledge.

MacAllister, J. (2016). *Reclaiming Discipline for Education: Knowledge, Relationships and the Birth of Community*. London: Routledge.

Marginson, S. (1997). *Markets in Education*. St. Leonards, NSW: Allen and Unwin.

Mautner, G. (2010). *Language and the Market Society: Critical Reflections on Discourse and Dominance*. London: Routledge.

May, T. (2012). *Friendship in an Age of Economics: Resisting the Forces of Neoliberalism*. Lanham, MD: Lexington Books.

Mayer, T. (2017). 'School Choice and the Urban Neighbourhood: Segregation Processes in the German Primary Sector with Special Reference to Private Schools'. In T. Koinzer, R. Nikolai and F. Waldow (eds), *Private Schools and School Choice in Compulsory Education* (pp. 153–75). Dordrecht: Springer.

McAfee, N. (2008). *Democracy and the Political Unconscious*. New York: Columbia University Press.

McGowan, T. (2013). *Enjoying What We Don't Have: The Political Project of Psychoanalysis*. Lincoln, NE: University of Nebraska Press.

McGowan, T. (2016). *Capitalism and Desire: The Psychic Cost of Free Markets*. New York: Columbia University Press.

McKenzie, M. (2012). 'Education for Y'all: Global Neoliberalism and the Case for a Politics of Scale in Sustainability Education Policy'. *Policy Futures in Education*, *10*(2), 165–77.

McNulty, T. (2014). *Wrestling with the Angel: Experiments in Symbolic Life*. New York: Columbia University Press.

McSwite, O. C. (1997). 'Jacques Lacan and the Theory of the Human Subject: How Psychoanalysis Can Help Public Administration'. *American Behavioral Scientist*, *41*(1), 43–63.

Means, A. (2013). *Schooling in the Age of Austerity: Urban Education and the Struggle for Democractic Life*. Basingstoke: Palgrave MacMillan.

Mercer, I. (2016). *The Trump Revolution: The Donald's Creative Destruction Deconstructed*. Issaquah, WA: Politically Incorrect Press.

Mirowski, P. (2009). 'Postface: Defining Neoliberalism'. In P. Mirowski and D. Plehwe (eds), *The Road from Mont Pèlerin: The Making of the Neoliberal Thought Collective* (pp. 417–55). Cambridge, MA: Harvard University Press.

Mirowski, P. (2013). *Never Let a Serious Crisis Go to Waste: How Neoliberalism Survived the Financial Meltdown*. London: Verso.

Mirowski, P., and Plehwe, D. (eds) (2009). *The Road from Mont Pèlerin: The Making of the Neoliberal Thought Collective*. Cambridge, MA: Harvard University Press.

Monbiot, G. (2016). *How Did We Get into This Mess? Politics, Equality, Nature*. London: Verso Books.

Monbiot, G. (2017). *Neoliberalism*. London: Routledge.

Monck, R. (2005). 'Neoliberalism and Politics: The Politics of Neoliberalism'. In A. Saad Filho and D. Johnston (eds), *Neoliberalism: A Critical Reader* (pp. 60–9). London: Pluto Press.

Moore, A. (2004). *The Good Teacher: Dominant Discourses in Teaching and Teacher Education*. London: Routledge.

Moore, A., and Clarke, M. (2016). ' "Cruel Optimism": Teacher Attachment to Professionalism in an Era of Performativity'. *Journal of Education Policy*, *31*(5), 666–77.

Morgan, G. (1980). 'Paradigms, Metaphors, and Puzzle Solving in Organization Theory'. *Administrative Science Quarterly*, *25*(4), 605–22.

Mouffe, C. (2005). *On the Political*. Abingdon: Routledge.

Muller, J. Z. (2018). *The Tyranny of Metrics*. Princeton, NJ: Princeton University Press.

Musil, R. (1995 [1940]). *The Man without Qualities* (S. Wilkins and B. Pike, trans.). London: Picador.

Mutton, T., Burn, K., and Menter, I. (2017). 'Deconstructing the Carter Review: Competing Conceptions of Quality in England's "School-Led" System of Initial Teacher Education'. *Journal of Education Policy*, *32*(1), 14–33.

National Commission on Excellence in Education (1983). *A Nation at Risk*. Washington, DC: US Government Printing Office.

Neill, C. (2011). *Without Ground: Lacanain Ethics and the Assumption of Subjectivity.* Basingstoke: Palgrave Macmillan.

Nobus, D., and Quinn, M. (2005). *Knowing Nothing, Staying Stupid: Elements for a Psychoanalytic Epistemology.* London: Routledge.

Oliver, K. (2004). *The Colonization of Psychic Space: A Psychoanalytic Social Theory of Oppression.* Minneapolis: University of Minnesota Press.

Olssen, M. (1996). 'In Defense of the Welfare State and of Publicly Provided Education'. *Journal of Education Policy, 11,* 337–62.

Opolot, S. (2003). 'Neo-Liberal Globalisation and EFA: Debunking Global Constraints to "Quality" Education for All in Africa'. *Network for Policy Research Review and Advice on Education and Training (NORRAG) News: Special Issue: Critical Perspectives on Education and Skills in Eastern Africa on Basic and Post-Basic Levels* (32), 29–31.

Osborne, D., and Gaebler, T. (1992). *Reinventing Government: How the Entrepreneurial Spirit Is Transforming the Public Sector.* Reading, MA: Addison-Wesley.

Ozga, J. (2007). 'Knowledge and Policy: Research and Knowledge Transfer'. *Critical Studies in Education, 48*(1), 63–78.

Panitch, L., and Gindin, S. (2012). *The Making of Global Capitalism: The Political Economy of American Empire.* New York: Verso Books.

Parekh, B. (1995). 'Liberalism and Colonialism: A Critique of Locke and Mill'. In J. N. Pieterse and B. Parekh (eds), *Decolonization of Imagination: Culture, Knowledge and Power* (pp. 81–98). London: Zed Books.

Parker, I. (2001a). 'Lacan, Psychology and the Discourse of the University'. *Psychoanalytic Studies, 3*(1), 67–78.

Parker, I. (2001b). 'What Is Wrong with the Discourse of the University in Psychotherapy Training?' *European Journal of Psychotherapy, Counselling and Health,* 4(1), 27–43.

Pavón-Cuéllar, D. (2011). *From the Conscious Interior to an Exterior Unconscious: Lacan, Discourse Analysis and Social Psychology.* London: Karnac Books.

Paxton, R. O. (2005). *The Anatomy of Fascism.* London: Penguin.

Peck, J. (2010). *Constructions of Neoliberal Reason.* Oxford: Oxford University Press.

Pesoa, F. (2001). *The Book of Disquiet* (R. Zenith, trans.). London: Penguin.

Peters, G. (2017). *Improvising Improvisation: From Out of Philosophy, Music, Dance and Literature.* Chicago: University of Chicago Press.

Phillips-Fein, K. (2018). *Fear City: New York's Fiscal Crisis and the Rise of Austerity Politics.* New York: Picador.

Piketty, T. (2014). *Capital in the Twenty-First Century.* Cambridge, MA: Belknap Harvard.

Polanyi, K. (1944). *The Great Transformation: Economic and Political Origins of Our Time.* New York: Rinehart.

Poovey, M. (1998). *A History of the Modern Fact.* Chicago: University of Chicago Press.

Poulantzas, N. (2008). 'The Political Crisis and the Crisis of the State' (J. W. Freiburg, trans., J. Martin, ed.), *The Poulantzas Reader: Marxism, Law and the State* (pp. 294–322). London: Verso.

Power, S., and Frandji, D. (2010). 'Education Markets, the New Politics of Recognition and the Increasing Fatalism towards Inequality'. *Journal of Education Policy*, 25(3), 385–96.

Preston, T. (2015). 'The Ethics of Cheating in UK Schools'. Paper presented at the Philosophy of Education Society of Great Britain Annual Conference, Oxford.

Price, D. (ed.) (2017). *Education Forward: Moving Schools into the Future*. London: Crux.

Pring, R. (2012). *The Life and Death of Secondary Education for All*. London: Routledge.

Prunty, J. (1984). *A Critical Reformulation of Educational Policy Analysis*. Geelong: Deakin University Press.

Prunty, J. (1985). 'Signposts for a Critical Education Policy'. *Australian Journal of Education*, 29(2), 133–40.

Rancière, J. (1999). *Disagreement: Politics and Philosophy* (J. Rose, trans.). Minneapolis: University of Minnesota Press.

Rancière, J. (2010a). *Dissensus: On Politics and Aesthetics*. London: Continuum.

Rancière, J. (2010b). 'On Ignorant Schoolmasters'. In C. Bingham and G. Biesta (eds), *Jacques Rancière: Education, Truth, Emancipation*. London: Continuum.

Ravitch, D. (2009). *The Death and Life of Great American School System: How Testing and Choice Are Undermining Education*. New York: Basic Books.

Ravitch, D. (2013). *Reign of Error: The Hoax of the Privatization Movement and the Danger to America's Public Schools*. New York: Vintage Books.

Reay, D. (2017). *Miseducation: Inequality, Education and the Working Classes*. Bristol: Policy Press.

Reay, D., and Lucey, H. (2003). 'The Limits of "Choice": Children and Inner City Schooling'. *Sociology*, 37(1), 121–42.

Reid, A. (2009). 'Is This a Revolution? A Critical Analysis of the Rudd Government's National Education Agenda'. *Curriculum Perspectives*, 29(3), 1–13.

Rhee, M. (2013). *Radical: Fighting to Put Students First*. New York: Harper Colins.

Rizvi, F., and Lingard, B. (2010). *Globalizing Education Policy*. New York: Routledge.

Roitman, J. (2014). *Anti-Crisis*. Durham, NC: Duke University Press.

Rolfe, G. (2002). '"A Lie That Helps Us See the Truth": Research, Truth and Fiction in the Helping Professions'. *Reflective Practice*, 3(1), 89–102.

Rönnberg, L. (2017). 'From National Policy-Making to Global Edu-Business: Swedish Edu-Preneurs on the Move', *Journal of Education Policy*, 32(2), 234–49.

Rothenberg, M. A. (2010). *The Excessive Subject: A New Theory of Social Change*. Cambridge: Polity Press.

Rothenberg, M. A. (2015). 'Changing the Subject: Rights, Revolution, and Capitalist Discourse'. In L. De Sutter (ed.), *Žižek and Law* (pp. 42–59). Abingdon: Routledge.

Royle, N. (2003). *The Uncanny*. Manchester: Manchester University Press.

Rudd, T., and Goodson, I. F. (eds) (2017). *Negotiating Neoliberalism: Developing Alternative Educational Visions*. Rotterdam: Sense.

Ruti, M. (2012). *The Singularity of Being: Lacan and the Immortal within*. New York: Fordham University Press.

Ruti, M. (2015). *Between Levinas and Lacan: Self, Other, Ethics*. New York: Bloomsbury.

Ruti, M. (2017). *The Ethics of Opting Out: Queer Theory's Defiant Subjects*. New York: Bloomsbury.

Rutkowski, D. J. (2007). 'Converging Us Softly: How Intergovernmental Organizations Promote Neoliberal Educational Policy'. *Critical Studies in Education*, *48*(2), 229–47.

Ryan, J. (2017). *Class and Psychoanalysis: Landscapes of Inequality*. London: Routledge.

Saad Filho, A., and Johnston, D. (2005). 'Introduction'. In A. Saad Filho and D. Johnston (eds), *Neoliberalism: A Critical Reader*. London: Pluto Press.

Sachs, J. (2001). 'Teacher Professional Identity: Competing Discourses, Competing Outcomes'. *Journal of Education Policy*, *16*(2), 149–61.

Saltman, K. J. (2014a). 'The Austerity School: Grit, Character, and the Privatization of Public Education'. *symploke*, *22*(1), 41–57.

Saltman, K. J. (2014b). *The Politics of Education: A Critical Introduction*. Boulder: Paradigm.

Samuels, R. (2017). *Educating Inequality: Beyond the Political Myths of Higher Education and the Job Market*. New York: Routledge.

Santner, E. (2011). *The Royal Remains: The People's Two Bodies and the Endgames of Sovereignty*. Chicago: University of Chicago Press.

Savage, G. (2011). 'When Worlds Collide: Excellent and Equitable Learning Communities? Australia's "Social Capitalist" Paradox?' *Journal of Education Policy*, *26*(1), 33–59.

Scharff, C. (2016). 'The Psychic Life of Neoliberalism: Mapping the Contours of Entrepreneurial Subjectivity'. *Theory, Culture & Society*, *33*(6), 107–22.

Schirato, T., and Yell, S. (1996). *Communication and Cultural Literacy: An Introduction*. St Leonards, NSW: Allen & Unwin.

Schroeder, J. L. (2008). *The Four Lacanian Discourses: Or Turning Law Inside Out*. London: Birkbeck Law Press.

Schuster, A. (2016). *The Trouble with Pleasure: Deleuze and Psychoanalysis*. Cambridge, MA: MIT Press.

Sellar, S., and Lingard, B. (2013). 'The OECD and Global Governance in Education'. *Journal of Education Policy*, *28*(5), 710–25.

Sellar, S., Thompson, G., and Rutkowski, D. (2017). *The Global Education Race: Taking the Measure of PISA and International Testing*. Edmonton, Canada: Brush Education.

Sennett, R. (2012). *Together: The Rituals, Pleasures and Politics of Cooperation*. New Haven: Yale University Press.

Seymour, R. (2014). *Against Austerity*. London: Pluto Press.

Shamir, R. (2008). 'The Age of Responsibilization: On Market-Embedded Morality'. *Economy and Society*, *37*(1), 1–19.

Shang, L., Li, J., Li, Y., Wang, T., and Siegrist, J. (2014). 'Stressful Psychosocial School Environment and Suicidal Ideation in Chinese Adolescents'. *Social Psychiatry and Psychiatric Epidemiology*, *49*(2), 205–10.

Sharpe, M., and Boucher, G. (2010). *Žižek and Politics: A Critical Introduction*. Edinburgh: Edinburgh University Press.

Shepherdson, C. (2008). *Lacan and the Limits of Language*. New York: Fordham University Press.

Showalter, E. (1998). *Hystories: Hysterical Epidemics and the Modern Media*. New York: Columbia University Press.

Singh, P. (2015). 'Performativity and Pedagogising Knowledge: Globalising Educational Policy Formation, Dissemination and Enactment'. *Journal of Education Policy*, *30*(3), 363–84.

Sleeter, C. (2010). 'Federal Education Policy and Social Justice Education'. In T. K. Chapman and N. Hobbel (eds), *Social Justice Pedagogy across the Curriculum: The Practice of Freedom* (pp. 36–58). New York: Routledge.

Stallybrass, P., and White, A. (1986). *The Politics and Poetics of Transgression*. Ithaca, NY: Cornell University Press.

Starr, P. (2001). '"Rien n'est tout": Lacan and the Legacy of May '68'. *L'Esprit Créateur*, *41*(1), 34–42.

Stavrakakis, Y. (1999). *Lacan and the Political*. London: Routledge.

Stedman Jones, D. (2012). *Masters of the Universe: Hayek, Friedman and the Birth of Neoliberal Politics*. Princeton, NJ: Princeton University Press.

Stern, J. P. (1968). 'War and the Comic Muse: *The Good Soldier Schweik* and *Catch-22*'. *Comparative Literature*, *20*(3), 193–216.

Stevenson, N. (2015). 'Revolution from above in English Schools: Neoliberalism, Democratic Commons and Education'. *Cultural Sociology*, 1–16.

Stiegler, B. (2015). *States of Shock: Stupidity and Knowledge in the 21st Century* (D. Ross, trans.). Cambridge: Polity Press.

Stobart, G. (2008). *Testing Times: The Uses and Abuses of Assessment*. New York: Routledge.

Strassheim, H., and Kettunen, P. (2014). 'When Does Evidence-Based Policy Turn into Policy-Based Evidence? Configurations, Contexts and Mechanisms'. *Evidence & Policy: A Journal of Research, Debate and Practice*, *10*(2), 259–77.

Stråth, B. (2005). 'The Monetary Issue and European Economic Policy in Historical Perspective'. In C. Joerges, B. Stråth and P. Wagner (eds), *The Economy as Polity: The Political Constitution of Contemporary Capitalism* (pp. 59–76). London: UCL Press.

Stronach, I. (2010). *Globalizing Education, Educating the Local: How Method Made Us Mad*. Abingdon: Routledge.

Sullivan, A., Johnson, B., and Lucas, B. (eds) (2016). *Challenging Dominant Views on Student Behaviour at School: Answering Back*. Dordrecht: Springer.

Tansel, C. B. (ed.) (2016). *States of Discipline: Authoritarian Neoliberalism and the Contested Reproduction of Capitalist Order*. Lanham, MD: Rowman & Littlefield.

Taubman, P. (2009). *Teaching by Numbers: Deconstructing the Discourse of Standards and Accountability in Education*. New York: Routledge.

Tell, S. (2016). *Charter School Report Card*. Charlotte, NC: Information Age.

Tharp, R., and Gallimore, R. (1988). *Rousing Minds to Life: Teaching, Learning and Schooling in Social Context*. Cambridge, MA: Cambridge University Press.

Tharp, R., and Gallimore, R. (1990). 'Teaching Mind in Society: Teaching, Schooling and Literate Discourse'. In L. Moll (ed.), *Vygotsky and Education: Instructional Implications and Applications of Sociohistorical Psychology* (pp. 175–205). Cambridge: Cambridge University Press.

Thompson, P., and Holdsworth, R. (2003). 'Theorizing Change in the Educational "Field": Re-Readings of "Student Participation" Projects'. *International Journal of Leadership in Education*, 6(4), 371–91.

Thorsen, D. E. (2010). 'The Neoliberal Challenge: What Is Neoliberalism?' *Contemporary Readings in Law and Social Justice*, 2(2), 188–214.

Thurston, L. (ed.) (2002). *Re-Inventing the Symptom: Essays on the Final Lacan*. New York: Other Press.

Tooley, J. (2000). *Reclaiming Education*. London: Continuum.

Tooley, J., and Darby, D. (1998). *Educational Research: A Critique. A Survey of Published Educational Research*. London: Office for Standards in Education London.

Toulmin, S. (1990). *Cosmopolis: The Hidden Agenda of Modernity*. Chicago: University of Chicago Press.

Tribe, K. (2009). 'Liberalism and Neoliberalism in Britain, 1930–1980'. In P. Mirowski and D. Plehwe (eds), *The Road from Mont Pèlerin: The Making of the Neoliberal Thought Collective* (pp. 68–97). Cambridge, MA: Harvard University Press.

Tribe, L. (1972). 'Policy Analysis: Science or Ideology?' *Philosophy & Public Affairs*, 2(1), 66–110.

Truss, E. (2013). *More Great Childcare: Raising Quality and Giving Parents More Choice*. London: The Stationary Office.

Tummers, L. (2013). *Policy Alienation and the Power of Professionals: Confronting New Policies*. Cheltenham: Edward Elgar.

Tummers, L., Bekkers, V., and Steijn, B. (2012). 'Policy Alienation of Public Professionals: A Comparative Case Study of Insurance Physicians and Secondary School Teachers'. *International Journal of Public Administration*, 35(4), 259–71.

UNESCO (2000). 'Education for All Movement'. Retrieved from http://www.unesco.org/new/en/archives/education/themes/leading-the-international-agenda/education-for-all/.

Vadolas, A. (2009). *Perversions of Fascism*. London: Karnac Books.

Van Haute, P. (2002). *Against Adaptation: Lacan's 'Subversion' of the Subject* (P. Crowe and P. Vankerk, trans.). New York: Other Press.

Varoufakis, Y. (2016). *And the Weak Suffer What They Must? Europe, Austerity and the Threat to Global Stability*. London: Vintage.

Verger, A., Lubienski, C., and Steiner-Khamsi, G. (eds) (2016). *World Yearbook of Education 2016: The Global Education Industry*. New York: Routledge.

Verhaeghe, P. (1995). 'From Impossibility to Inability: Lacan's Theory on the Four Discourses'. *The Letter: Lacanian Perspectives on Psychoanalysis, 3*, 76–99.

Verhaeghe, P. (2008). *On Being Normal and Other Disorders: A Manual for Clinical Psychodiagnostics*. London: Karnac Books.

Verhaeghe, P., and Declerq, F. (2002). 'Lacan's Analytic Goal: *Le sinthome* of the Feminine Way'. In L. Thurston (ed.), *Re-inventing the Symptom: Essays on the Final Lacan* (pp. 59–82). New York: Other Press.

Vighi, F. (2010). *On Žižek's Dialectics: Surplus, Subtraction, Sublimation*. London: Continuum.

Vygotsky, L. (1986). *Thought and Language* (A. Kozulin, trans.). Cambridge, MA: MIT Press.

Warren, S., Webb, D., Franklin, A., and Bowers-Brown, J. (2012). 'Trust Schools and the Politics of Persuasion and the Mobilisation of Interest'. *Journal of Education Policy, 26*(6), 839–53.

Watkins, W. (2015). *The Assault on Public Education: Confronting the Politics of Corporate School Reform*. Columbia: Teachers College Press.

Webb, P. T. (2014). 'Policy Problematization'. *International Journal of Qualitative Studies in Education, 27*(3), 364–76.

White, S. K. (2000). *Sustaining Affirmation: The Strengths of Weak Ontology in Political Theory*. Princeton: Princeton University Press.

Wildavsky, A. (1979). *Speaking Truth to Power: The Art and Craft of Policy Analysis*. Boston: Little, Brown.

Wilder, B. (Writer) (1960). *The Apartment*. Hollywood, CA: United Artists.

Wiliam, D. (2018). *Creating the Schools Our Children Need: Why What We're Doing Now Won't Help Much (and What We Can Do Instead)*. West Palm Beach: Learning Sciences International.

Wilkins, A. (2017). 'Rescaling the Local: Multi-Academy Trusts, Private Monopoly and Statecraft in England'. *Journal of Educational Administration and History, 49*(2), 171–85.

Wilkinson, R., and Pickett, K. (2009). *The Spirit Level: Why More Equal Societies Almost Always Do Better*. London: Allen Lane.

Wilson, J. K. (1995). *The Myth of Political Correctness: The Conservative Attack on Higher Education*. Durham: Duke University Press.

Winch, C., and Gingell, J. (2004). *Philosophy and Educational Policy: A Critical Introduction*. London: Routledge.

Wolf, A. (2002). *Does Education Matter: Myths about Education and Economic Growth*. London: Penguin.

Wright, C. (2015). 'Discourse and the Master's Lining: A Lacanian Critique of the Globalizing (Bio)politics of the *Diagnostic and Statistical Manual*'. In S. Tomšič (ed.), *Jacques Lacan: Between Psychoanalysis and Politics* (pp. 131–45). Abingdon: Routledge.

Wrigley, T. (2017). 'Canonical Knowledge and Common Culture: In Search of Curricular Justice'. *European Journal of Curriculum Studies*, 4(1), 536–55.

Wrigley, T. (2018). '"Knowledge", Curriculum and Social Justice'. *The Curriculum Journal*, 29(1), 4–24.

Wyn, J., Turnbull, M., and Grimshaw, L. (2014). *The Experience of Education: The Impacts of High Stakes Testing on School Students and Their Families*. Retrieved from http://citeseerx.ist.psu.edu/viewdoc/download?doi=10.1.1.737.8428&rep=rep1&type=pdf. Sydney, NSW.

Youdell, D. (2011). *School Trouble: Identity, Power and Politics in Education*. London: Routledge.

Zipin, L. (2017). 'Pursuing a Problematic-Based Curriculum Approach for the Sake of Social Justice'. *Journal of Education*, 69, 67–92.

Žižek, S. (1989). *The Sublime Object of Ideology*. London: Verso Books.

Žižek, S. (1992). *Looking Awry: An Introduction to Jacques Lacan through Popular Culture*. Cambridge, MA: MIT Press.

Žižek, S. (1996a). 'The Fetish of the Party'. In W. Apollon and R. Feldstein (eds), *Lacan, Politics, Aesthetics*. Albany: State University of New York Press.

Žižek, S. (1996b). *The Indivisible Remainder: An Essay on Schelling and Related Matters*. London: Verso.

Žižek, S. (1997). *The Plague of Fantasies*. London: Verso.

Žižek, S. (1998). 'Four Discourses, Four Subjects'. In S. Žižek (ed.), *Cogito and the Unconscious* (pp. 74–113). Durham, NC: Duke University Press.

Žižek, S. (2002). 'The Real of Sexual Difference'. In S. Barnard and B. Fink (eds), *Reading Seminar XX: Lacan's Major Work on Love, Knowledge and Feminine Sexuality*. Albany, NY: SUNY Press.

Žižek, S. (2006). *The Parallax View*. Cambridge, MA: MIT Press.

Žižek, S. (2008 [1992]). *Enjoy Your Symptom! Jacques Lacan in Hollywood and Out*. London: Routledge.

Zupančič, A. (2006). 'When Surplus Enjoyment Meets Surplus Value'. In J. Clemens and R. Grigg (eds), *Jacques Lacan and the Other Side of Psychoanalysis* (pp. 155–78). Durham, NC: Duke University Press.

Index